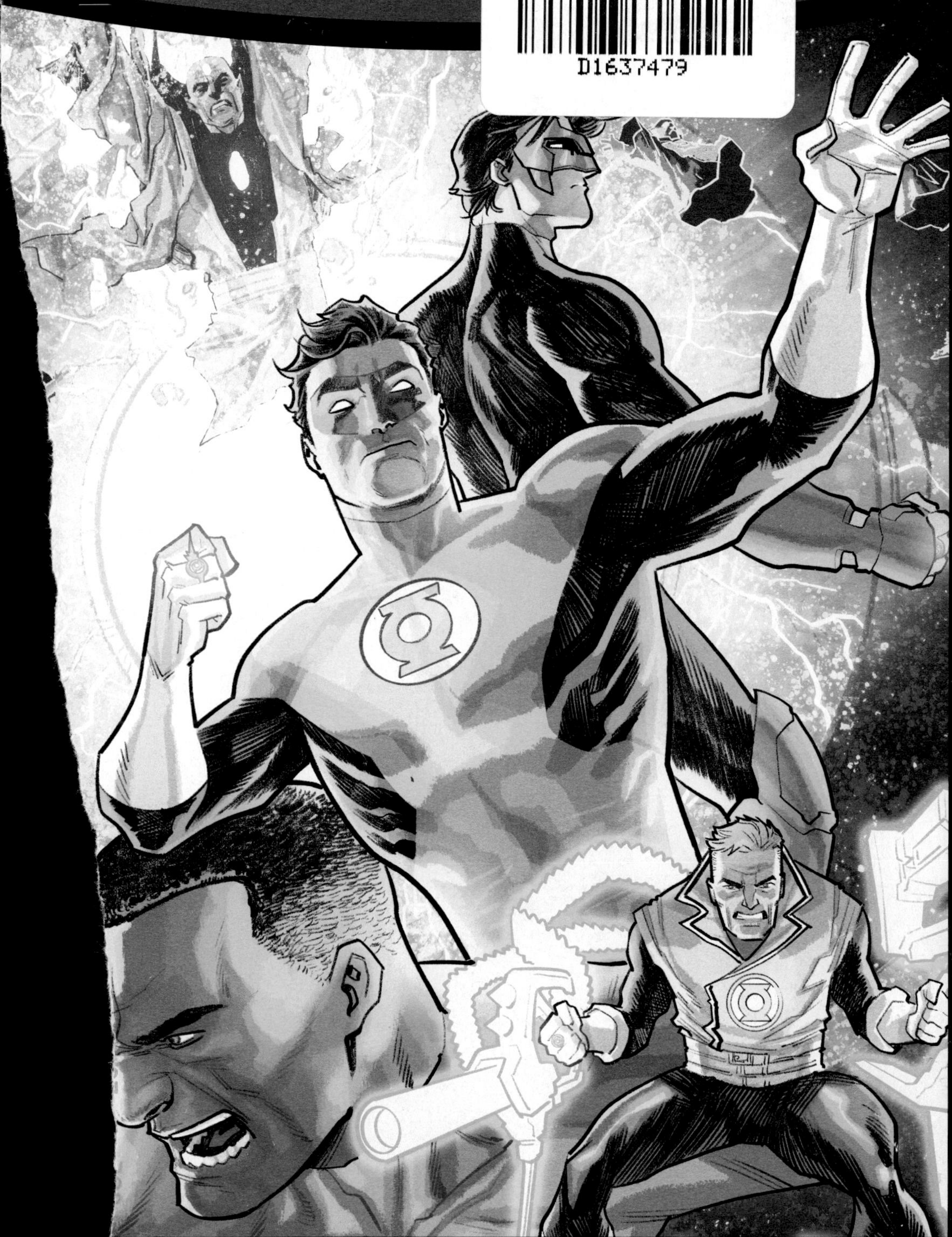

ORDAN AND THE GREEN LANTERN CORPS
VOL.5 TWILIGHT OF THE GUARDIANS

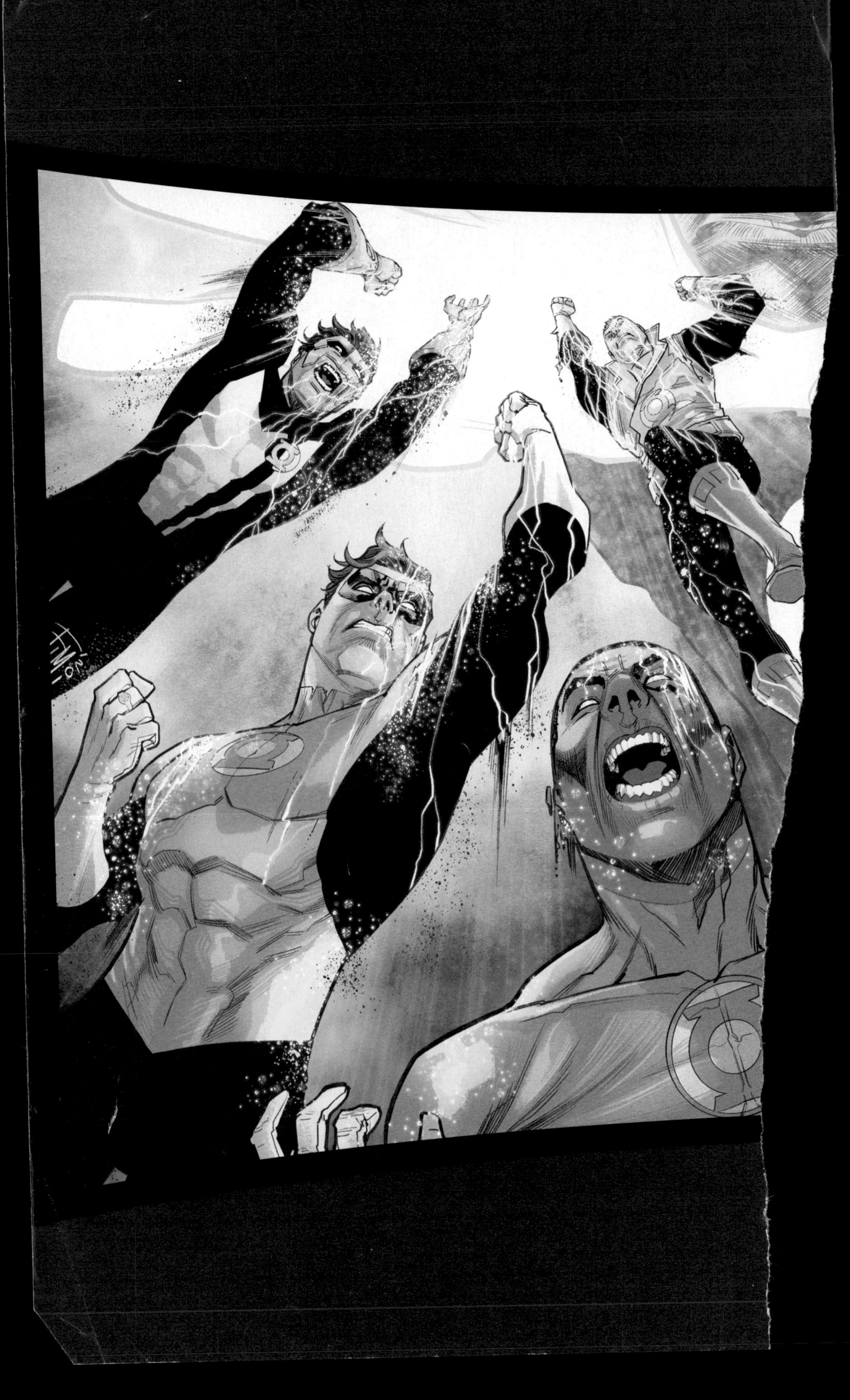

HAL JORDAN AND THE GREEN LANTERN CORPS
VOL.5 TWILIGHT OF THE GUARDIANS

ROBERT VENDITTI
writer

PATRICK ZIRCHER * **JACK HERBERT** * **TOM DERENICK**
JOSÉ LUÍS * **MICK GRAY** * **CAM SMITH**
artists

JASON WRIGHT
colorist

DAVE SHARPE
letterer

ETHAN VAN SCIVER and **JASON WRIGHT**
collection cover artists

SUPERMAN created by **JERRY SIEGEL** and **JOE SHUSTER**
By special arrangement with the Jerry Siegel family

MIKE COTTON Editor - Original Series ✻ **ANDREW MARINO** Assistant Editor - Original Series ✻ **JEB WOODARD** Group Editor - Collected Editions
ERIKA ROTHBERG Editor - Collected Edition ✻ **STEVE COOK** Design Director - Books ✻ **LOUIS PRANDI** Publication Design

BOB HARRAS Senior VP - Editor-in-Chief, DC Comics ✻ **PAT McCALLUM** Executive Editor, DC Comics

DIANE NELSON President ✻ **DAN DiDIO** Publisher ✻ **JIM LEE** Publisher ✻ **GEOFF JOHNS** President & Chief Creative Officer
AMIT DESAI Executive VP - Business & Marketing Strategy, Direct to Consumer & Global Franchise Management
SAM ADES Senior VP & General Manager, Digital Services ✻ **BOBBIE CHASE** VP & Executive Editor, Young Reader & Talent Development
MARK CHIARELLO Senior VP - Art, Design & Collected Editions ✻ **JOHN CUNNINGHAM** Senior VP - Sales & Trade Marketing
ANNE DePIES Senior VP - Business Strategy, Finance & Administration ✻ **DON FALLETTI** VP - Manufacturing Operations
LAWRENCE GANEM VP - Editorial Administration & Talent Relations ✻ **ALISON GILL** Senior VP - Manufacturing & Operations
HANK KANALZ Senior VP - Editorial Strategy & Administration ✻ **JAY KOGAN** VP - Legal Affairs ✻ **JACK MAHAN** VP - Business Affairs
NICK J. NAPOLITANO VP - Manufacturing Administration ✻ **EDDIE SCANNELL** VP - Consumer Marketing
COURTNEY SIMMONS Senior VP - Publicity & Communications ✻ **JIM (SKI) SOKOLOWSKI** VP - Comic Book Specialty Sales & Trade Marketing
NANCY SPEARS VP - Mass, Book, Digital Sales & Trade Marketing ✻ **MICHELE R. WELLS** VP - Content Strategy

HAL JORDAN AND THE GREEN LANTERN CORPS VOL. 5: TWILIGHT OF THE GUARDIANS

Published by DC Comics. Compilation and all new material Copyright © 2018 DC Comics. All Rights Reserved. Originally published in single
form in HAL JORDAN AND THE GREEN LANTERN CORPS 30-31, 33-36. Copyright © 2017, 2018 DC Comics. All Rights Reserved. All character
distinctive likenesses and related elements featured in this publication are trademarks of DC Comics. The stories, characters and incide
featured in this publication are entirely fictional. DC Comics does not read or accept unsolicited submissions of ideas, stories or artw

DC Comics, 2900 West Alameda Ave., Burbank, CA 91505
Printed by LSC Communications, Kendallville, IN, USA. 5/4/18. First Printing.
ISBN: 978-1-4012-8037-6

Library of Congress Cataloging-in-Publication Data is available.

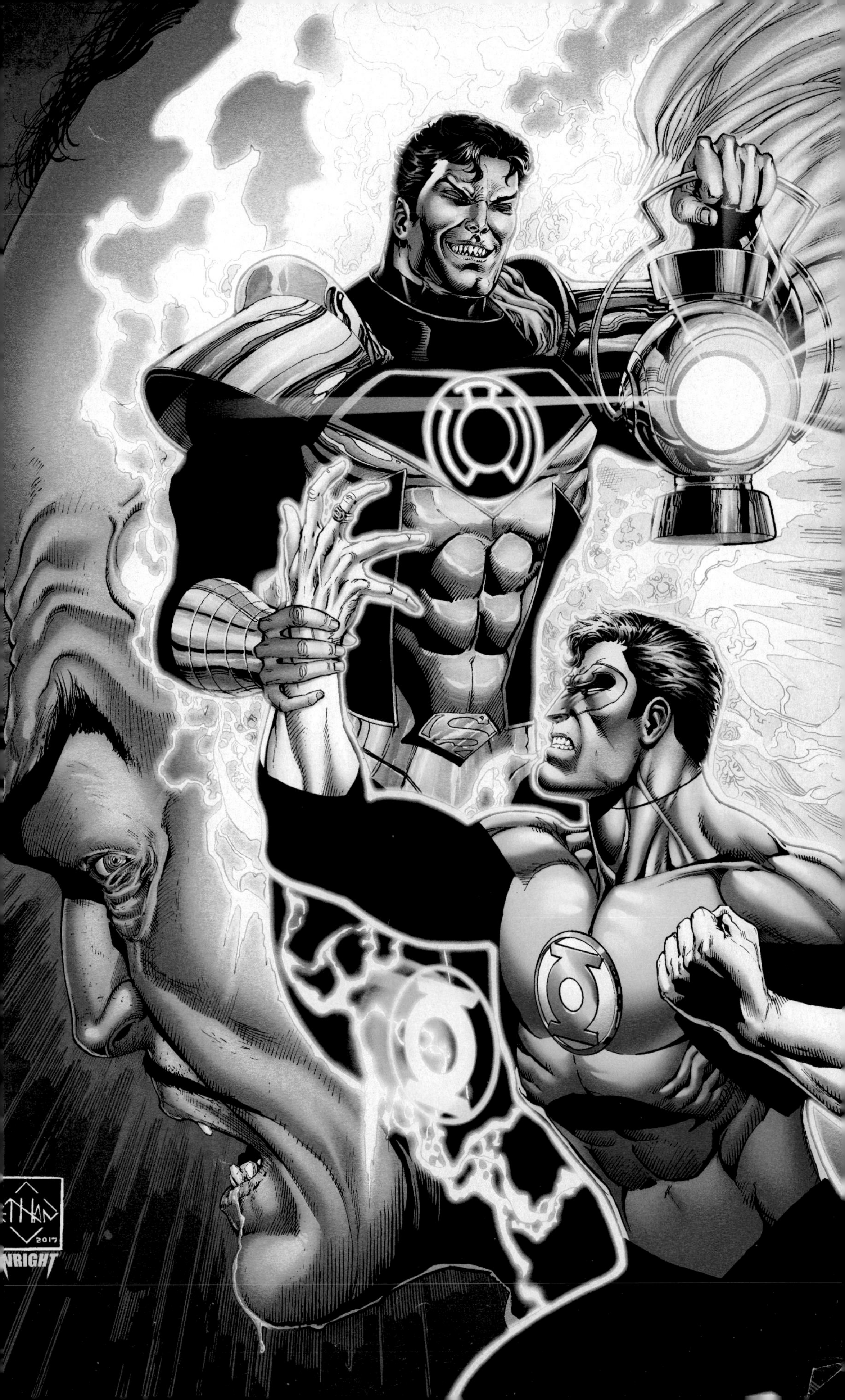

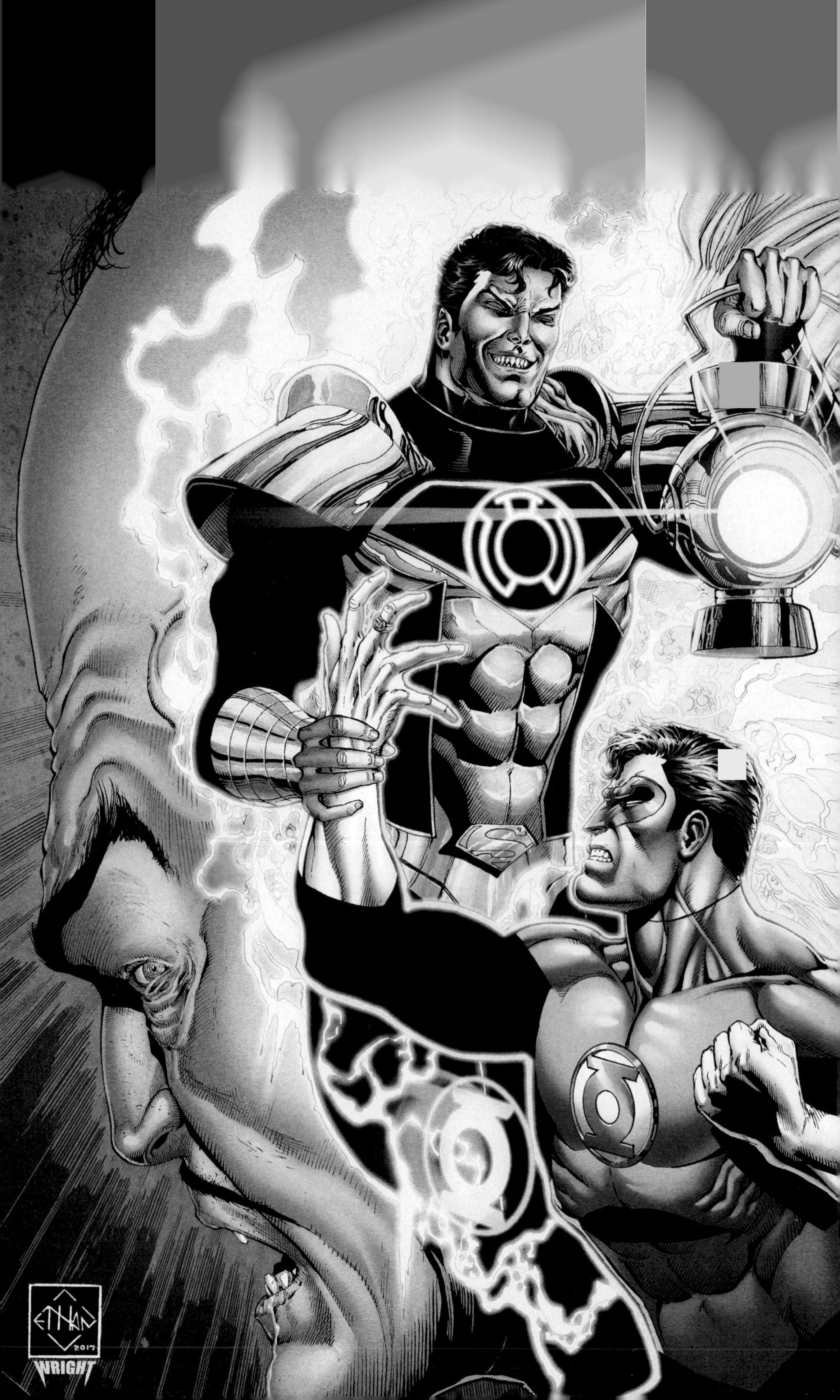
2017
WRIGHT

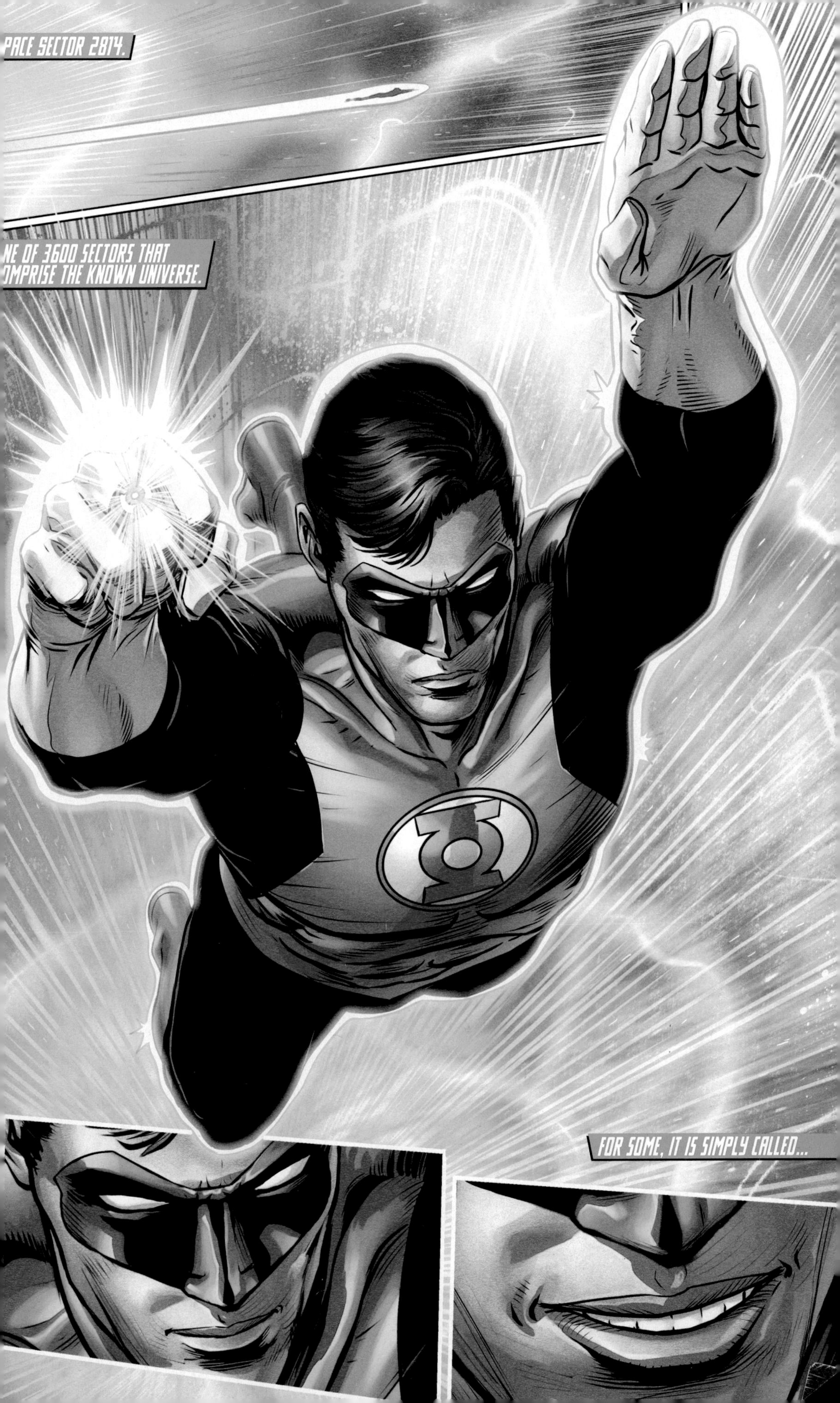
PACE SECTOR 2814.
NE OF 3600 SECTORS THAT
OMPRISE THE KNOWN UNIVERSE.
FOR SOME, IT IS SIMPLY CALLED...

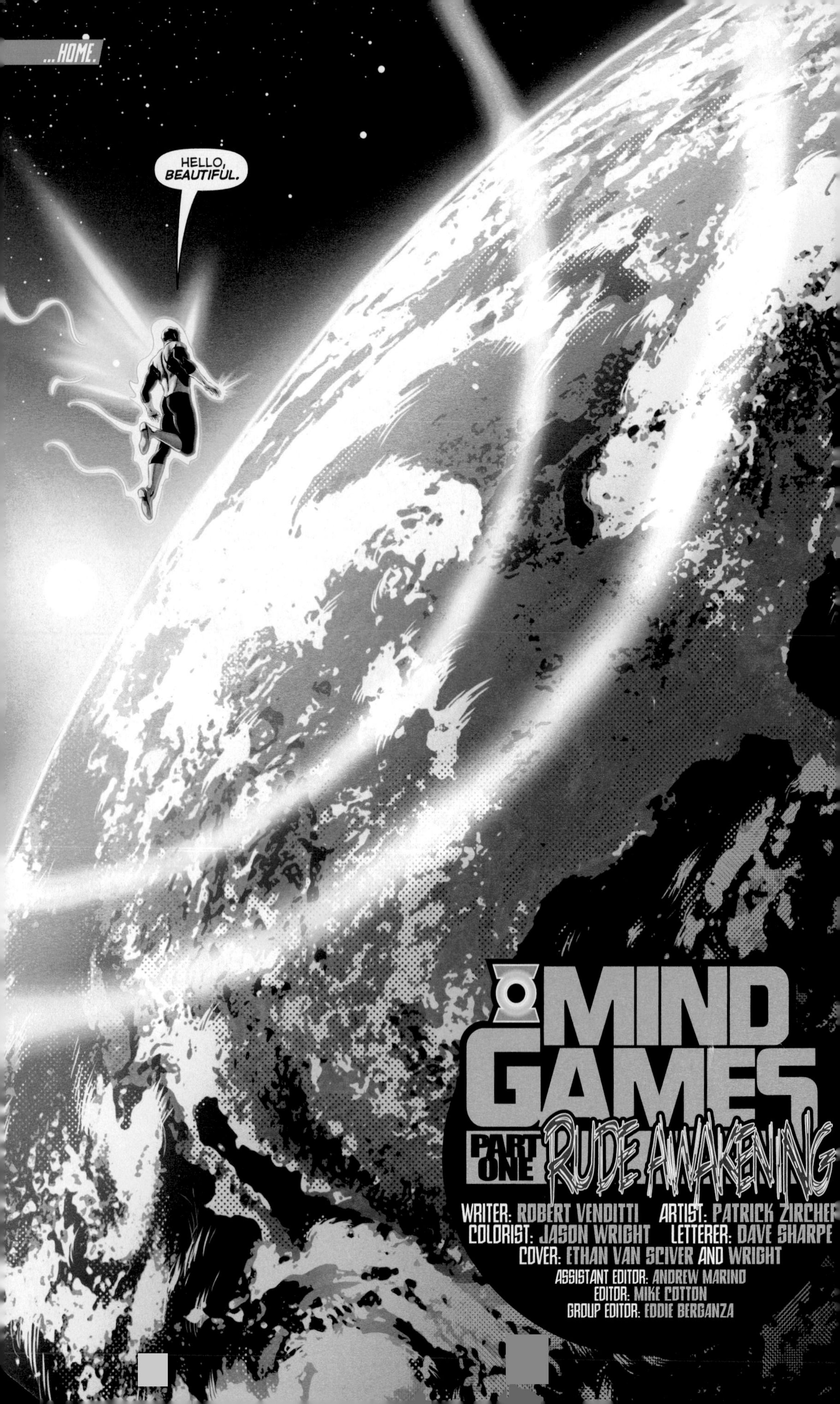
...HOME.
HELLO, BEAUTIFUL.
MIND GAMES
PART ONE RUDE AWAKENING
WRITER: ROBERT VENDITTI ARTIST: PATRICK ZIRCHER
COLORIST: JASON WRIGHT LETTERER: DAVE SHARPE
COVER: ETHAN VAN SCIVER AND WRIGHT
ASSISTANT EDITOR: ANDREW MARINO
EDITOR: MIKE COTTON
GROUP EDITOR: EDDIE BERGANZA

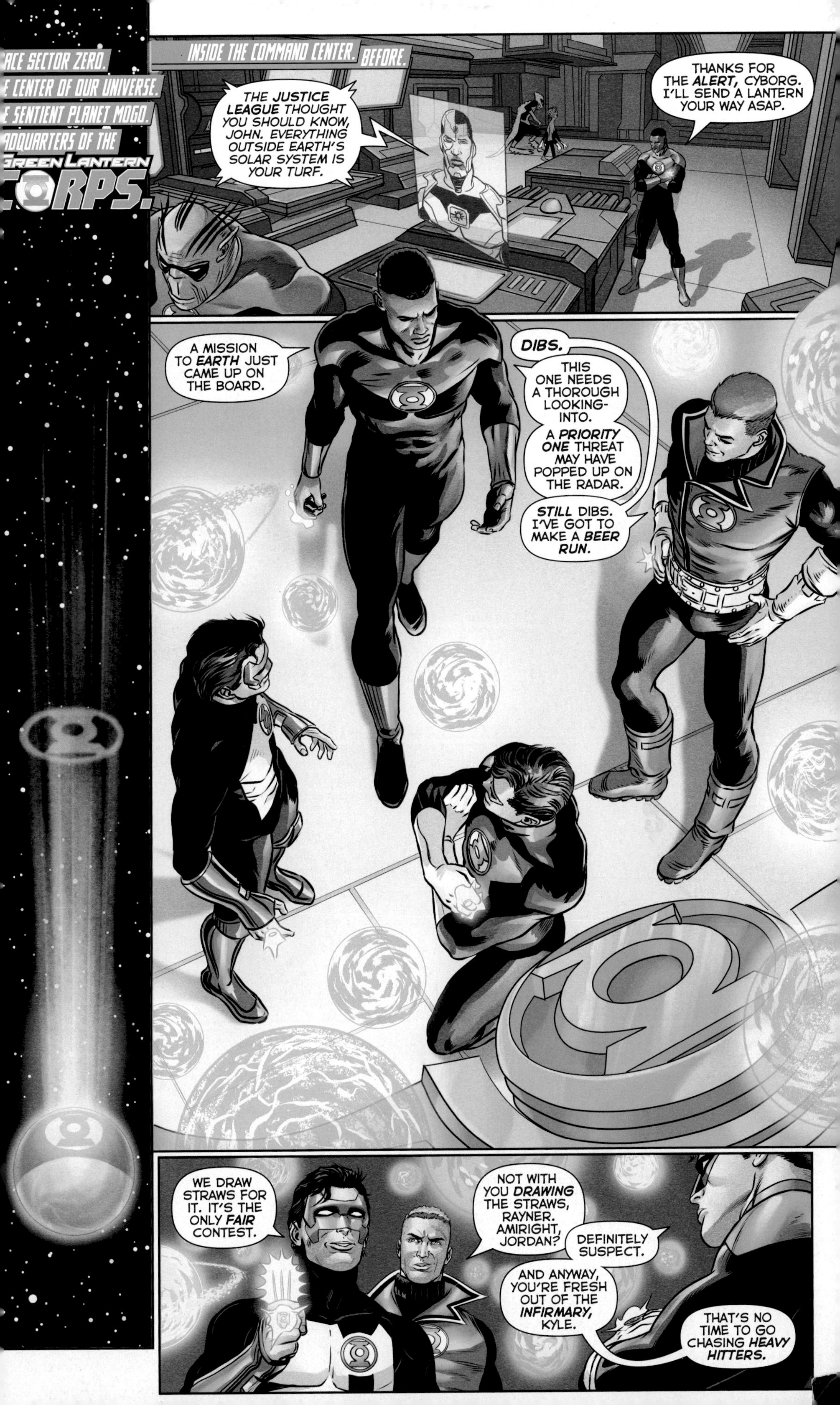

ACE SECTOR ZERO.
E CENTER OF OUR UNIVERSE.
E SENTIENT PLANET MOGO.
ADQUARTERS OF THE
GREEN LANTERN
CORPS.
INSIDE THE COMMAND CENTER. BEFORE.
THE JUSTICE LEAGUE THOUGHT YOU SHOULD KNOW, JOHN. EVERYTHING OUTSIDE EARTH'S SOLAR SYSTEM IS YOUR TURF.
THANKS FOR THE ALERT, CYBORG. I'LL SEND A LANTERN YOUR WAY ASAP.
A MISSION TO EARTH JUST CAME UP ON THE BOARD.
DIBS.
THIS ONE NEEDS A THOROUGH LOOKING-INTO.
A PRIORITY ONE THREAT MAY HAVE POPPED UP ON THE RADAR.
STILL DIBS. I'VE GOT TO MAKE A BEER RUN.
WE DRAW STRAWS FOR IT. IT'S THE ONLY FAIR CONTEST.
NOT WITH YOU DRAWING THE STRAWS, RAYNER. AMIRIGHT, JORDAN?
DEFINITELY SUSPECT.
AND ANYWAY, YOU'RE FRESH OUT OF THE INFIRMARY, KYLE.
THAT'S NO TIME TO GO CHASING HEAVY HITTERS.

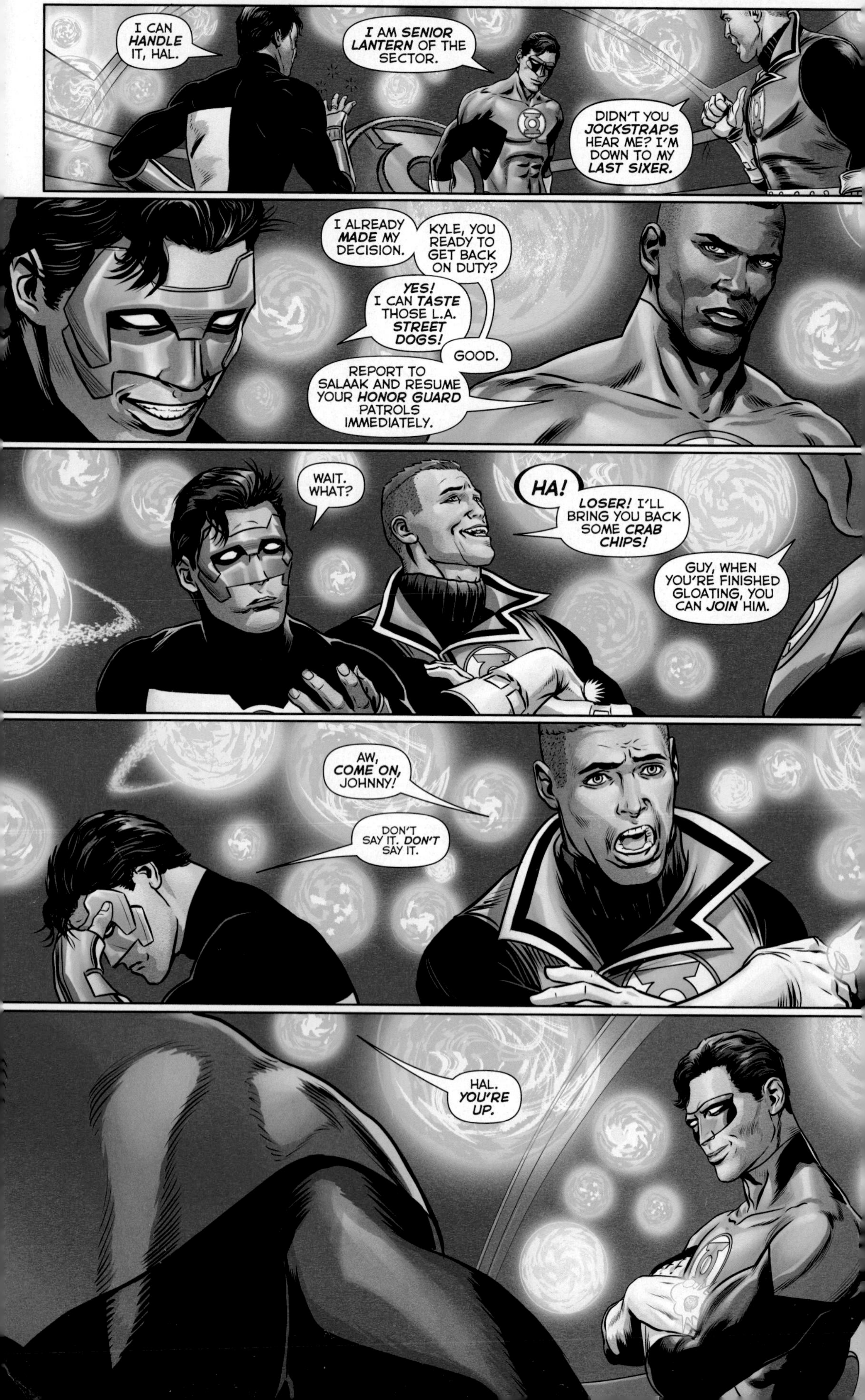

I CAN HANDLE IT, HAL.
I AM SENIOR LANTERN OF THE SECTOR.
DIDN'T YOU JOCKSTRAPS HEAR ME? I'M DOWN TO MY LAST SIXER.
I ALREADY MADE MY DECISION.
KYLE, YOU READY TO GET BACK ON DUTY?
YES! I CAN TASTE THOSE L.A. STREET DOGS!
GOOD.
REPORT TO SALAAK AND RESUME YOUR HONOR GUARD PATROLS IMMEDIATELY.
WAIT. WHAT?
HA!
LOSER! I'LL BRING YOU BACK SOME CRAB CHIPS!
GUY, WHEN YOU'RE FINISHED GLOATING, YOU CAN JOIN HIM.
AW, COME ON, JOHNNY!
DON'T SAY IT. DON'T SAY IT.
HAL. YOU'RE UP.

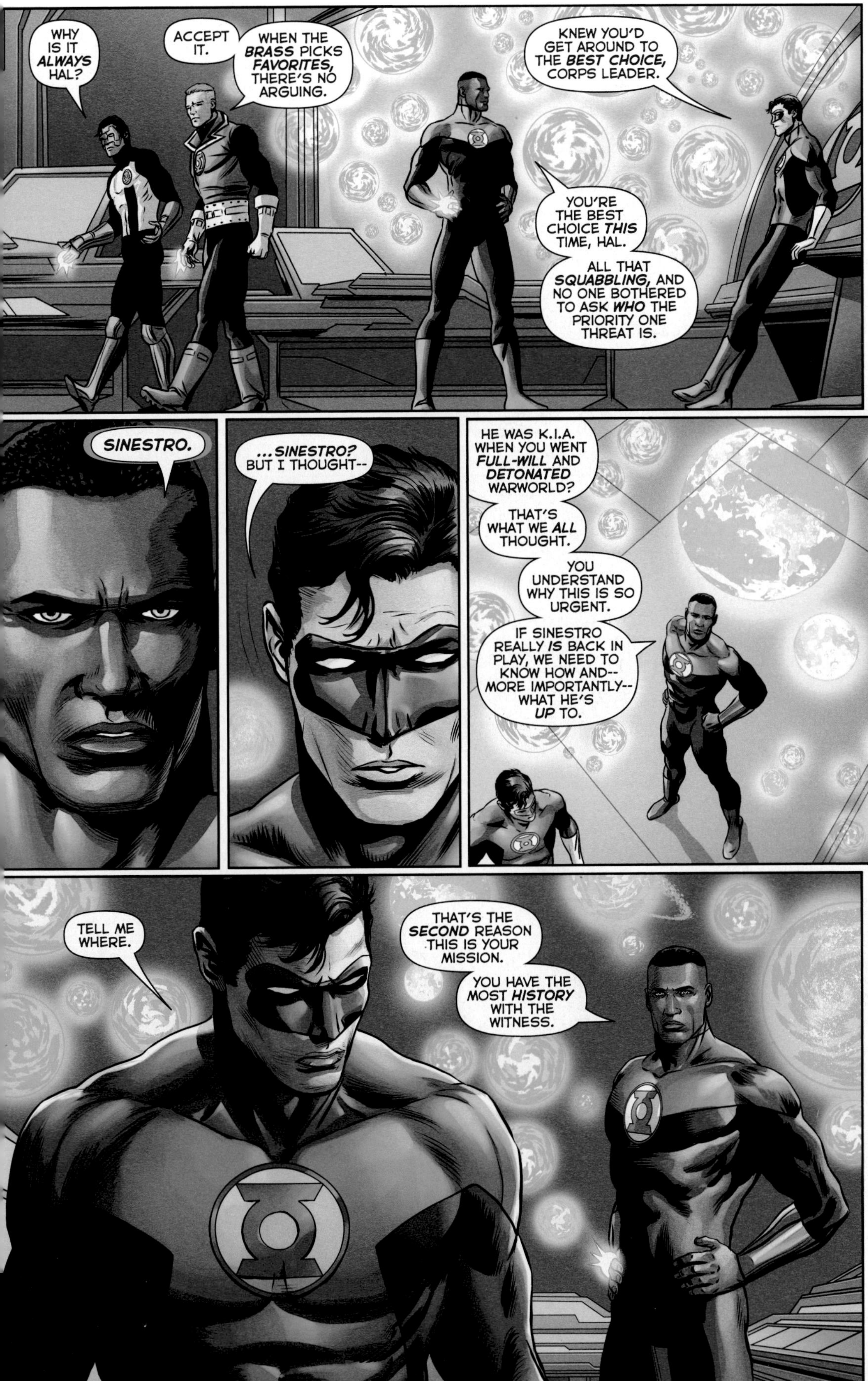
WHY IS IT ALWAYS HAL?
ACCEPT IT.
WHEN THE BRASS PICKS FAVORITES, THERE'S NO ARGUING.
KNEW YOU'D GET AROUND TO THE BEST CHOICE, CORPS LEADER.
YOU'RE THE BEST CHOICE THIS TIME, HAL.
ALL THAT SQUABBLING, AND NO ONE BOTHERED TO ASK WHO THE PRIORITY ONE THREAT IS.
SINESTRO.
...SINESTRO? BUT I THOUGHT--
HE WAS K.I.A. WHEN YOU WENT FULL-WILL AND DETONATED WARWORLD?
THAT'S WHAT WE ALL THOUGHT.
YOU UNDERSTAND WHY THIS IS SO URGENT.
IF SINESTRO REALLY IS BACK IN PLAY, WE NEED TO KNOW HOW AND--MORE IMPORTANTLY--WHAT HE'S UP TO.
TELL ME WHERE.
THAT'S THE SECOND REASON THIS IS YOUR MISSION.
YOU HAVE THE MOST HISTORY WITH THE WITNESS.

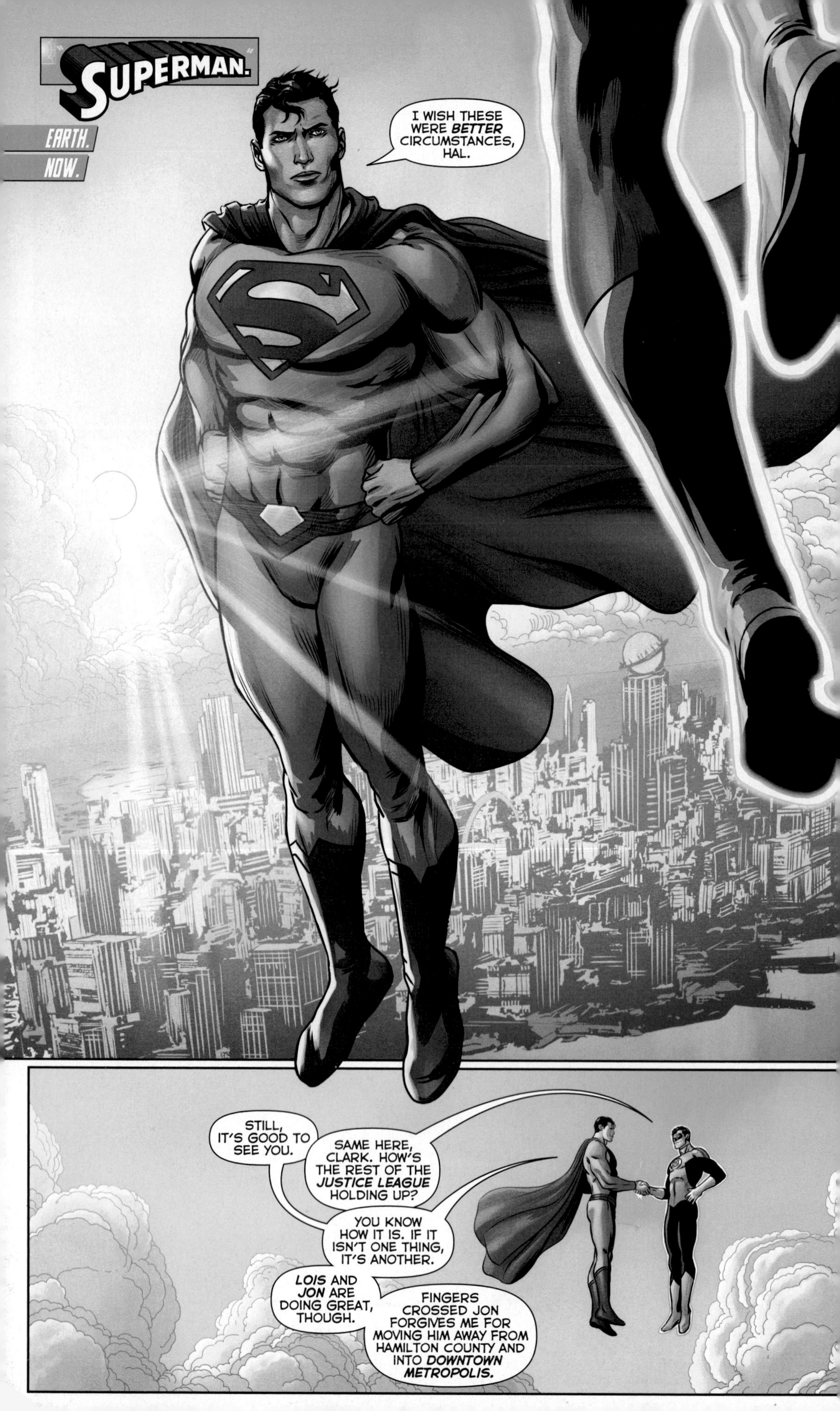
SUPERMAN.
EARTH.
NOW.
I WISH THESE WERE BETTER CIRCUMSTANCES, HAL.
STILL, IT'S GOOD TO SEE YOU.
SAME HERE, CLARK. HOW'S THE REST OF THE JUSTICE LEAGUE HOLDING UP?
YOU KNOW HOW IT IS. IF IT ISN'T ONE THING, IT'S ANOTHER.
LOIS AND JON ARE DOING GREAT, THOUGH.
FINGERS CROSSED JON FORGIVES ME FOR MOVING HIM AWAY FROM HAMILTON COUNTY AND INTO DOWNTOWN METROPOLIS.

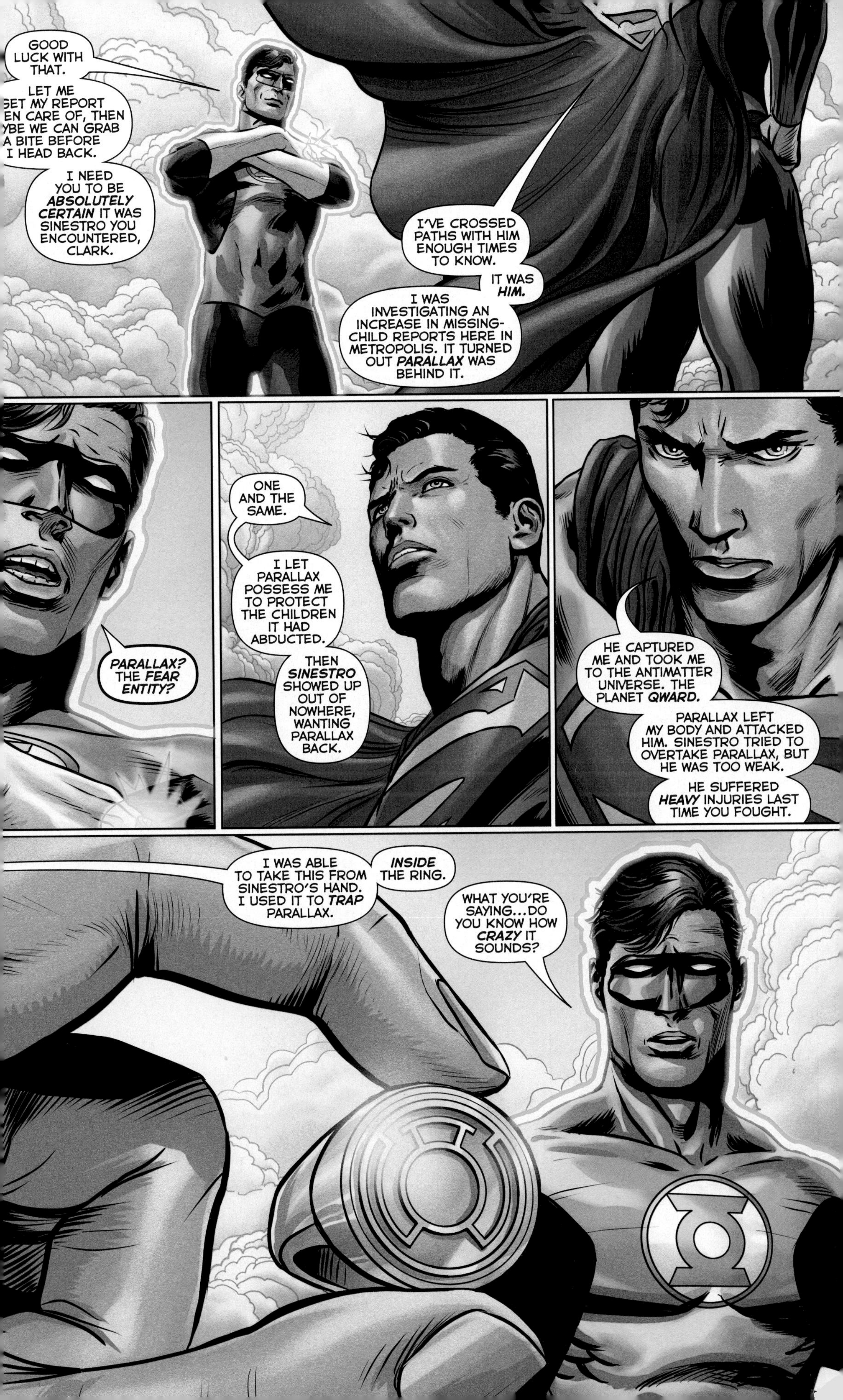
GOOD LUCK WITH THAT.
LET ME GET MY REPORT EN CARE OF, THEN YBE WE CAN GRAB A BITE BEFORE I HEAD BACK.
I NEED YOU TO BE ABSOLUTELY CERTAIN IT WAS SINESTRO YOU ENCOUNTERED, CLARK.
I'VE CROSSED PATHS WITH HIM ENOUGH TIMES TO KNOW.
IT WAS HIM.
I WAS INVESTIGATING AN INCREASE IN MISSING-CHILD REPORTS HERE IN METROPOLIS. IT TURNED OUT PARALLAX WAS BEHIND IT.
PARALLAX? THE FEAR ENTITY?
ONE AND THE SAME.
I LET PARALLAX POSSESS ME TO PROTECT THE CHILDREN IT HAD ABDUCTED.
THEN SINESTRO SHOWED UP OUT OF NOWHERE, WANTING PARALLAX BACK.
HE CAPTURED ME AND TOOK ME TO THE ANTIMATTER UNIVERSE. THE PLANET QWARD.
PARALLAX LEFT MY BODY AND ATTACKED HIM. SINESTRO TRIED TO OVERTAKE PARALLAX, BUT HE WAS TOO WEAK.
HE SUFFERED HEAVY INJURIES LAST TIME YOU FOUGHT.
I WAS ABLE TO TAKE THIS FROM SINESTRO'S HAND. I USED IT TO TRAP PARALLAX.
INSIDE THE RING.
WHAT YOU'RE SAYING...DO YOU KNOW HOW CRAZY IT SOUNDS?

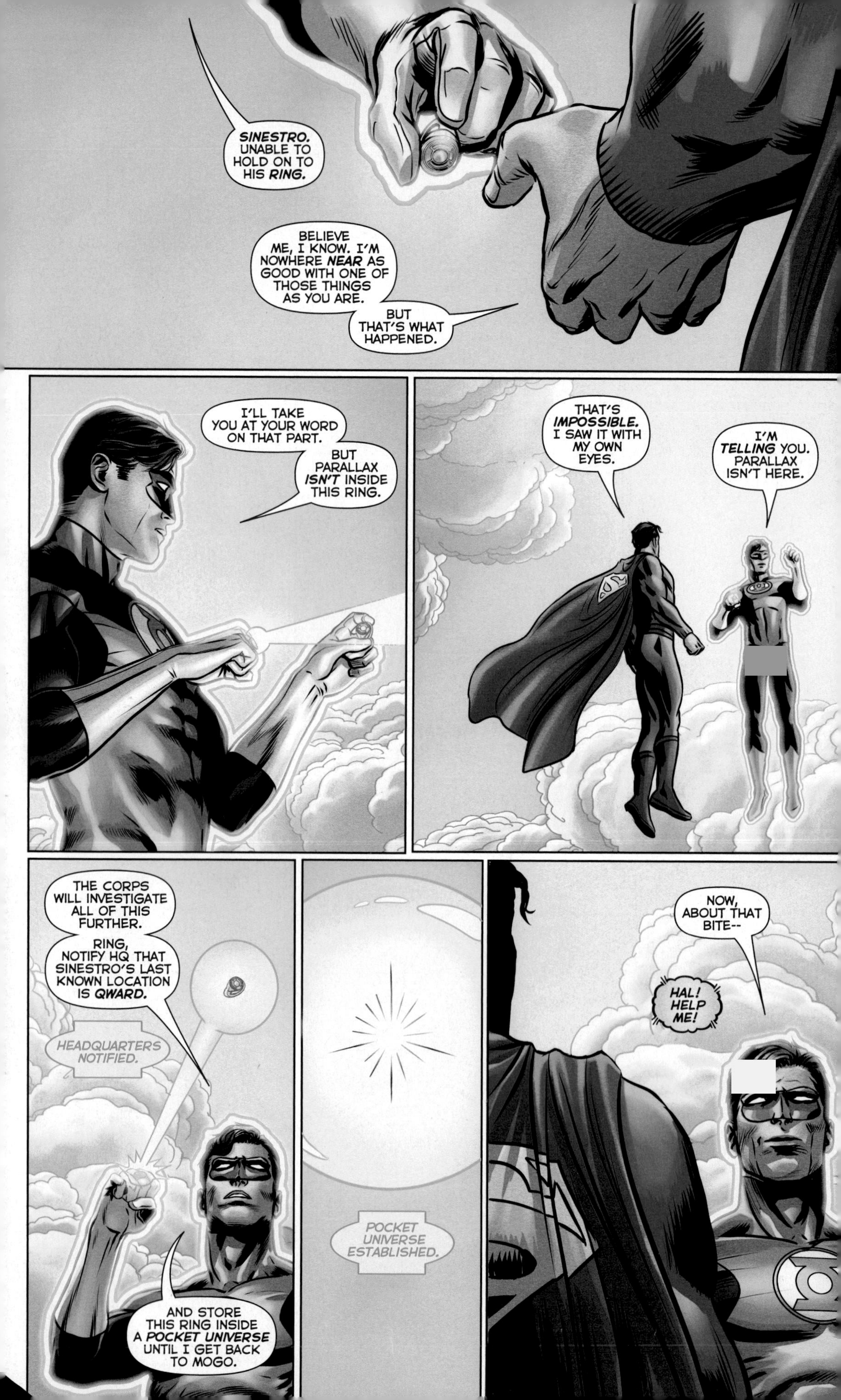
SINESTRO. UNABLE TO HOLD ON TO HIS RING.
BELIEVE ME, I KNOW. I'M NOWHERE NEAR AS GOOD WITH ONE OF THOSE THINGS AS YOU ARE.
BUT THAT'S WHAT HAPPENED.
I'LL TAKE YOU AT YOUR WORD ON THAT PART.
BUT PARALLAX ISN'T INSIDE THIS RING.
THAT'S IMPOSSIBLE. I SAW IT WITH MY OWN EYES.
I'M TELLING YOU. PARALLAX ISN'T HERE.
THE CORPS WILL INVESTIGATE ALL OF THIS FURTHER.
RING, NOTIFY HQ THAT SINESTRO'S LAST KNOWN LOCATION IS QWARD.
HEADQUARTERS NOTIFIED.
AND STORE THIS RING INSIDE A POCKET UNIVERSE UNTIL I GET BACK TO MOGO.
POCKET UNIVERSE ESTABLISHED.
NOW, ABOUT THAT BITE--
HAL! HELP ME!

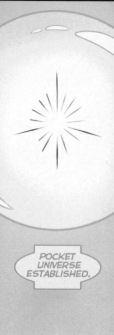

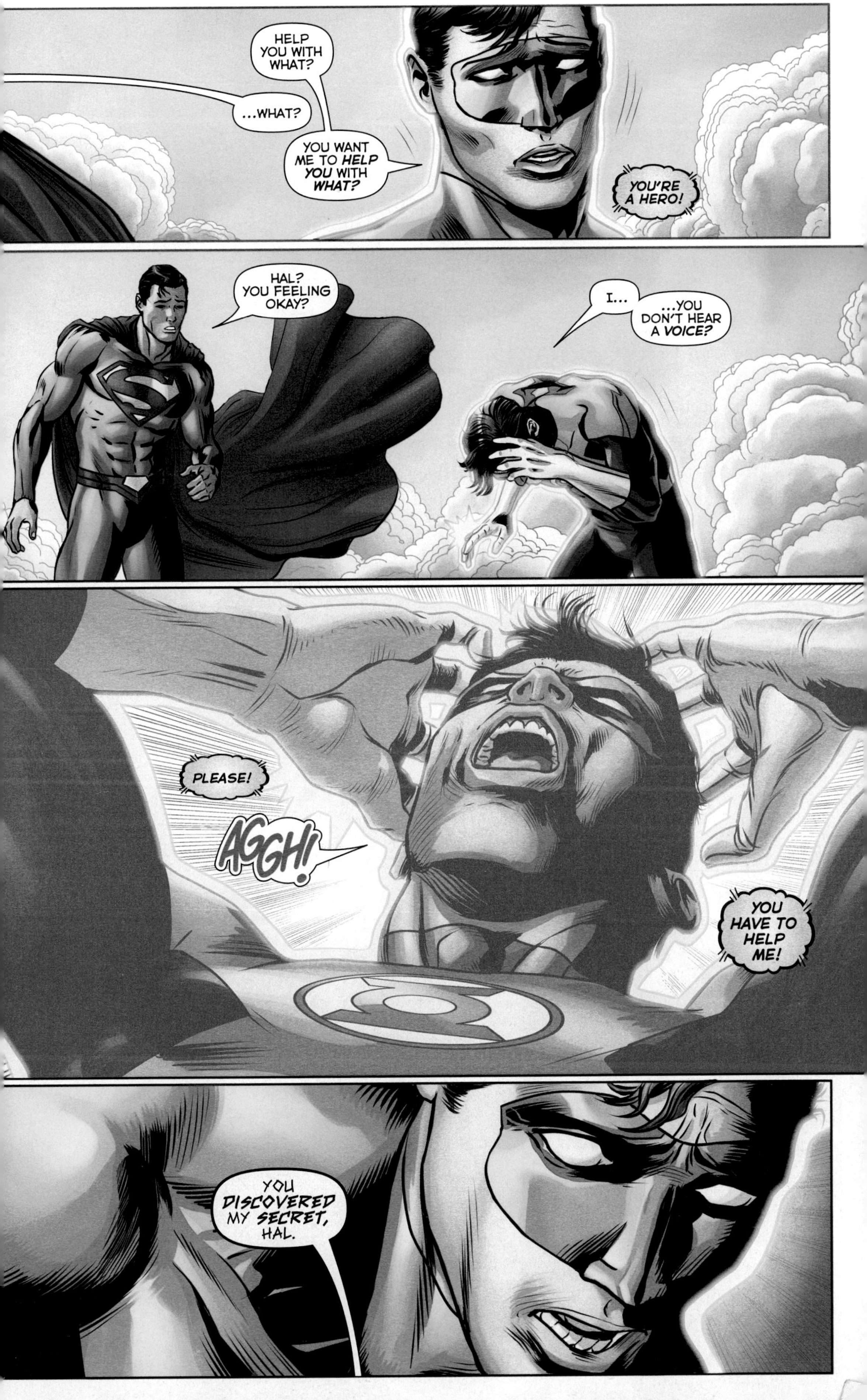
HELP YOU WITH WHAT?
...WHAT?
YOU WANT ME TO HELP YOU WITH WHAT?
YOU'RE A HERO!
HAL? YOU FEELING OKAY?
I...
...YOU DON'T HEAR A VOICE?
PLEASE!
AGGH!
YOU HAVE TO HELP ME!
YOU DISCOVERED MY SECRET, HAL.

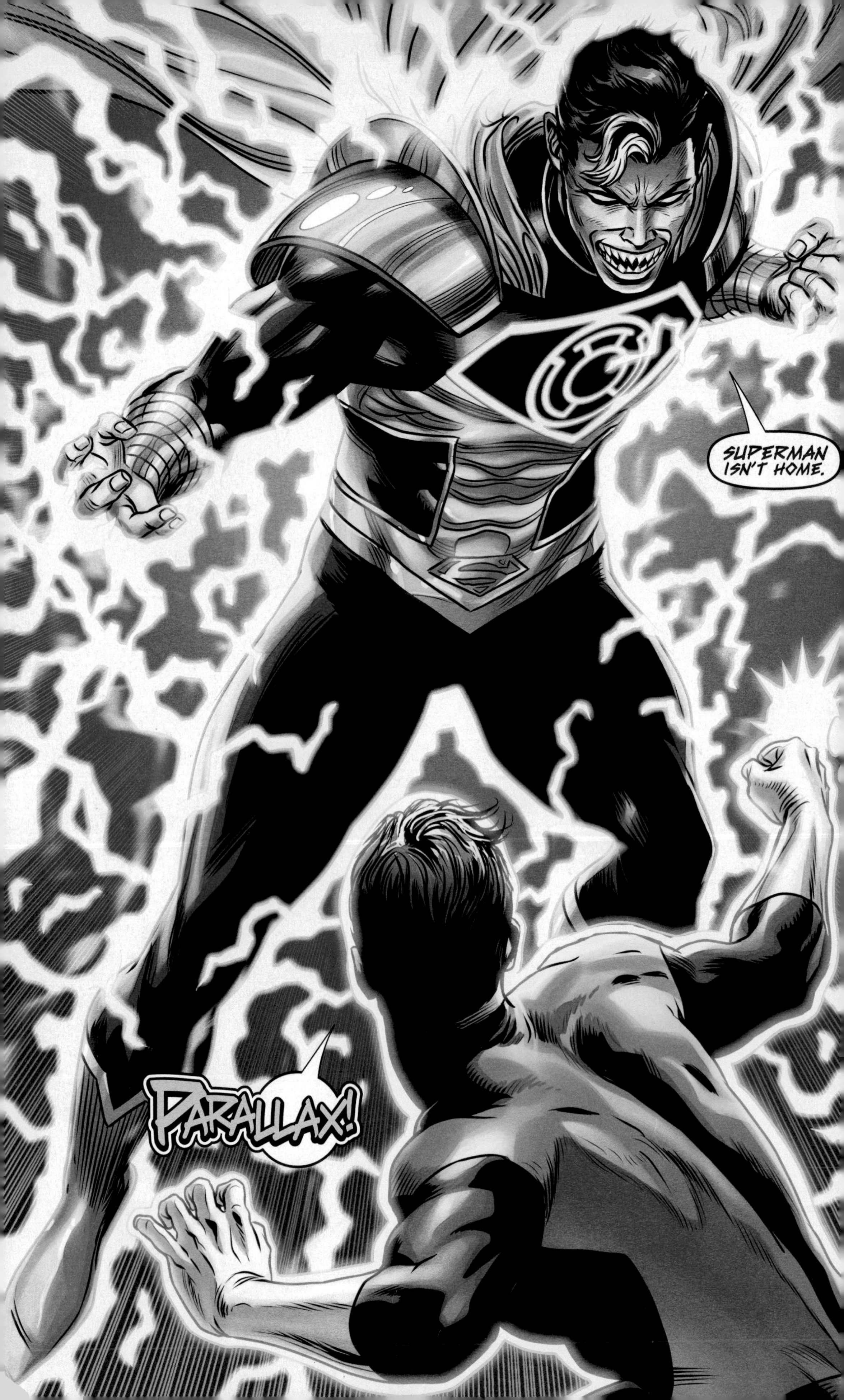
SUPERMAN ISN'T HOME.
PARALLAX!

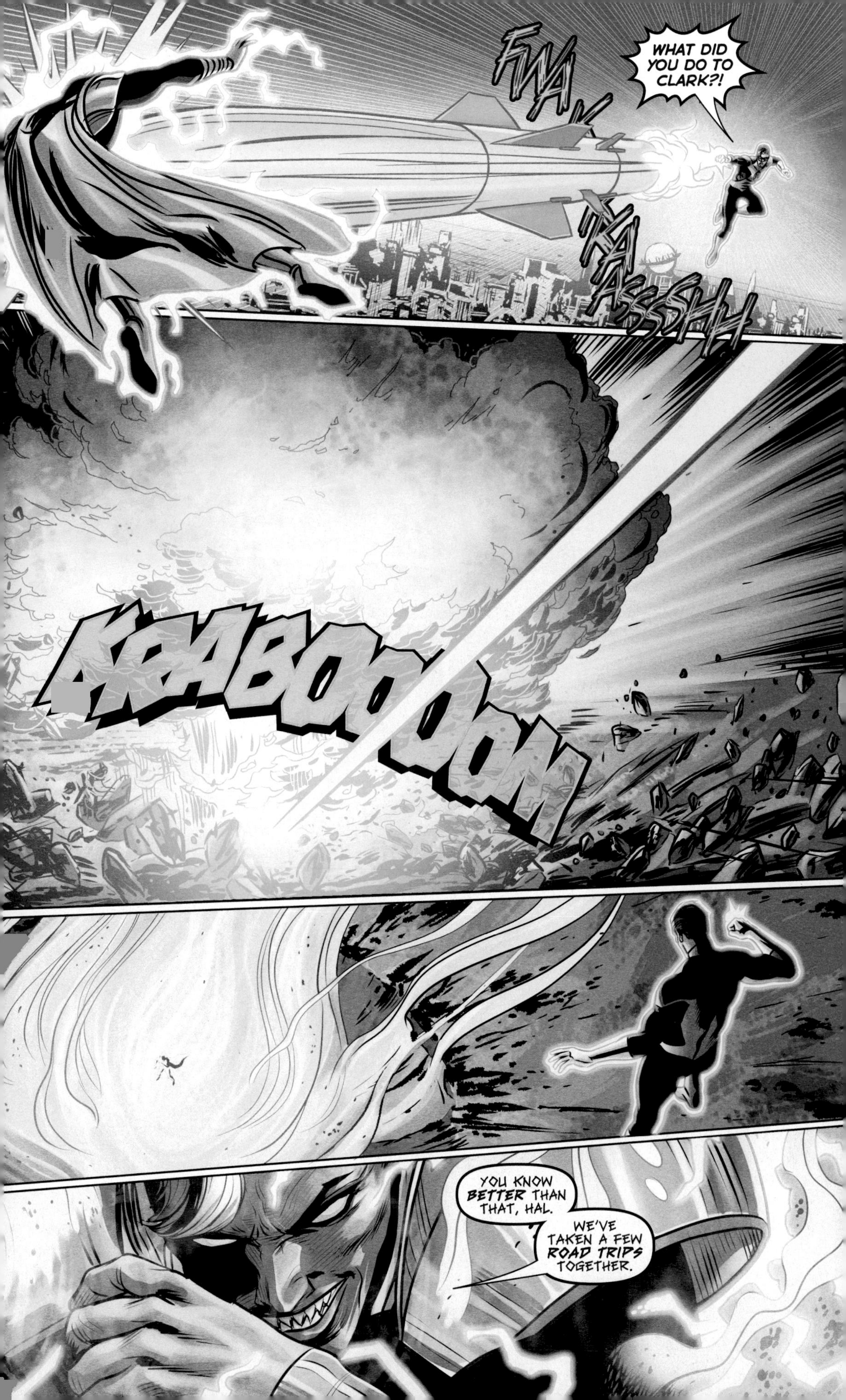
FWAAK
WHAT DID YOU DO TO CLARK?!
KRAASSSHH
KRABOOOOOM
YOU KNOW BETTER THAN THAT, HAL.
WE'VE TAKEN A FEW ROAD TRIPS TOGETHER.

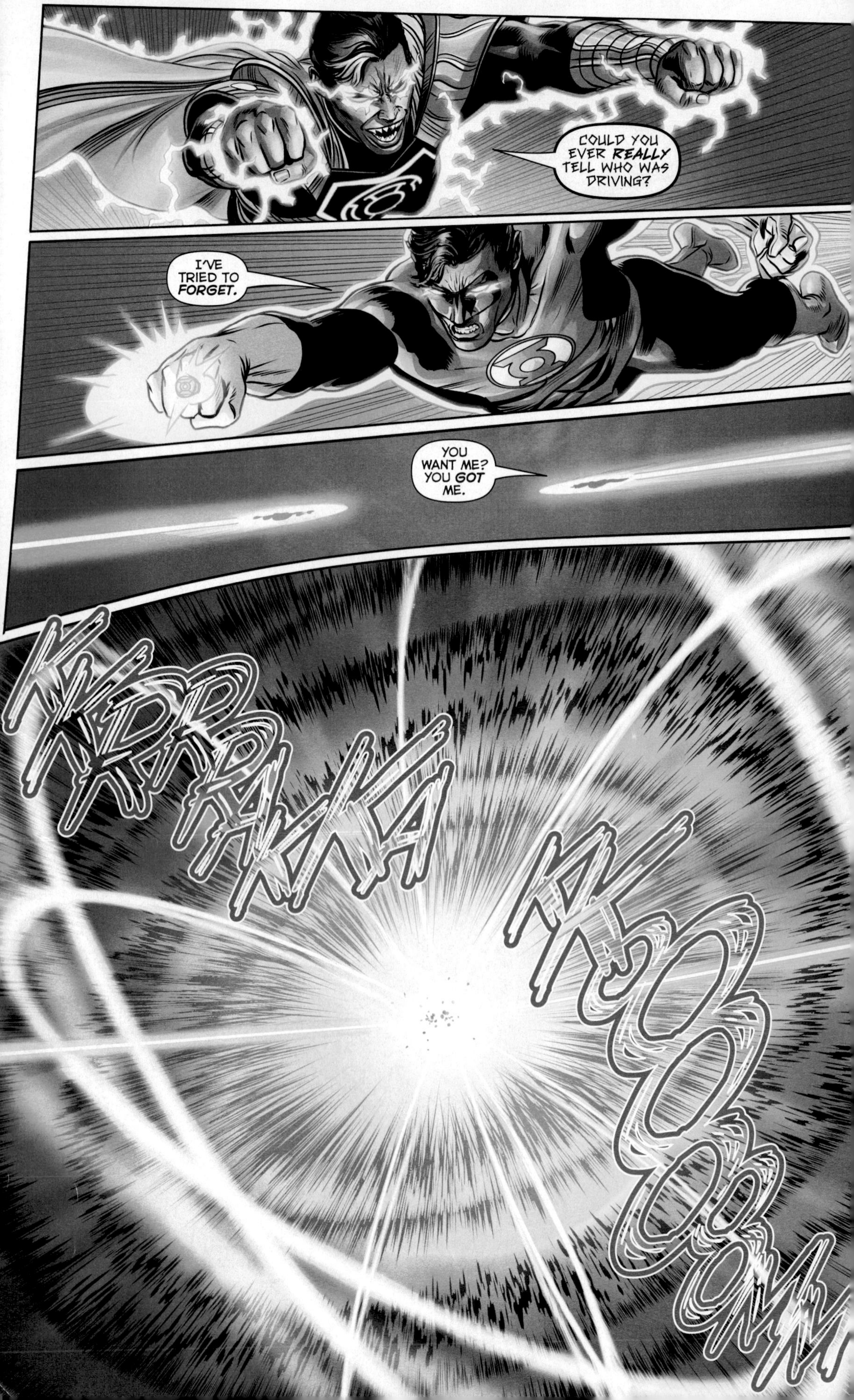
COULD YOU EVER REALLY TELL WHO WAS DRIVING?
I'VE TRIED TO FORGET.
YOU WANT ME? YOU GOT ME.

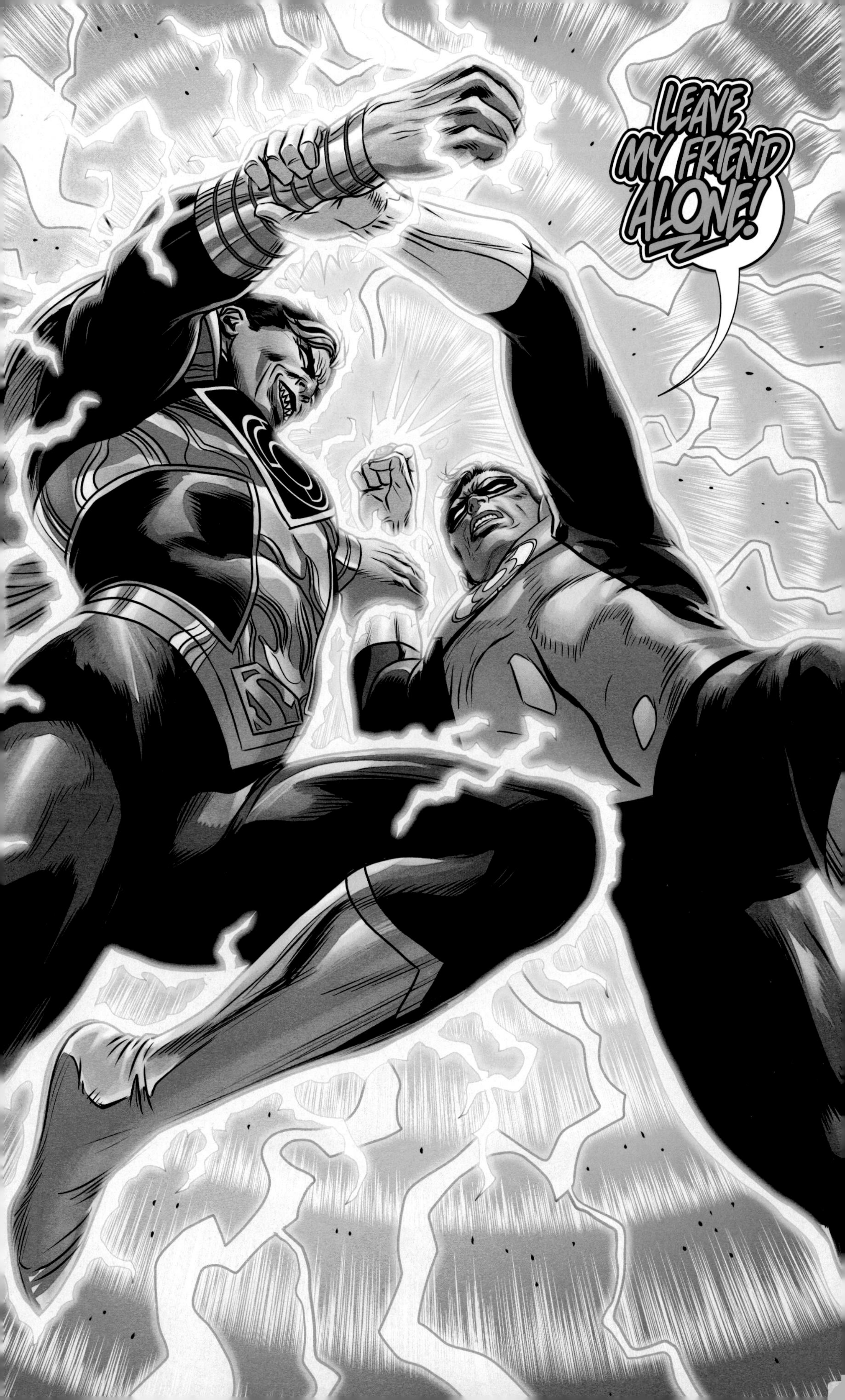
LEAVE MY FRIEND ALONE!

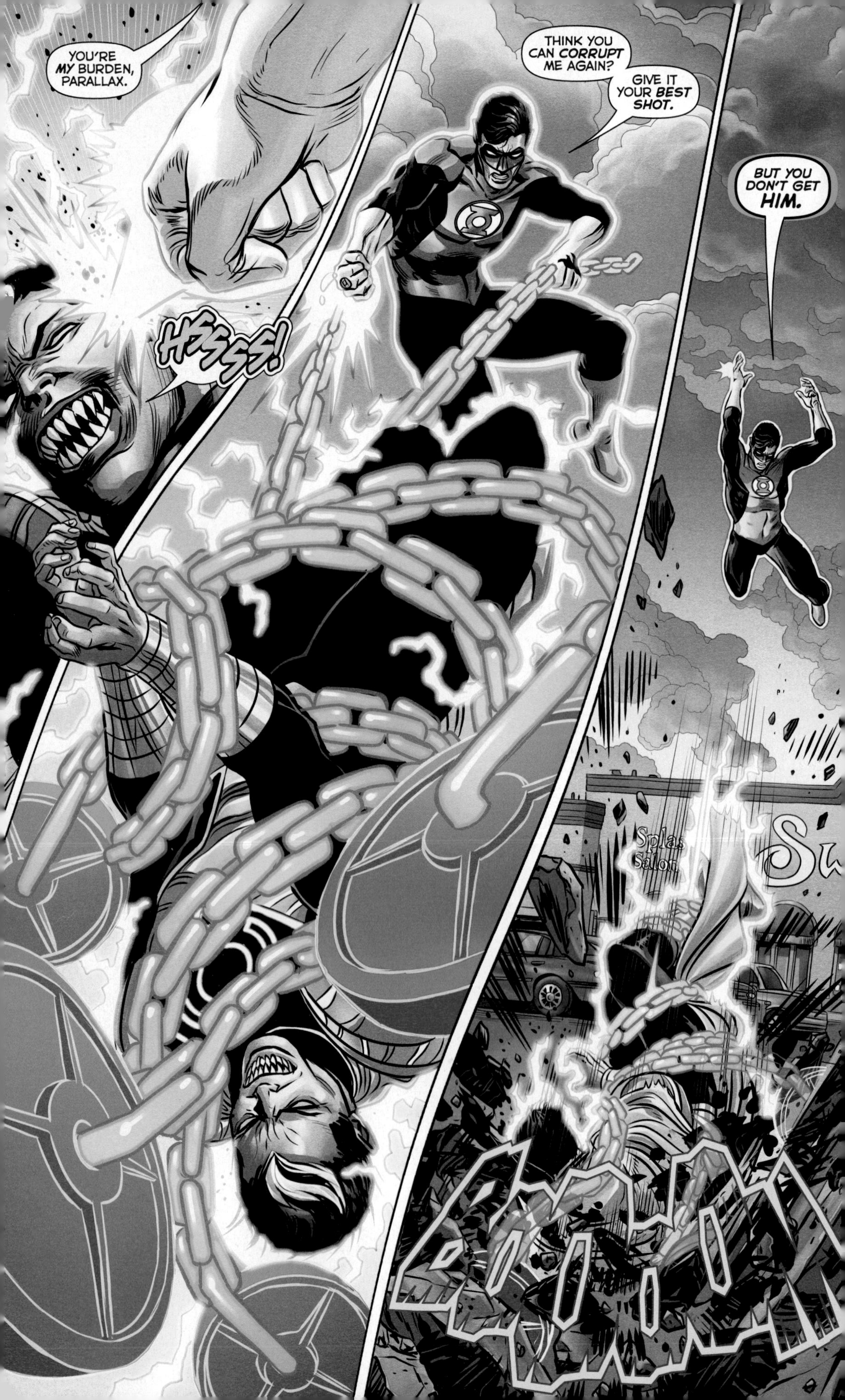
YOU'RE MY BURDEN, PARALLAX.
HSSSS!
THINK YOU CAN CORRUPT ME AGAIN?
GIVE IT YOUR BEST SHOT.
BUT YOU DON'T GET HIM.
Splas
Salon

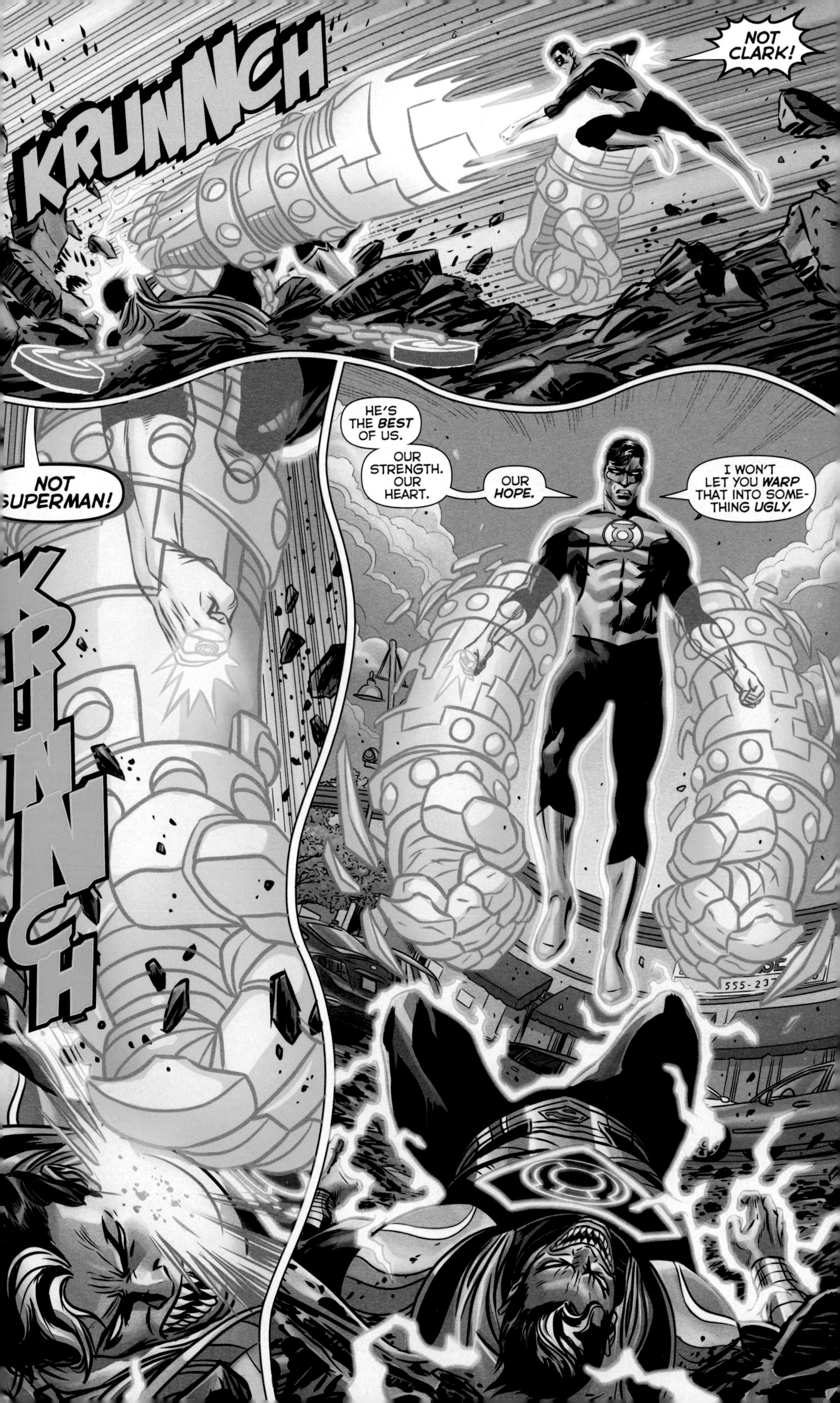
KRUNNCH
NOT CLARK!
NOT SUPERMAN!
KRUNNCH
HE'S THE BEST OF US.
OUR STRENGTH. OUR HEART.
OUR HOPE.
I WON'T LET YOU WARP THAT INTO SOMETHING UGLY.
555-237

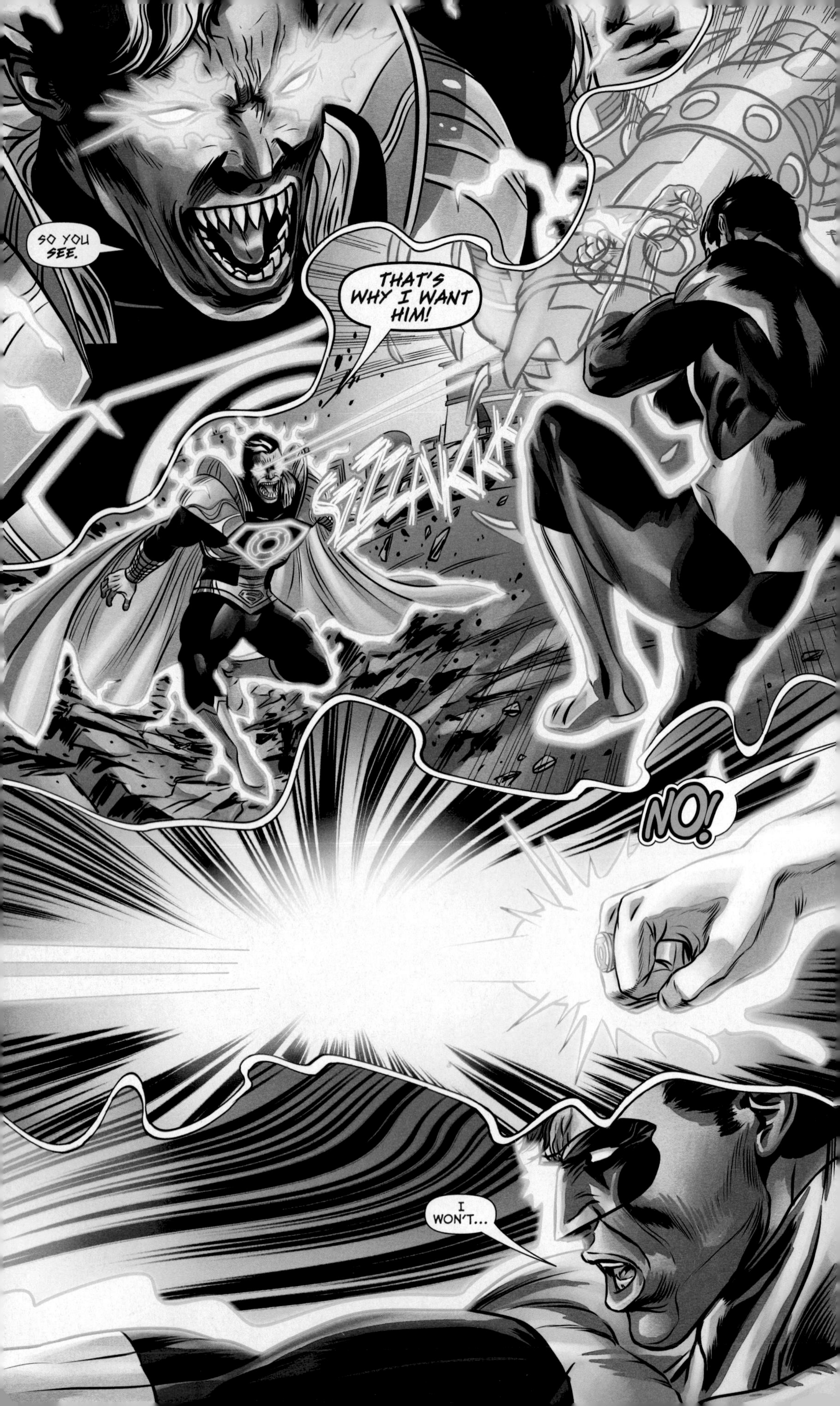
SO YOU SEE.
THAT'S WHY I WANT HIM!
SZZZAKKK
NO!
I WON'T...

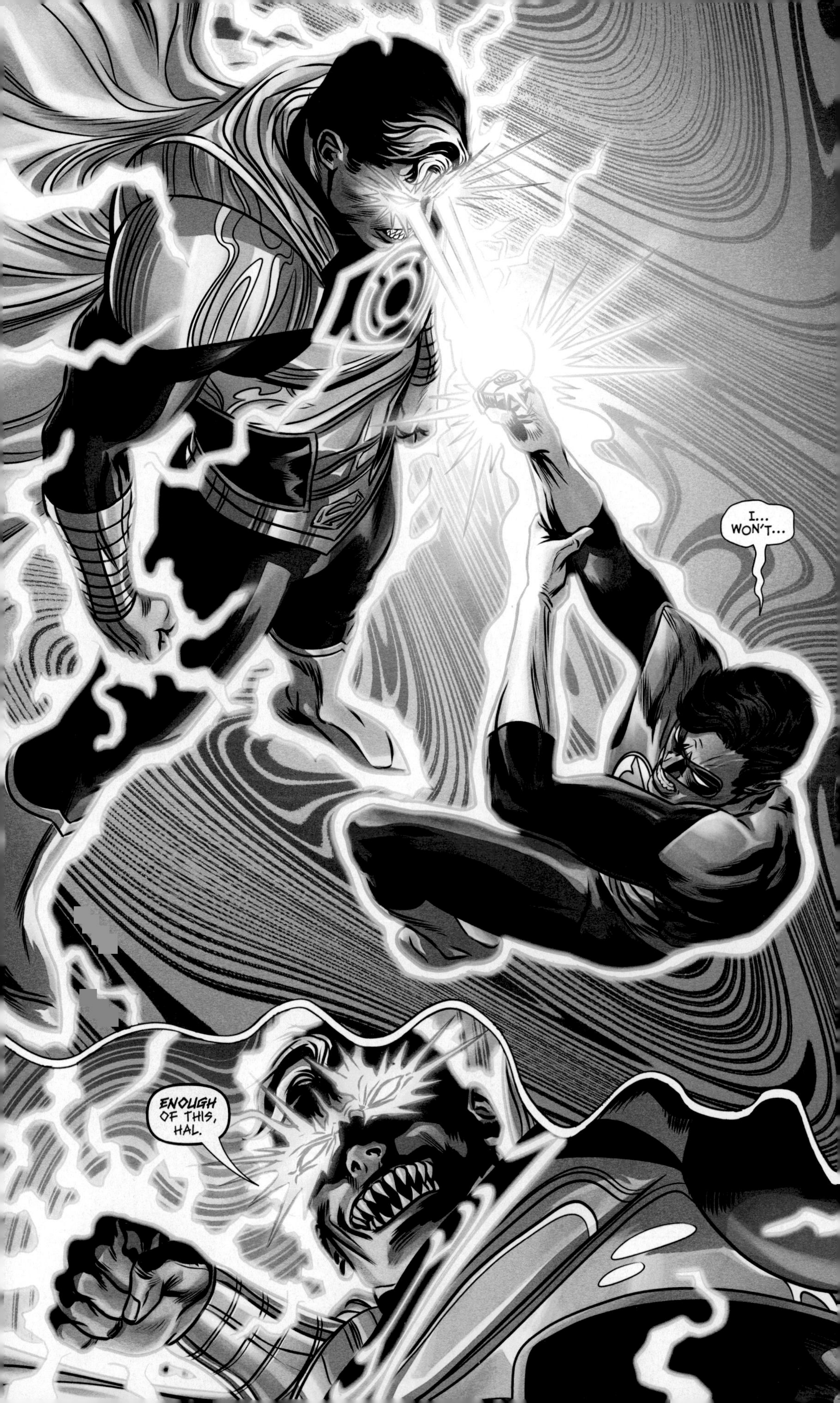
I... WON'T...
ENOUGH OF THIS, HAL.

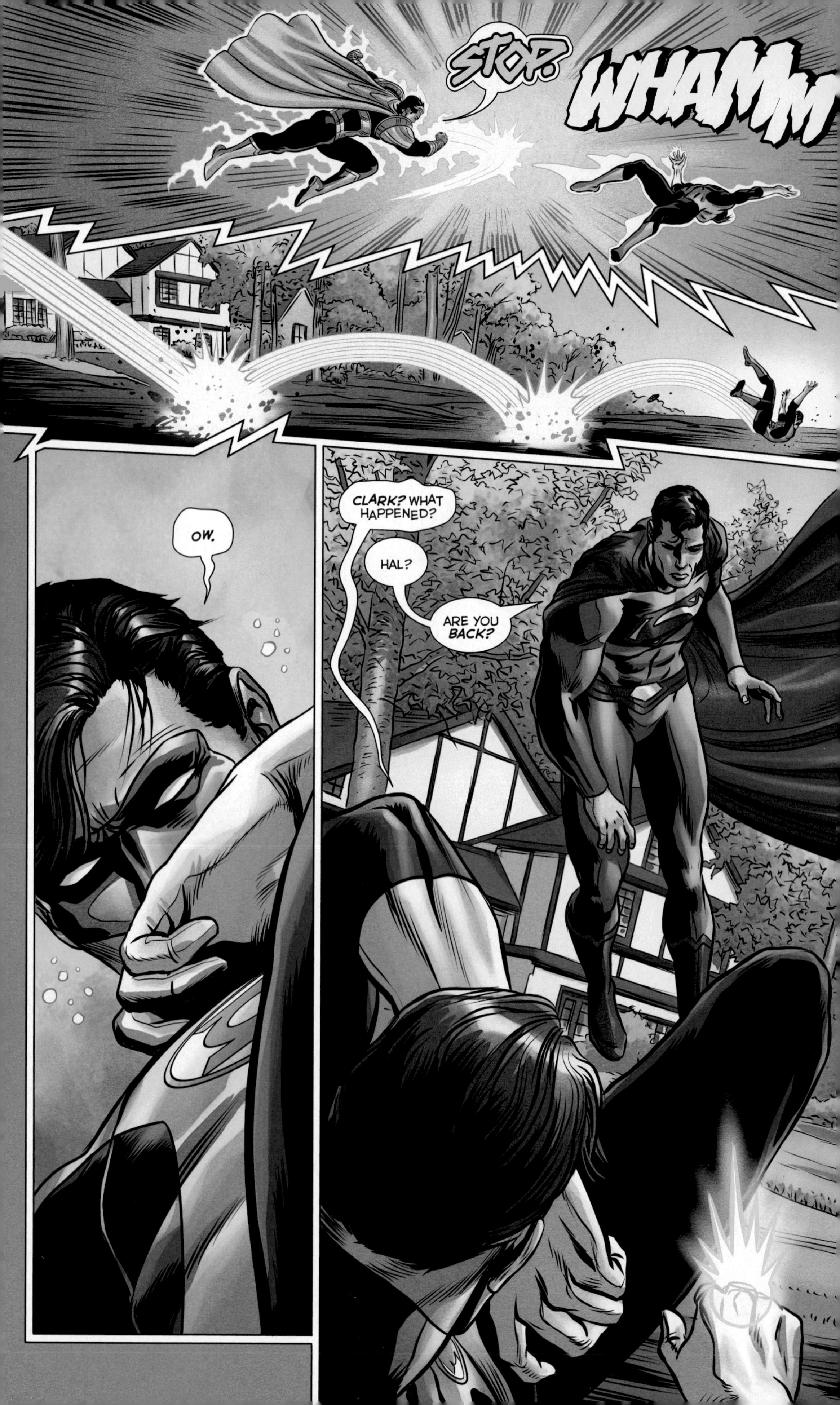
STOP.
WHAMM
OW.
CLARK? WHAT HAPPENED?
HAL?
ARE YOU BACK?

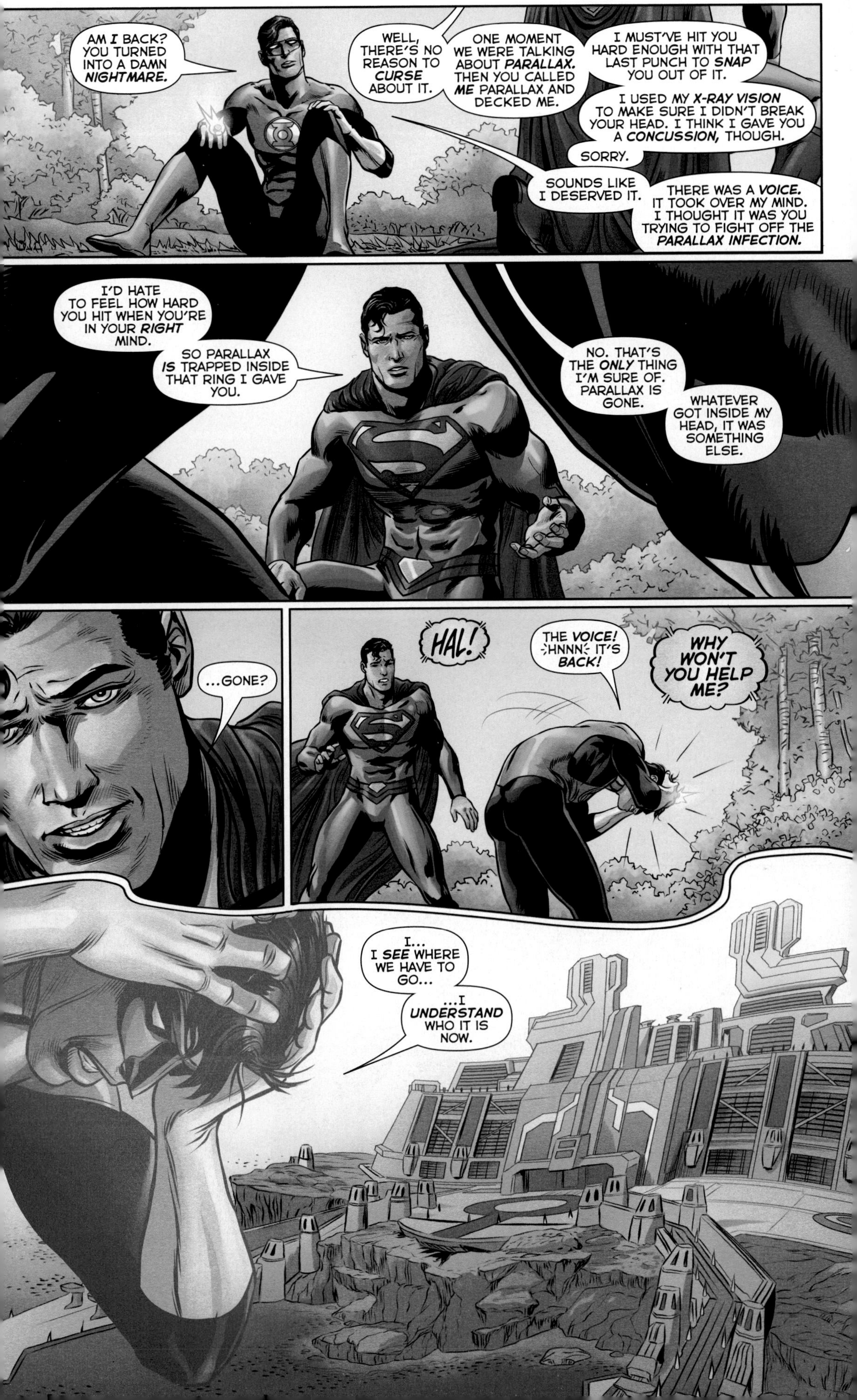

AM I BACK? YOU TURNED INTO A DAMN NIGHTMARE.
WELL, THERE'S NO REASON TO CURSE ABOUT IT.
ONE MOMENT WE WERE TALKING ABOUT PARALLAX. THEN YOU CALLED ME PARALLAX AND DECKED ME.
I MUST'VE HIT YOU HARD ENOUGH WITH THAT LAST PUNCH TO SNAP YOU OUT OF IT.
I USED MY X-RAY VISION TO MAKE SURE I DIDN'T BREAK YOUR HEAD. I THINK I GAVE YOU A CONCUSSION, THOUGH.
SORRY.
SOUNDS LIKE I DESERVED IT.
THERE WAS A VOICE. IT TOOK OVER MY MIND. I THOUGHT IT WAS YOU TRYING TO FIGHT OFF THE PARALLAX INFECTION.
I'D HATE TO FEEL HOW HARD YOU HIT WHEN YOU'RE IN YOUR RIGHT MIND.
SO PARALLAX IS TRAPPED INSIDE THAT RING I GAVE YOU.
NO. THAT'S THE ONLY THING I'M SURE OF. PARALLAX IS GONE.
WHATEVER GOT INSIDE MY HEAD, IT WAS SOMETHING ELSE.
...GONE?
HAL!
THE VOICE! HNNN IT'S BACK!
WHY WON'T YOU HELP ME?
I... I SEE WHERE WE HAVE TO GO...
...I UNDERSTAND WHO IT IS NOW.

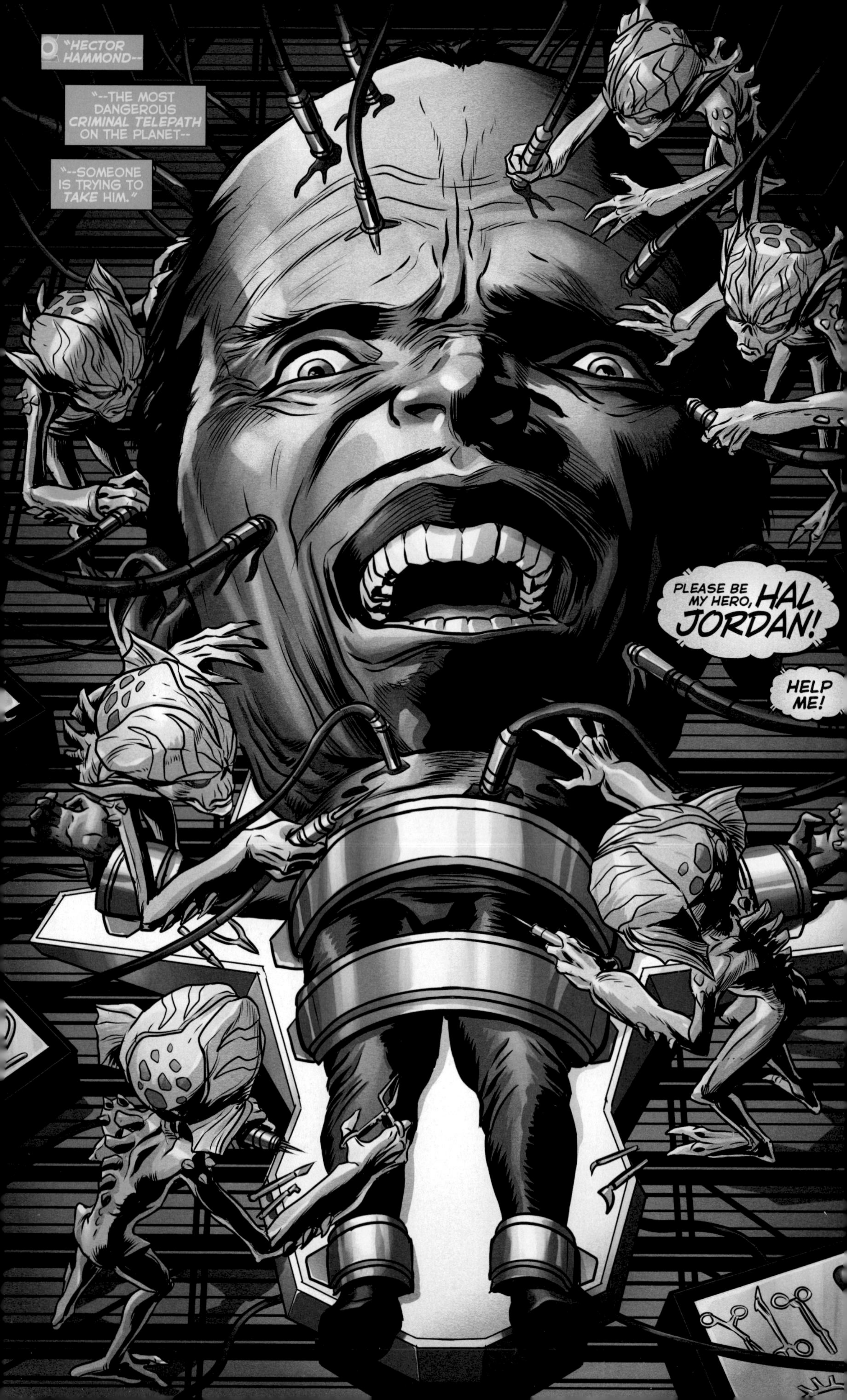
"HECTOR HAMMOND--
"--THE MOST DANGEROUS CRIMINAL TELEPATH ON THE PLANET--
"--SOMEONE IS TRYING TO TAKE HIM."
PLEASE BE MY HERO, HAL JORDAN!
HELP ME!

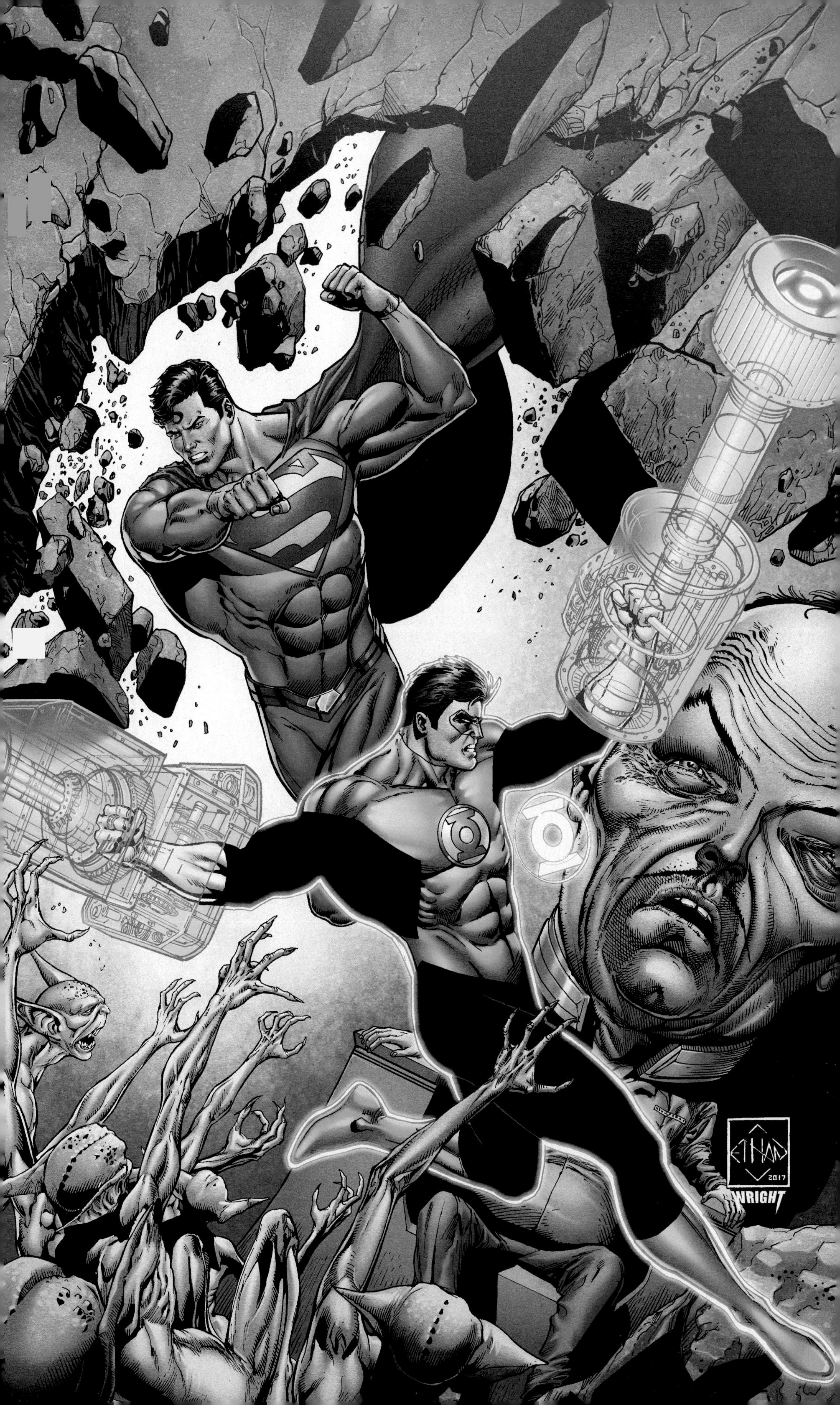

ETHAN
2017
WRIGHT

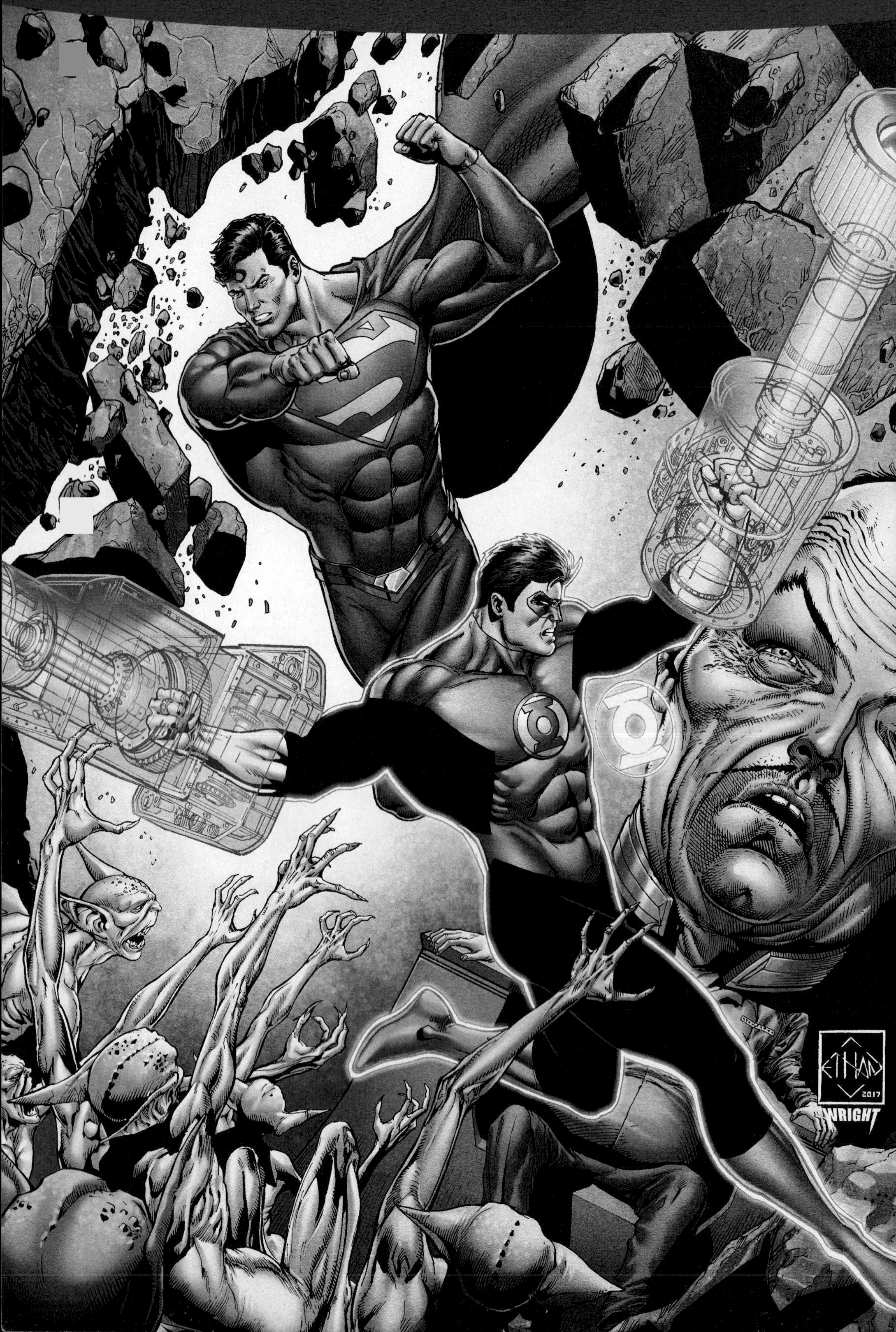
2017
WRIGHT

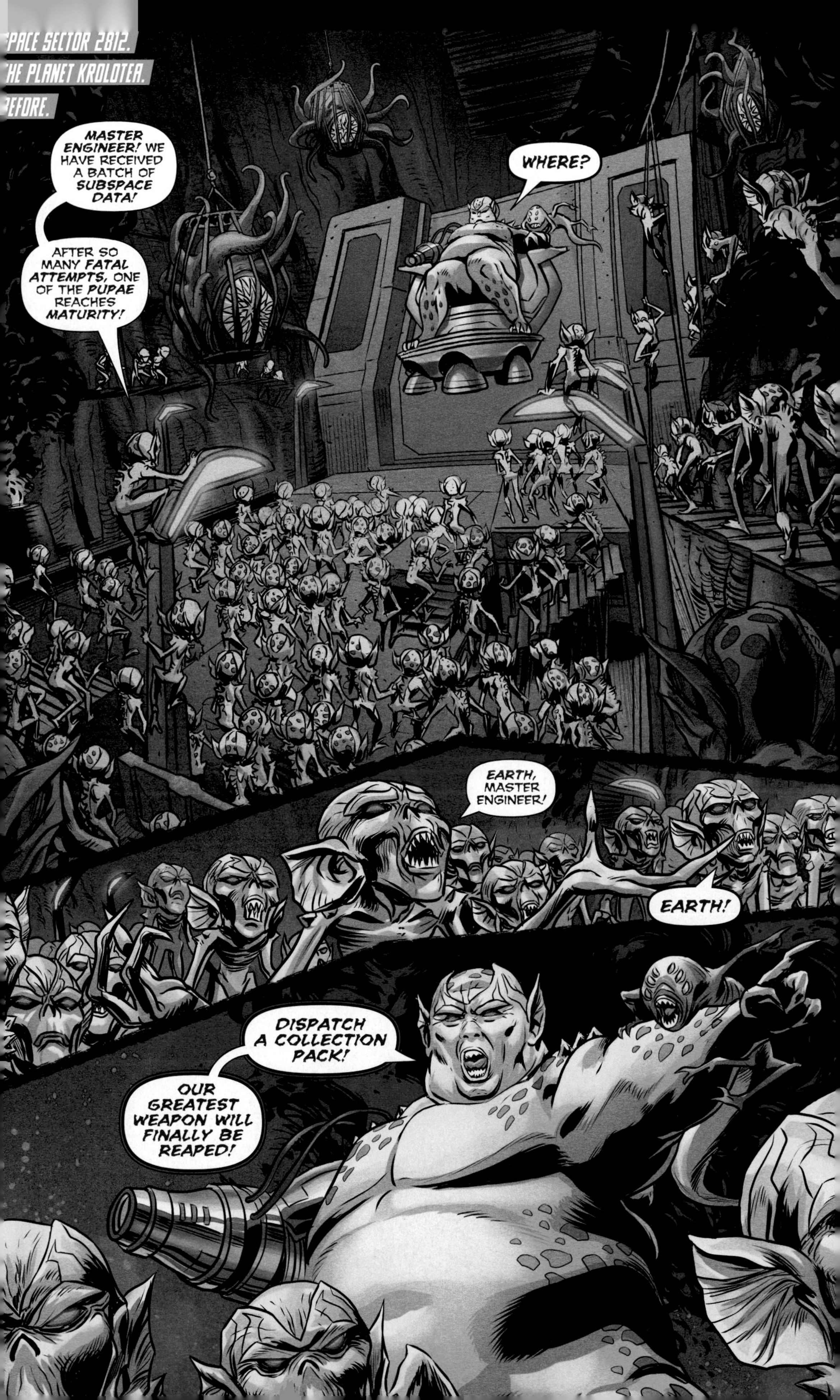
PACE SECTOR 2812.
HE PLANET KROLOTER.
EFORE.
MASTER ENGINEER! WE HAVE RECEIVED A BATCH OF SUBSPACE DATA!
AFTER SO MANY FATAL ATTEMPTS, ONE OF THE PUPAE REACHES MATURITY!
WHERE?
EARTH, MASTER ENGINEER!
EARTH!
DISPATCH A COLLECTION PACK!
OUR GREATEST WEAPON WILL FINALLY BE REAPED!

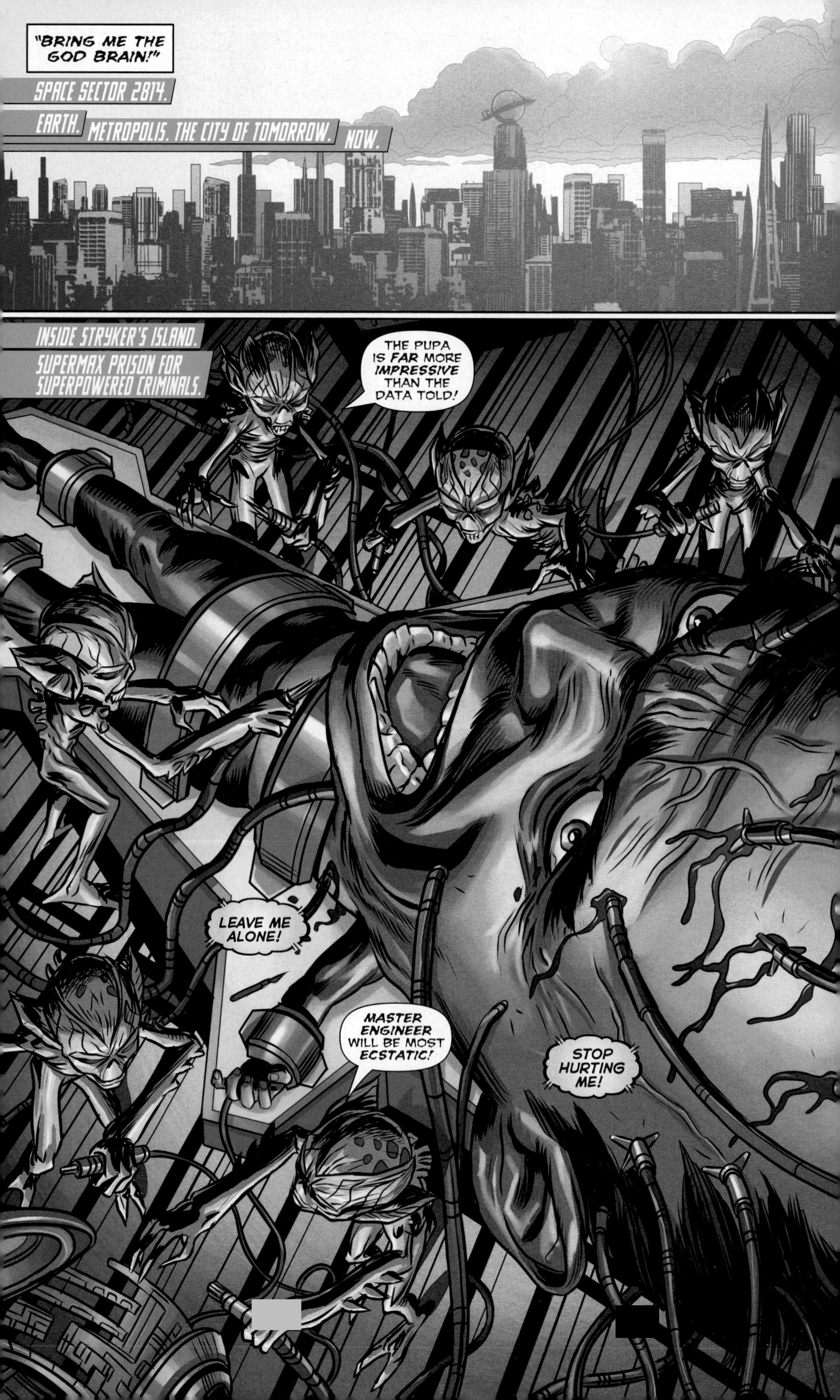

"BRING ME THE GOD BRAIN!"
SPACE SECTOR 2814.
EARTH.
METROPOLIS. THE CITY OF TOMORROW.
NOW.
INSIDE STRYKER'S ISLAND.
SUPERMAX PRISON FOR SUPERPOWERED CRIMINALS.
THE PUPA IS FAR MORE IMPRESSIVE THAN THE DATA TOLD!
LEAVE ME ALONE!
MASTER ENGINEER WILL BE MOST ECSTATIC!
STOP HURTING ME!
[redacted]

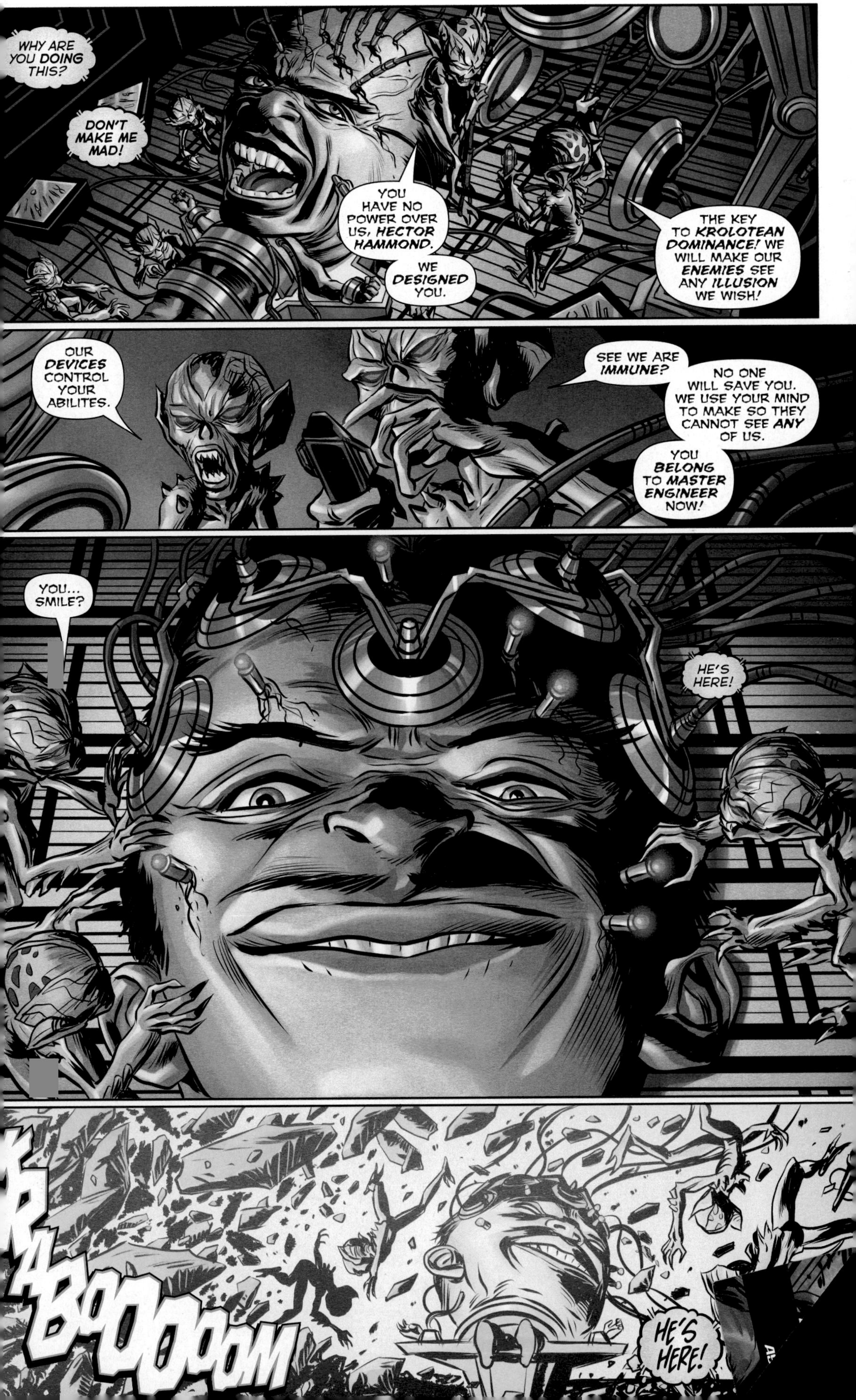

WHY ARE YOU DOING THIS?
DON'T MAKE ME MAD!
YOU HAVE NO POWER OVER US, HECTOR HAMMOND.
WE DESIGNED YOU.
THE KEY TO KROLOTEAN DOMINANCE! WE WILL MAKE OUR ENEMIES SEE ANY ILLUSION WE WISH!
OUR DEVICES CONTROL YOUR ABILITES.
SEE WE ARE IMMUNE?
NO ONE WILL SAVE YOU. WE USE YOUR MIND TO MAKE SO THEY CANNOT SEE ANY OF US.
YOU BELONG TO MASTER ENGINEER NOW!
YOU... SMILE?
HE'S HERE!
KRABOOOOOM
HE'S HERE!

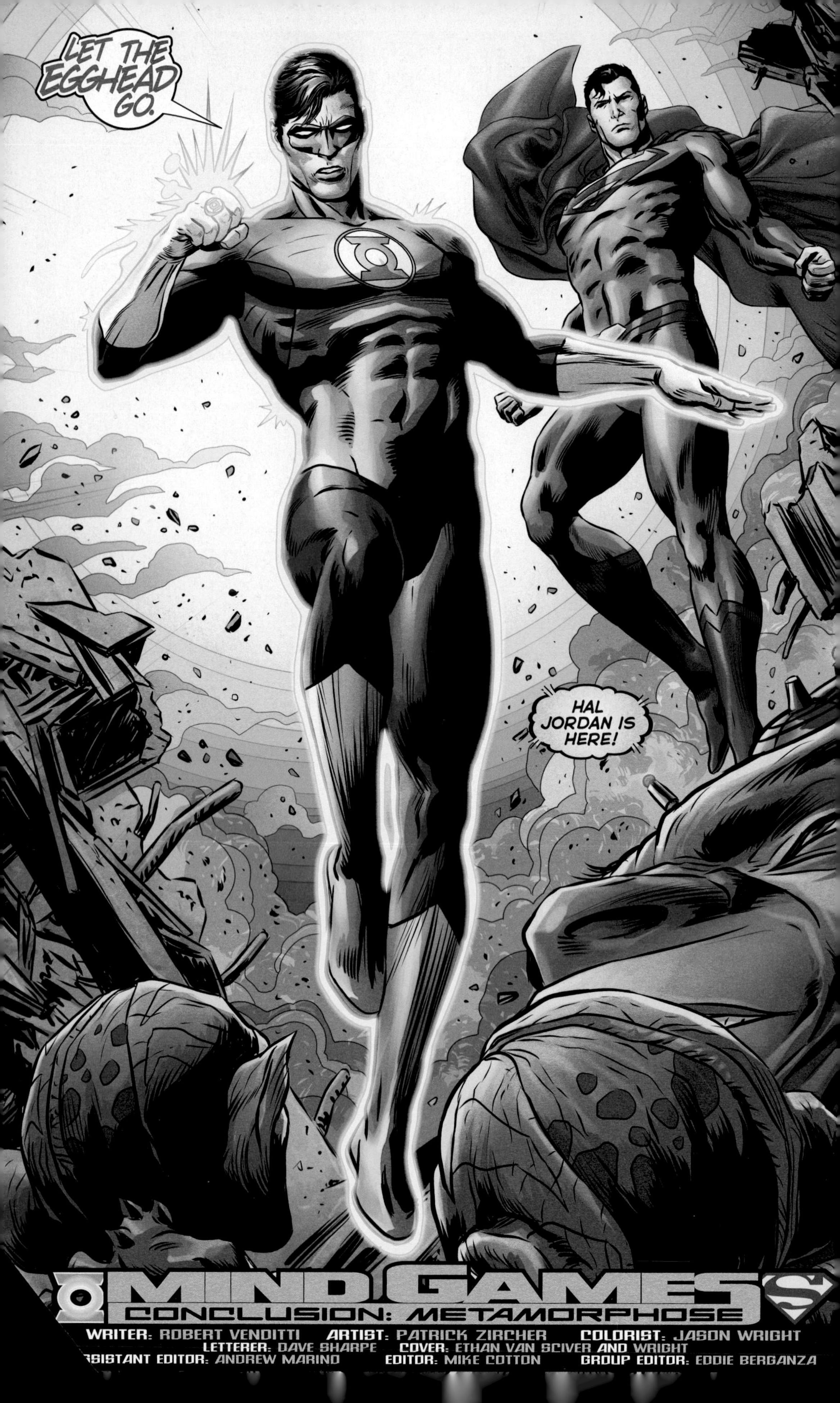

LET THE EGGHEAD GO.
HAL JORDAN IS HERE!
MIND GAMES
CONCLUSION: METAMORPHOSE
WRITER: ROBERT VENDITTI ARTIST: PATRICK ZIRCHER COLORIST: JASON WRIGHT
LETTERER: DAVE SHARPE COVER: ETHAN VAN SCIVER AND WRIGHT
SSISTANT EDITOR: ANDREW MARINO EDITOR: MIKE COTTON GROUP EDITOR: EDDIE BERGANZA

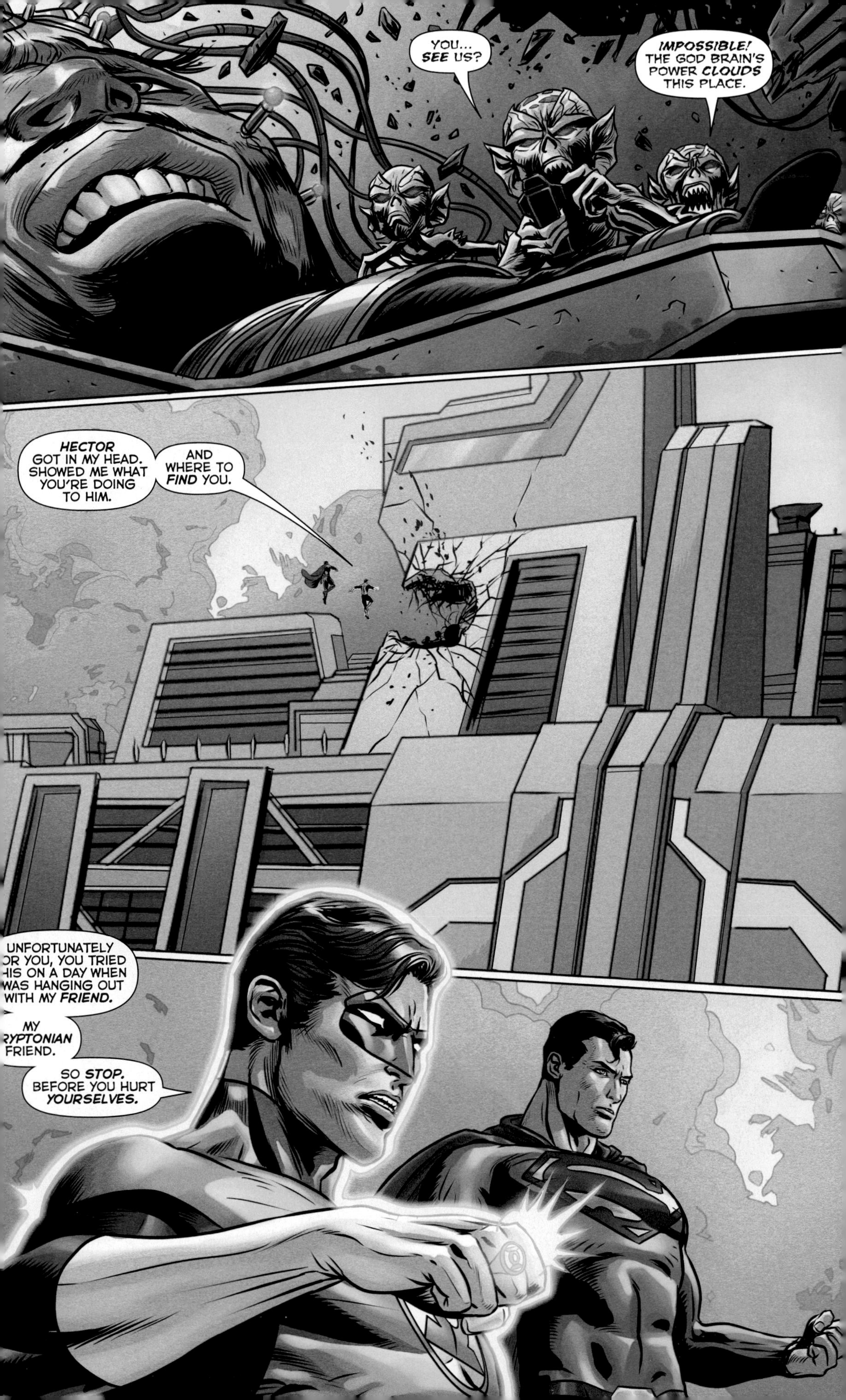

YOU... SEE US?
IMPOSSIBLE! THE GOD BRAIN'S POWER CLOUDS THIS PLACE.
HECTOR GOT IN MY HEAD. SHOWED ME WHAT YOU'RE DOING TO HIM.
AND WHERE TO FIND YOU.
UNFORTUNATELY OR YOU, YOU TRIED HIS ON A DAY WHEN WAS HANGING OUT WITH MY FRIEND.
MY RYPTONIAN FRIEND.
SO STOP. BEFORE YOU HURT YOURSELVES.

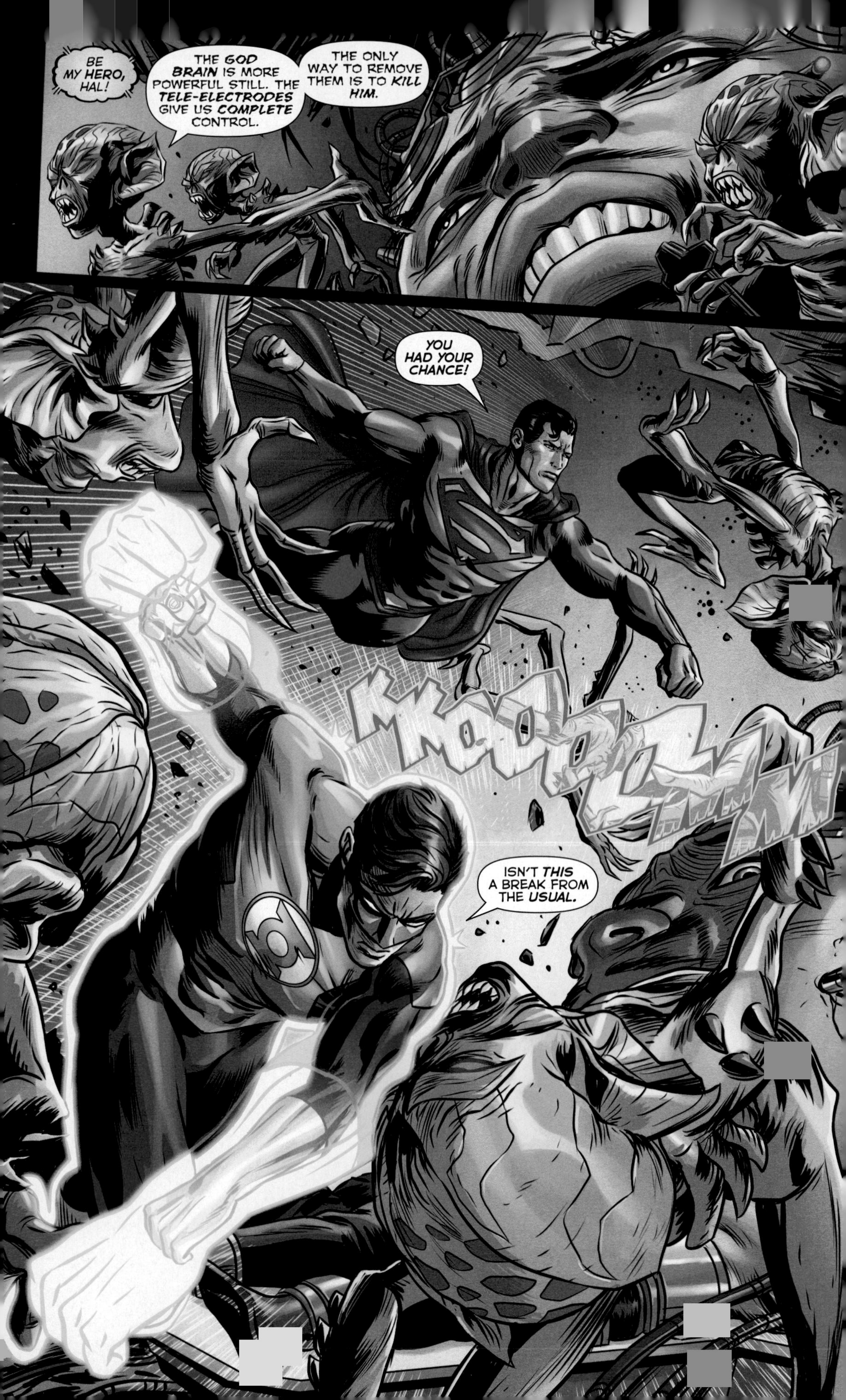
BE MY HERO, HAL!
THE GOD BRAIN IS MORE POWERFUL STILL. THE TELE-ELECTRODES GIVE US COMPLETE CONTROL.
THE ONLY WAY TO REMOVE THEM IS TO KILL HIM.
YOU HAD YOUR CHANCE!
ISN'T THIS A BREAK FROM THE USUAL.

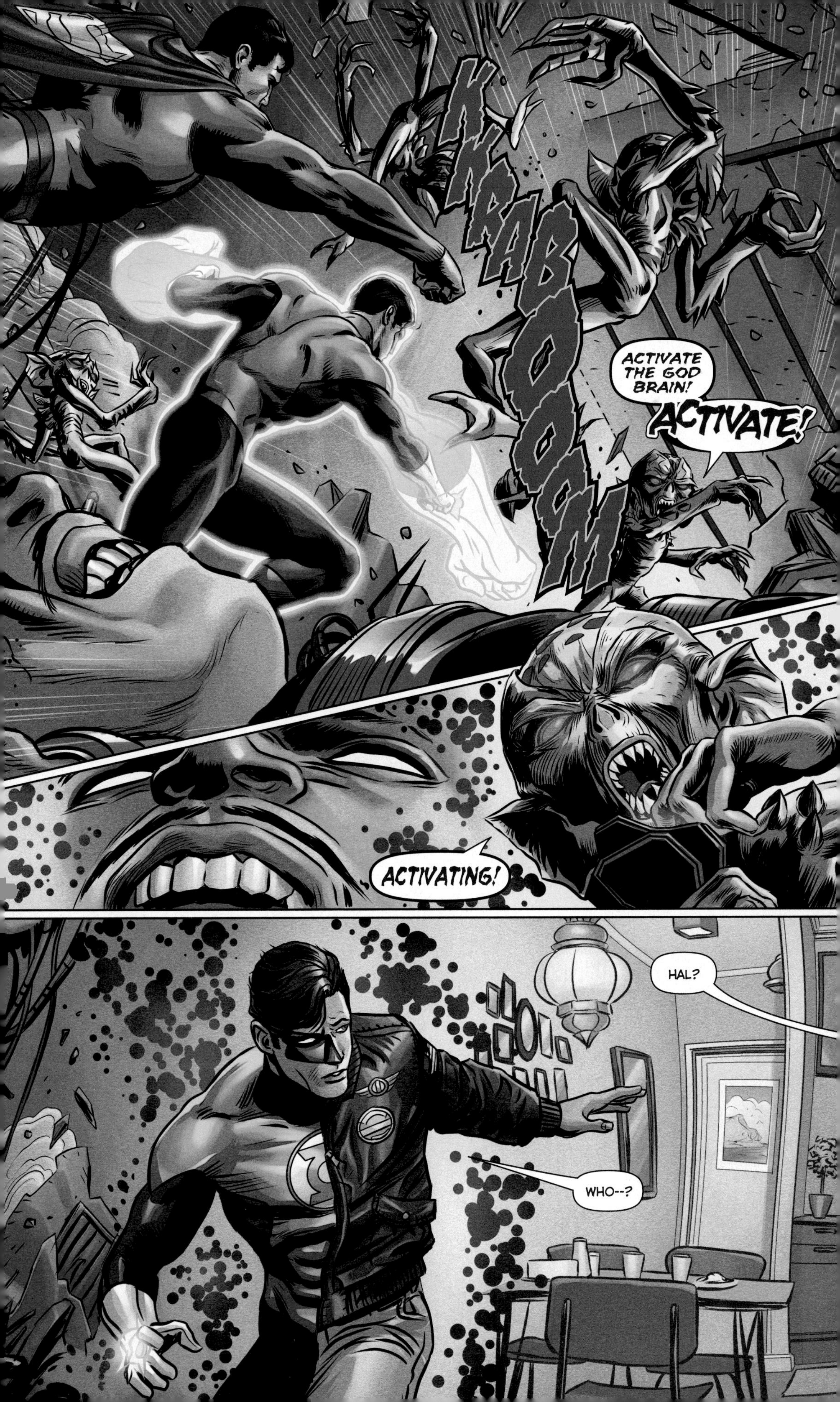
KKRABOOOOM
ACTIVATE THE GOD BRAIN!
ACTIVATE!
ACTIVATING!
HAL?
WHO--?

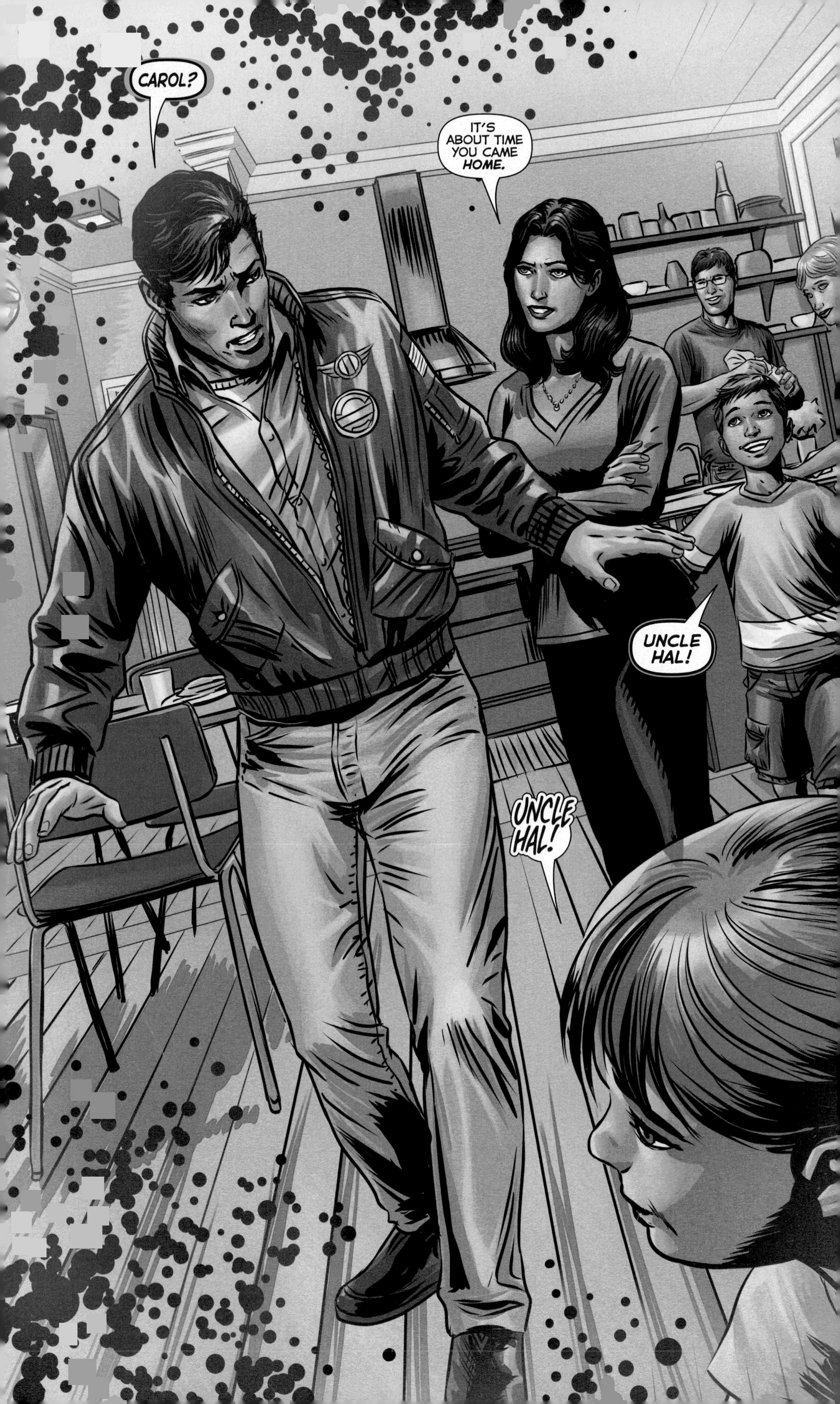
CAROL?
IT'S ABOUT TIME YOU CAME HOME.
UNCLE HAL!
UNCLE HAL!

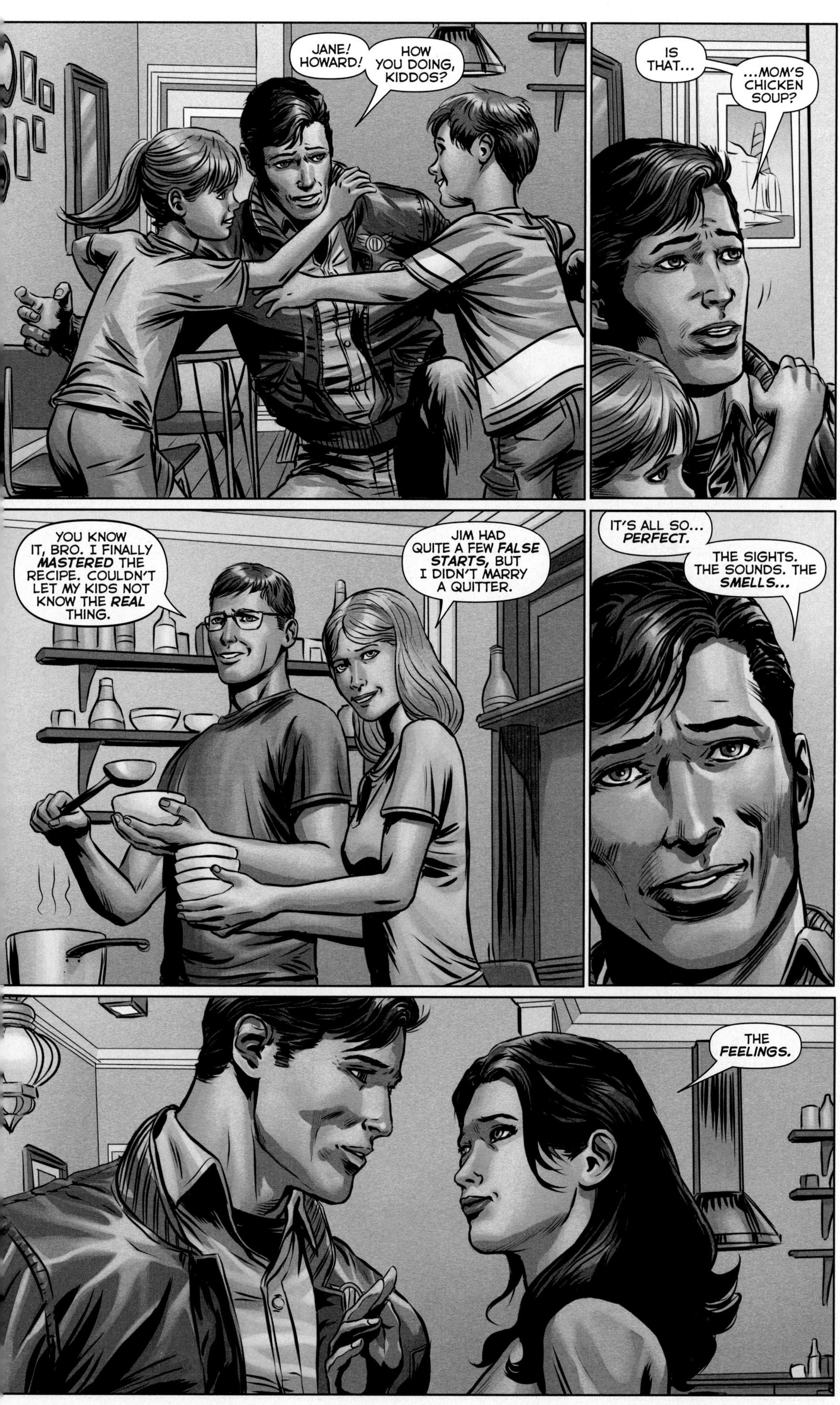
JANE! HOWARD!
HOW YOU DOING, KIDDOS?
IS THAT...
...MOM'S CHICKEN SOUP?
YOU KNOW IT, BRO. I FINALLY MASTERED THE RECIPE. COULDN'T LET MY KIDS NOT KNOW THE REAL THING.
JIM HAD QUITE A FEW FALSE STARTS, BUT I DIDN'T MARRY A QUITTER.
IT'S ALL SO... PERFECT.
THE SIGHTS. THE SOUNDS. THE SMELLS...
THE FEELINGS.

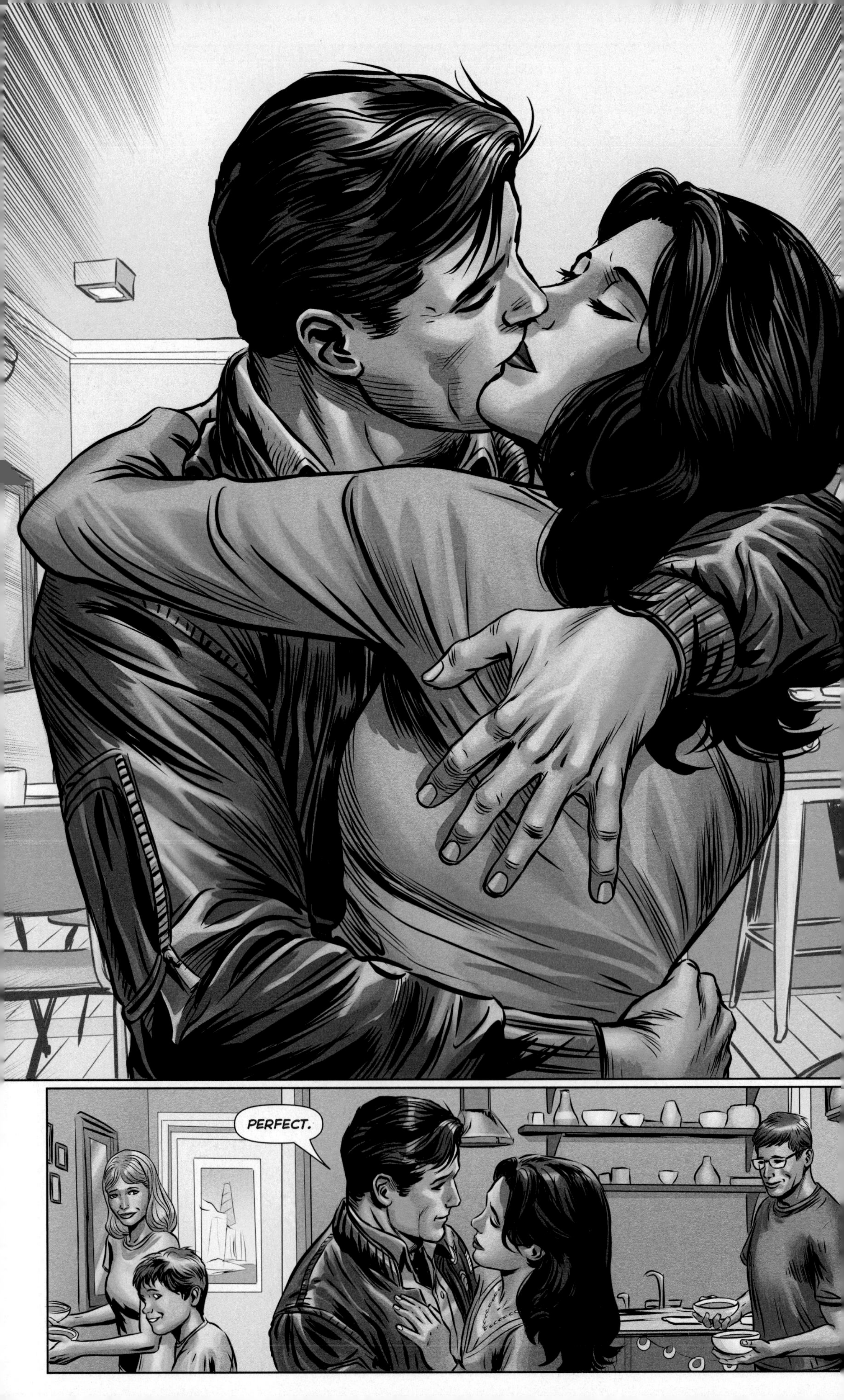
PERFECT.

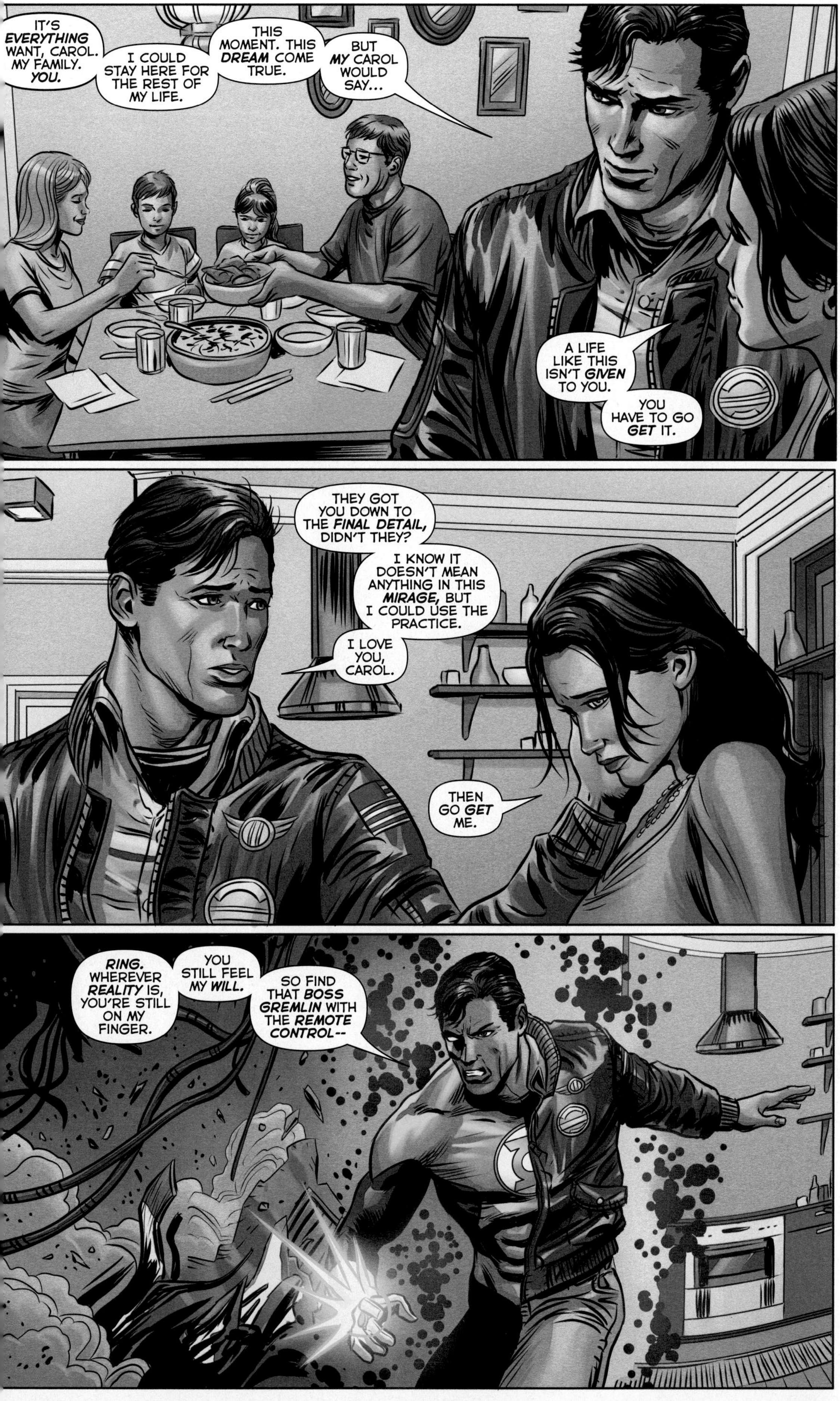
IT'S EVERYTHING I WANT, CAROL. MY FAMILY. YOU.
I COULD STAY HERE FOR THE REST OF MY LIFE.
THIS MOMENT. THIS DREAM COME TRUE.
BUT MY CAROL WOULD SAY...
A LIFE LIKE THIS ISN'T GIVEN TO YOU.
YOU HAVE TO GO GET IT.
THEY GOT YOU DOWN TO THE FINAL DETAIL, DIDN'T THEY?
I KNOW IT DOESN'T MEAN ANYTHING IN THIS MIRAGE, BUT I COULD USE THE PRACTICE.
I LOVE YOU, CAROL.
THEN GO GET ME.
RING. WHEREVER REALITY IS, YOU'RE STILL ON MY FINGER.
YOU STILL FEEL MY WILL.
SO FIND THAT BOSS GREMLIN WITH THE REMOTE CONTROL--

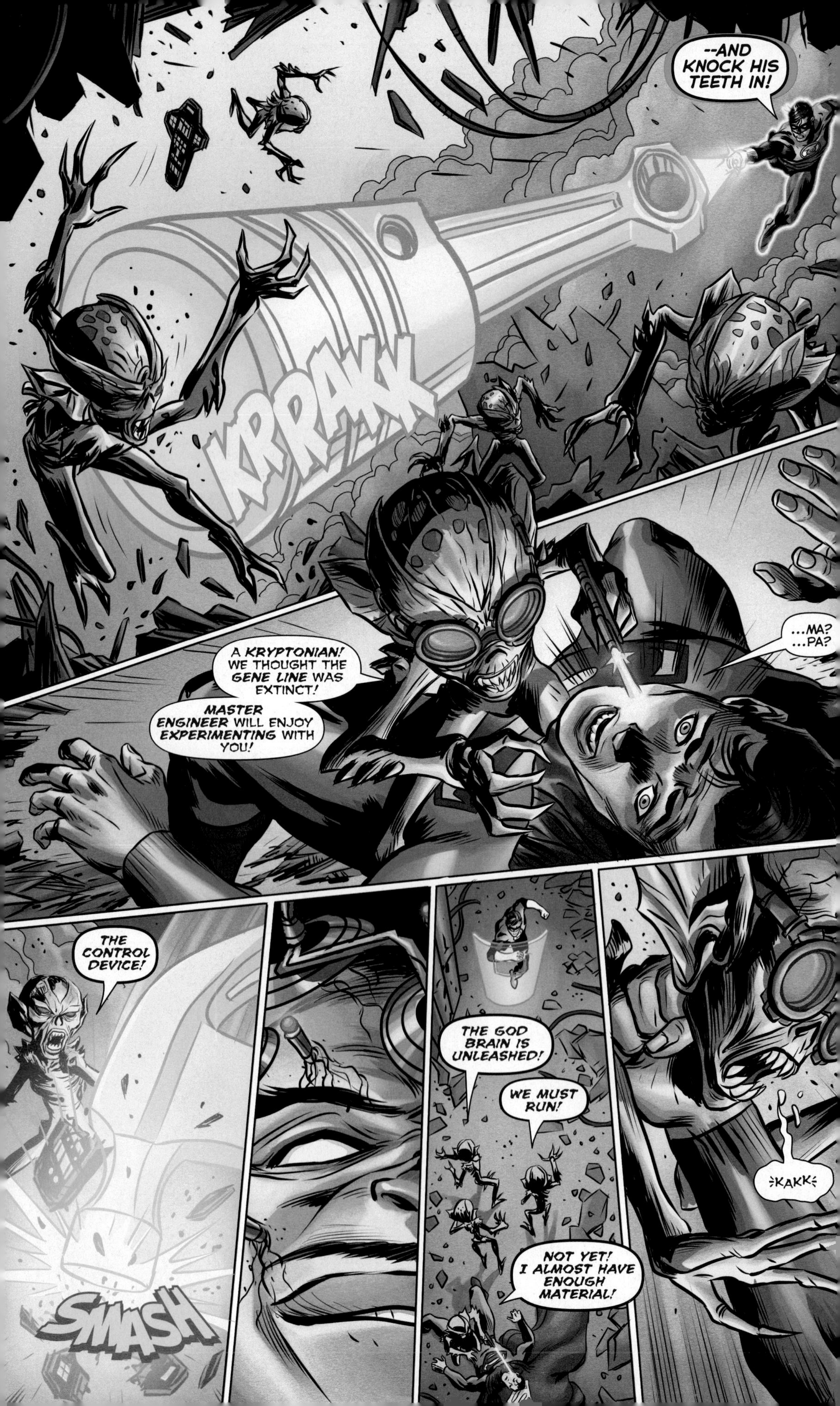
--AND KNOCK HIS TEETH IN!
KRRAKK
A KRYPTONIAN! WE THOUGHT THE GENE LINE WAS EXTINCT!
MASTER ENGINEER WILL ENJOY EXPERIMENTING WITH YOU!
...MA? ...PA?
THE CONTROL DEVICE!
SMASH
THE GOD BRAIN IS UNLEASHED!
WE MUST RUN!
NOT YET! I ALMOST HAVE ENOUGH MATERIAL!
KAKK

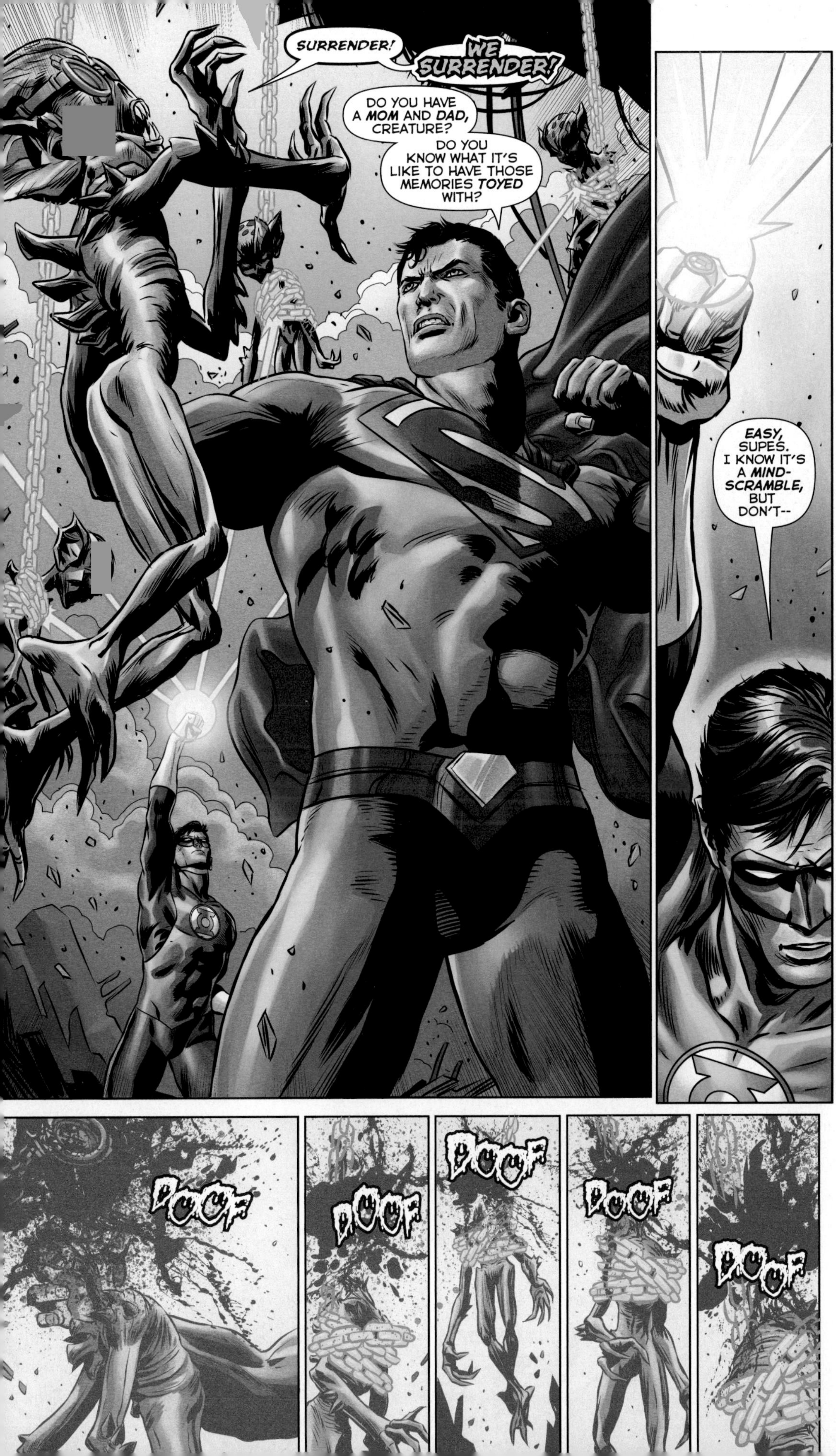
SURRENDER!
WE SURRENDER!
DO YOU HAVE A MOM AND DAD, CREATURE?
DO YOU KNOW WHAT IT'S LIKE TO HAVE THOSE MEMORIES TOYED WITH?
EASY, SUPES. I KNOW IT'S A MIND-SCRAMBLE, BUT DON'T--
DOOF
DOOF
DOOF
DOOF
DOOF

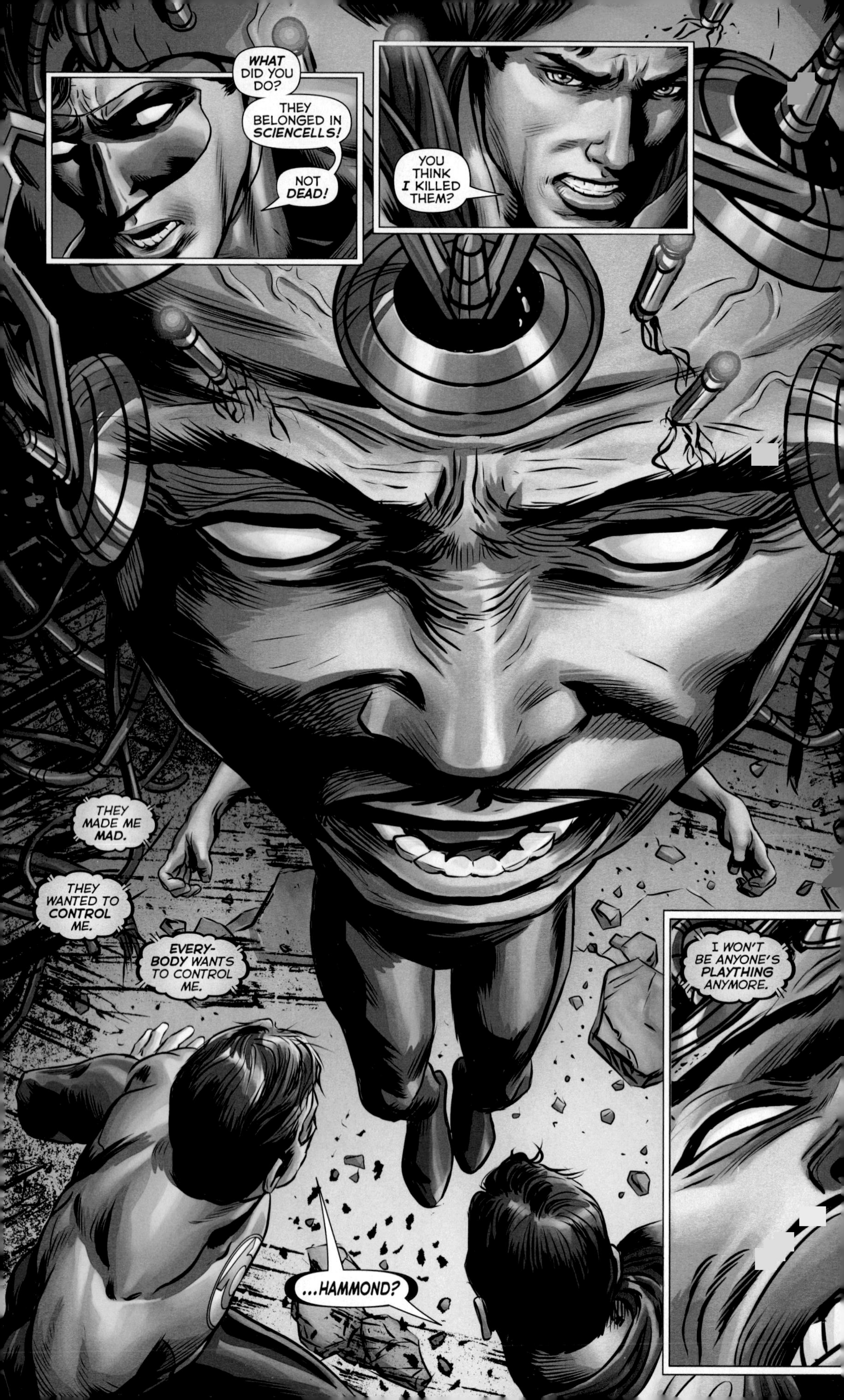
WHAT DID YOU DO?
THEY BELONGED IN SCIENCELLS!
NOT DEAD!
YOU THINK I KILLED THEM?
THEY MADE ME MAD.
THEY WANTED TO CONTROL ME.
EVERY-BODY WANTS TO CONTROL ME.
I WON'T BE ANYONE'S PLAYTHING ANYMORE.
...HAMMOND?

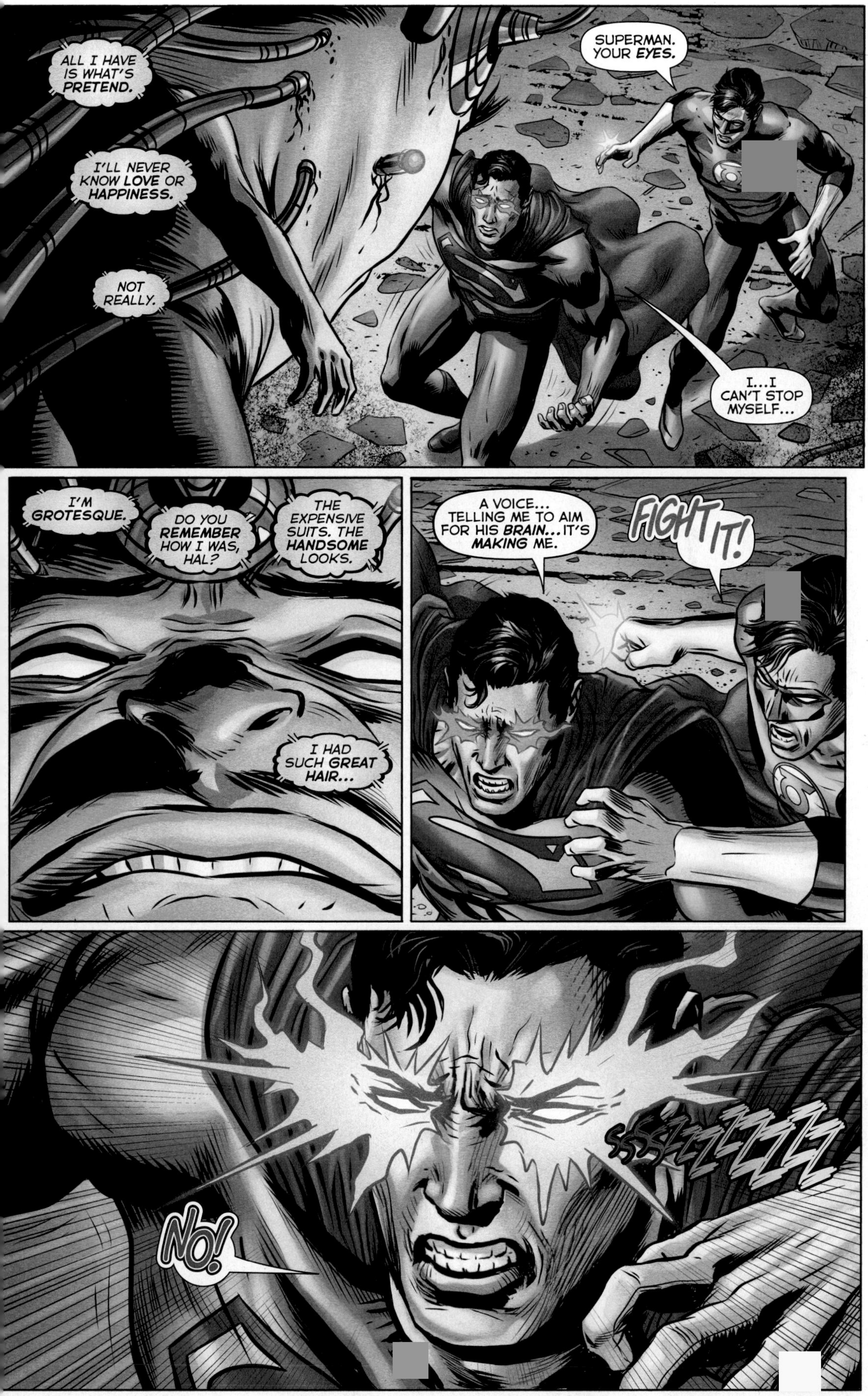
ALL I HAVE IS WHAT'S PRETEND.
SUPERMAN. YOUR EYES.
I'LL NEVER KNOW LOVE OR HAPPINESS.
NOT REALLY.
I...I CAN'T STOP MYSELF...
I'M GROTESQUE.
DO YOU REMEMBER HOW I WAS, HAL?
THE EXPENSIVE SUITS. THE HANDSOME LOOKS.
I HAD SUCH GREAT HAIR...
A VOICE... TELLING ME TO AIM FOR HIS BRAIN... IT'S MAKING ME.
FIGHT IT!
SSSSZZZZZZZ
NO!

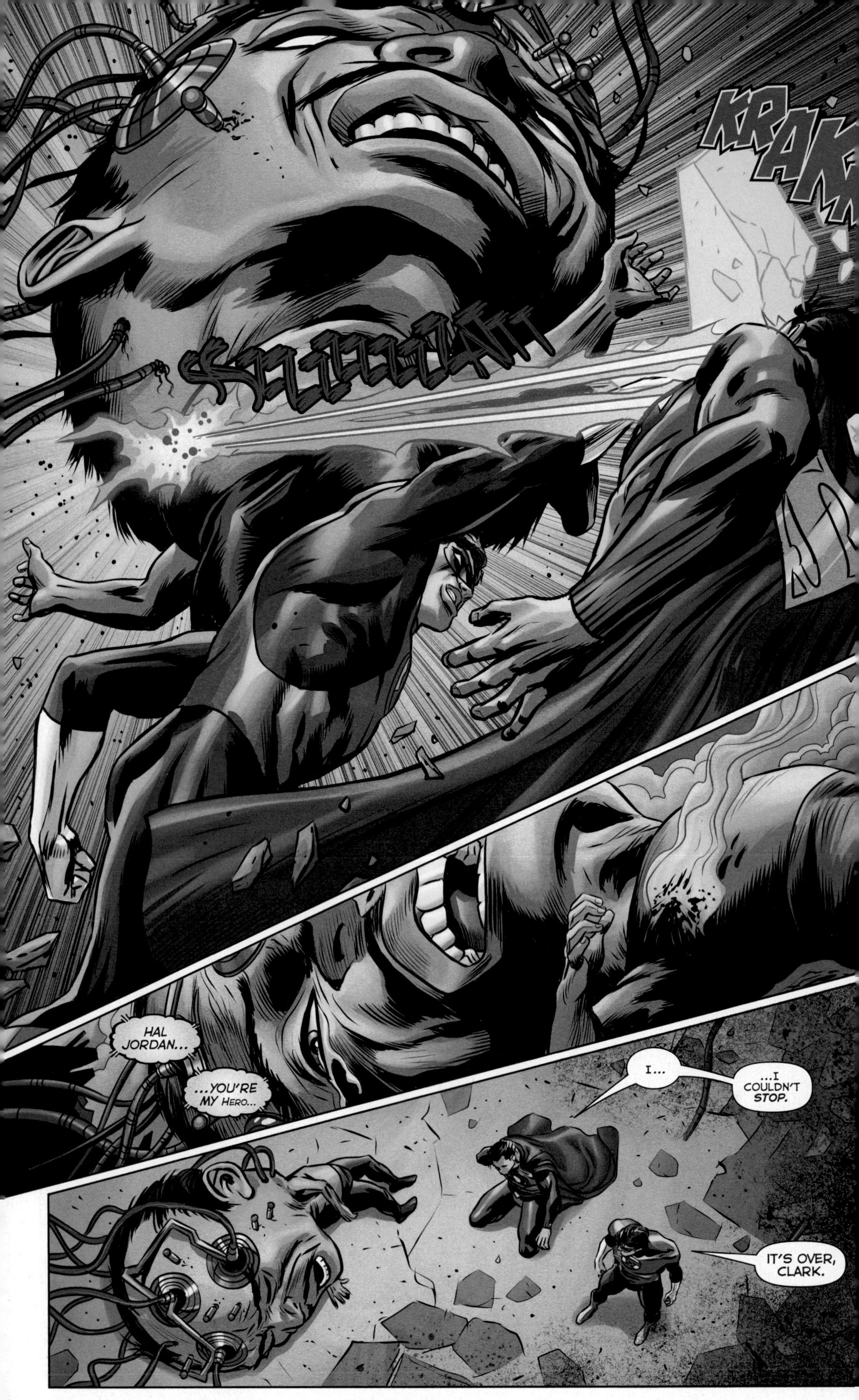
KRAK
HAL JORDAN...
...YOU'RE MY HERO...
I...
...I COULDN'T STOP.
IT'S OVER, CLARK.

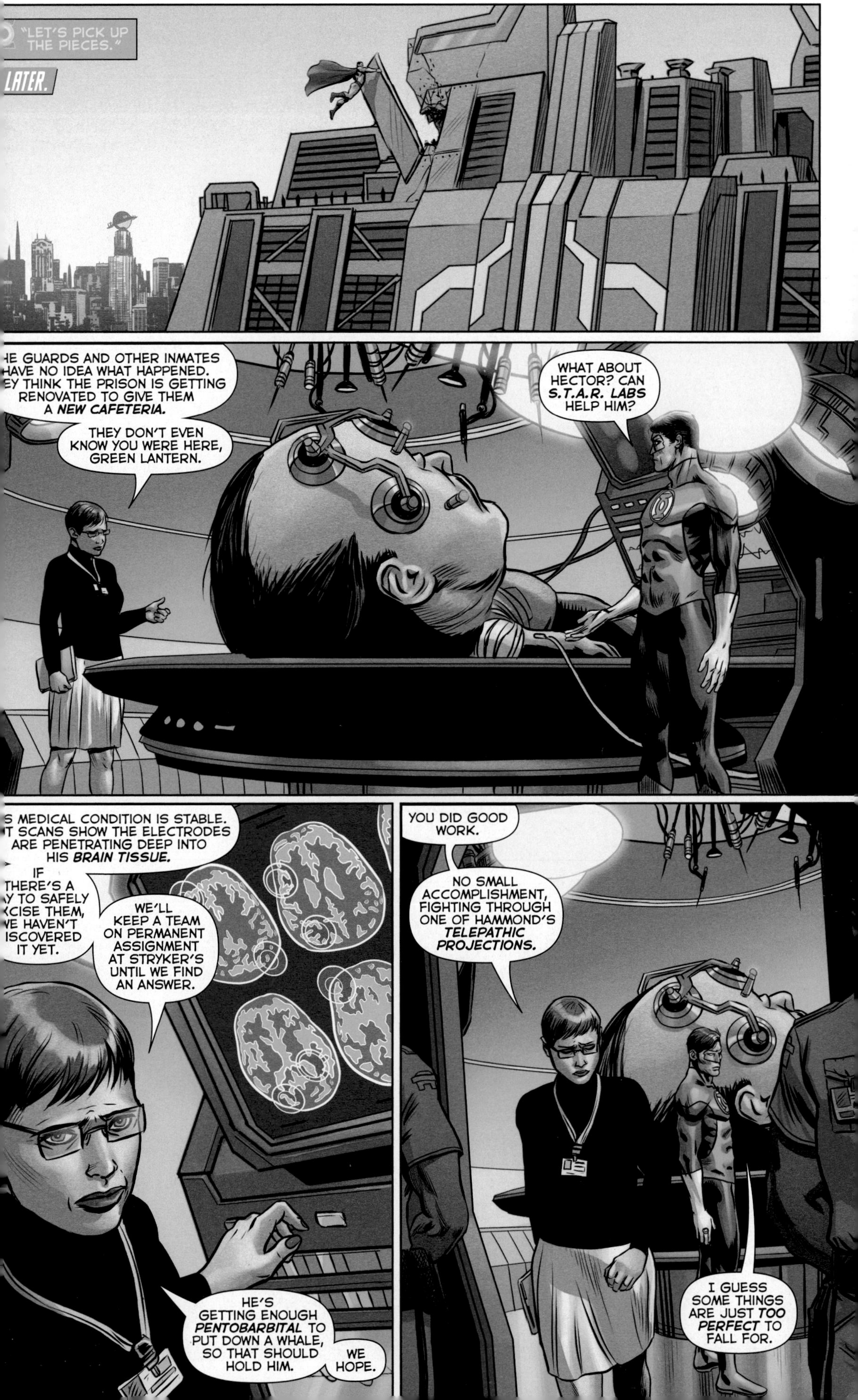

"LET'S PICK UP THE PIECES."
LATER.
IE GUARDS AND OTHER INMATES HAVE NO IDEA WHAT HAPPENED. EY THINK THE PRISON IS GETTING RENOVATED TO GIVE THEM A NEW CAFETERIA.
THEY DON'T EVEN KNOW YOU WERE HERE, GREEN LANTERN.
WHAT ABOUT HECTOR? CAN S.T.A.R. LABS HELP HIM?
S MEDICAL CONDITION IS STABLE. T SCANS SHOW THE ELECTRODES ARE PENETRATING DEEP INTO HIS BRAIN TISSUE.
IF THERE'S A Y TO SAFELY XCISE THEM, VE HAVEN'T ISCOVERED IT YET.
WE'LL KEEP A TEAM ON PERMANENT ASSIGNMENT AT STRYKER'S UNTIL WE FIND AN ANSWER.
HE'S GETTING ENOUGH PENTOBARBITAL TO PUT DOWN A WHALE, SO THAT SHOULD HOLD HIM.
WE HOPE.
YOU DID GOOD WORK.
NO SMALL ACCOMPLISHMENT, FIGHTING THROUGH ONE OF HAMMOND'S TELEPATHIC PROJECTIONS.
I GUESS SOME THINGS ARE JUST TOO PERFECT TO FALL FOR.

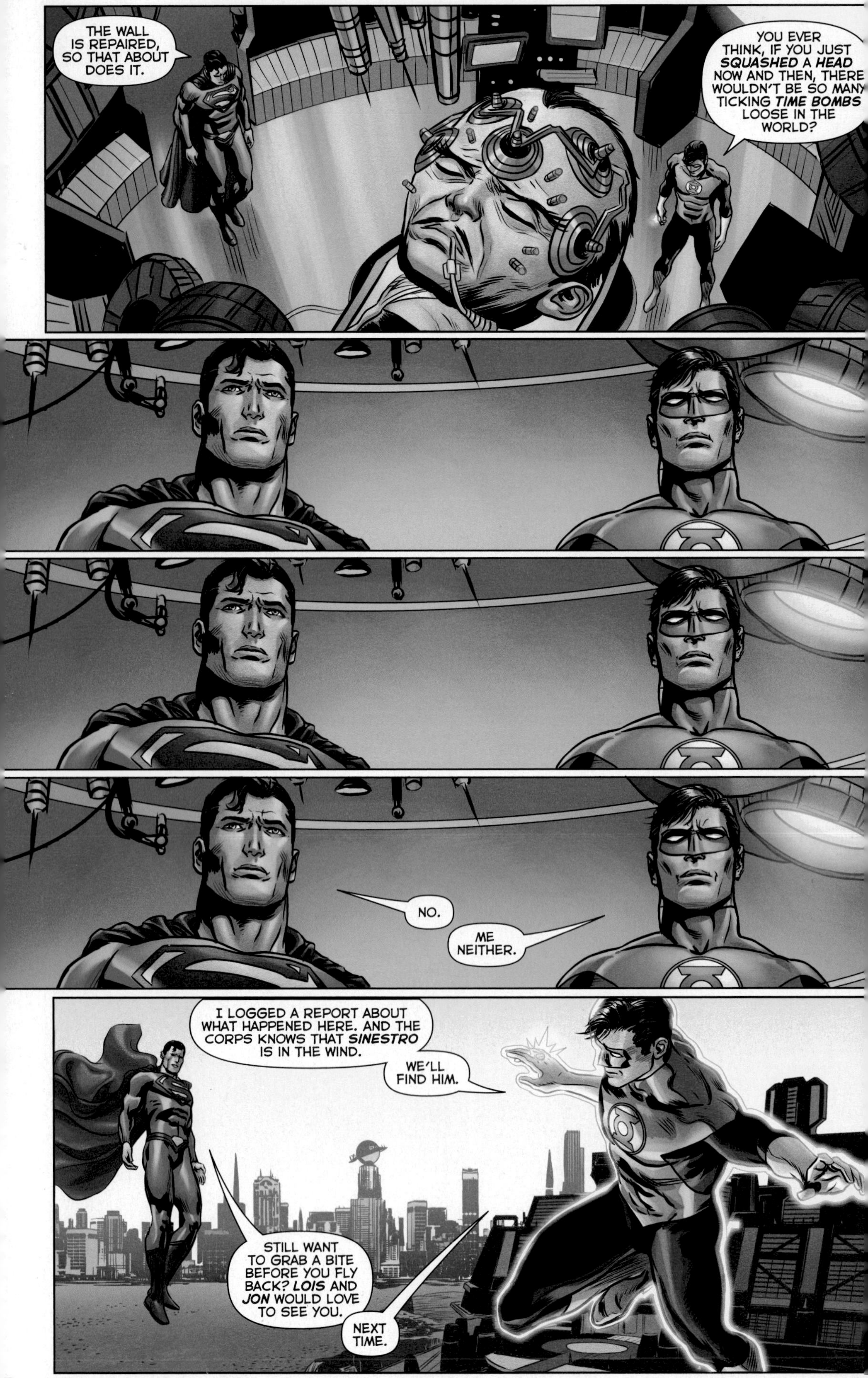
THE WALL IS REPAIRED, SO THAT ABOUT DOES IT.
YOU EVER THINK, IF YOU JUST SQUASHED A HEAD NOW AND THEN, THERE WOULDN'T BE SO MANY TICKING TIME BOMBS LOOSE IN THE WORLD?
NO.
ME NEITHER.
I LOGGED A REPORT ABOUT WHAT HAPPENED HERE. AND THE CORPS KNOWS THAT SINESTRO IS IN THE WIND.
WE'LL FIND HIM.
STILL WANT TO GRAB A BITE BEFORE YOU FLY BACK? LOIS AND JON WOULD LOVE TO SEE YOU.
NEXT TIME.

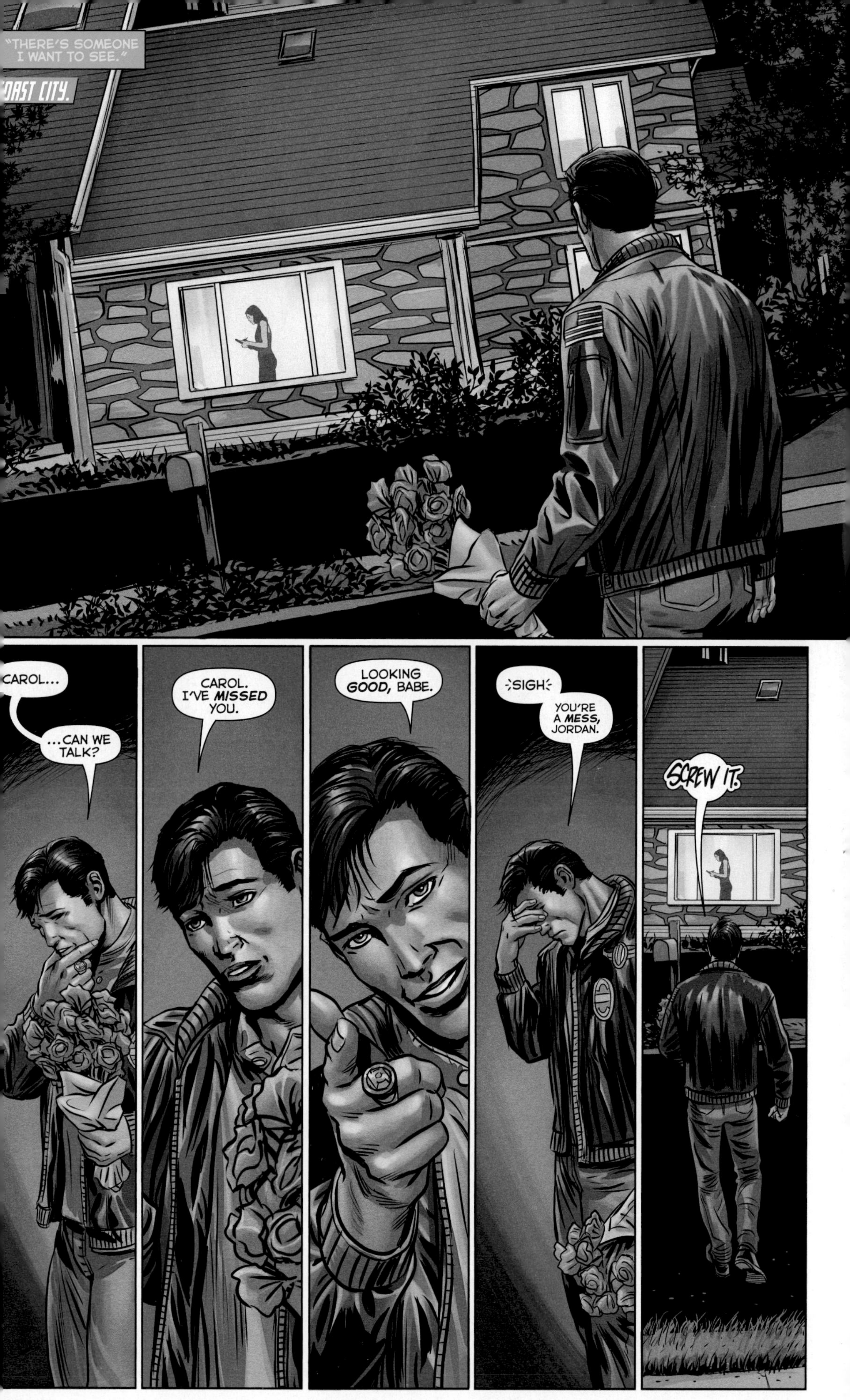
"THERE'S SOMEONE I WANT TO SEE."
OAST CITY.
CAROL...
...CAN WE TALK?
CAROL. I'VE MISSED YOU.
LOOKING GOOD, BABE.
SIGH
YOU'RE A MESS, JORDAN.
SCREW IT.

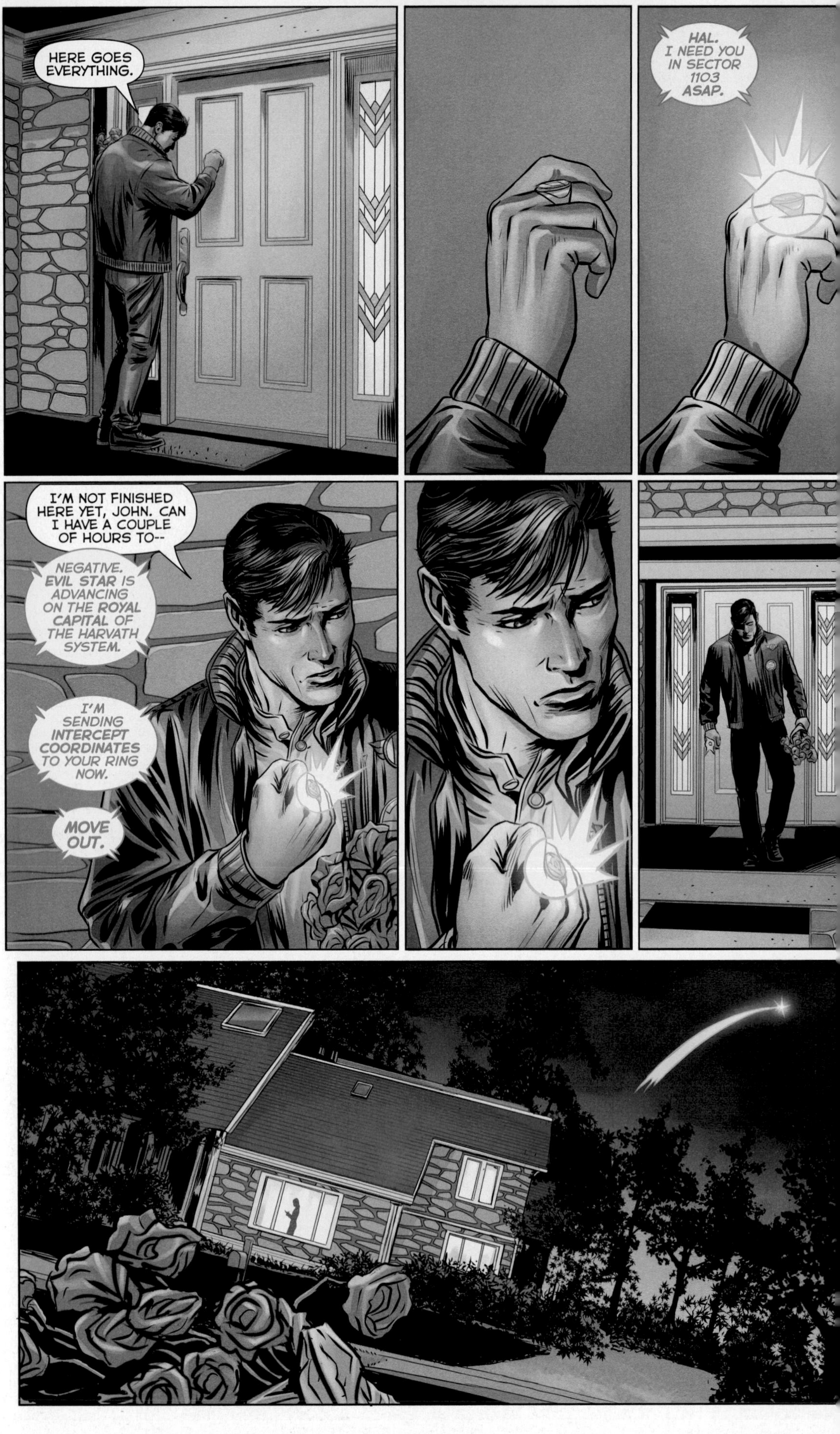
HERE GOES EVERYTHING.
HAL. I NEED YOU IN SECTOR 1103 ASAP.
I'M NOT FINISHED HERE YET, JOHN. CAN I HAVE A COUPLE OF HOURS TO--
NEGATIVE. EVIL STAR IS ADVANCING ON THE ROYAL CAPITAL OF THE HARVATH SYSTEM.
I'M SENDING INTERCEPT COORDINATES TO YOUR RING NOW.
MOVE OUT.

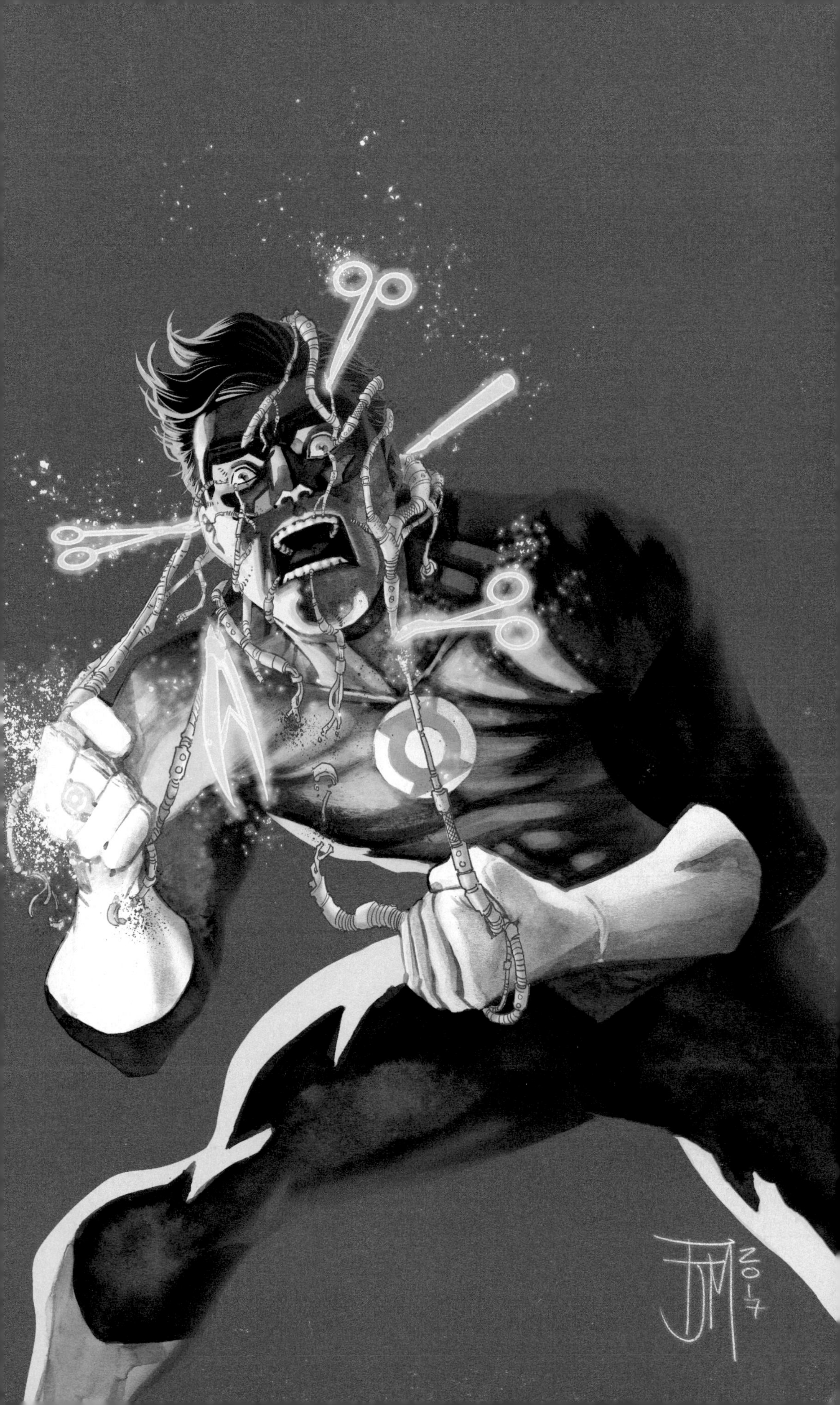

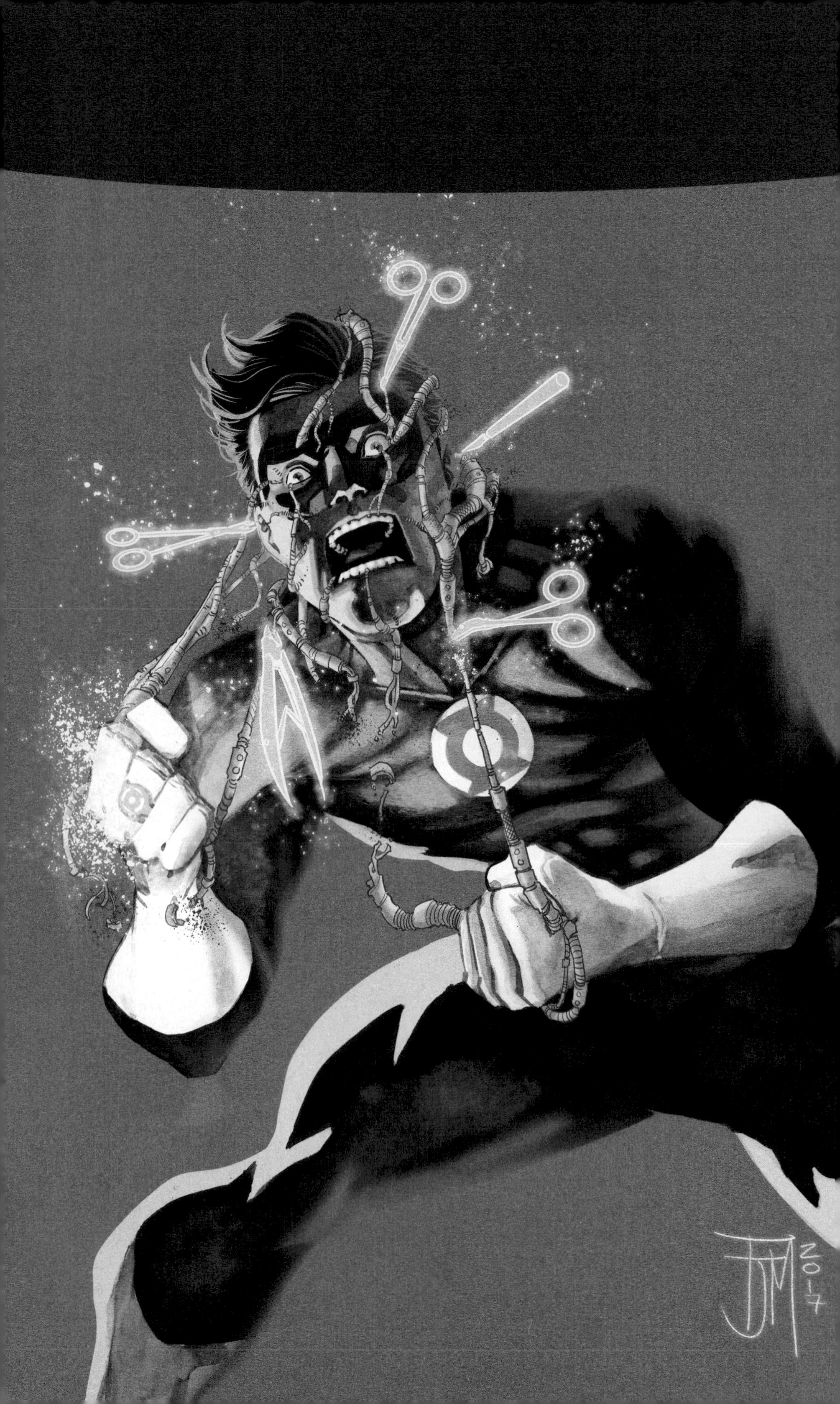

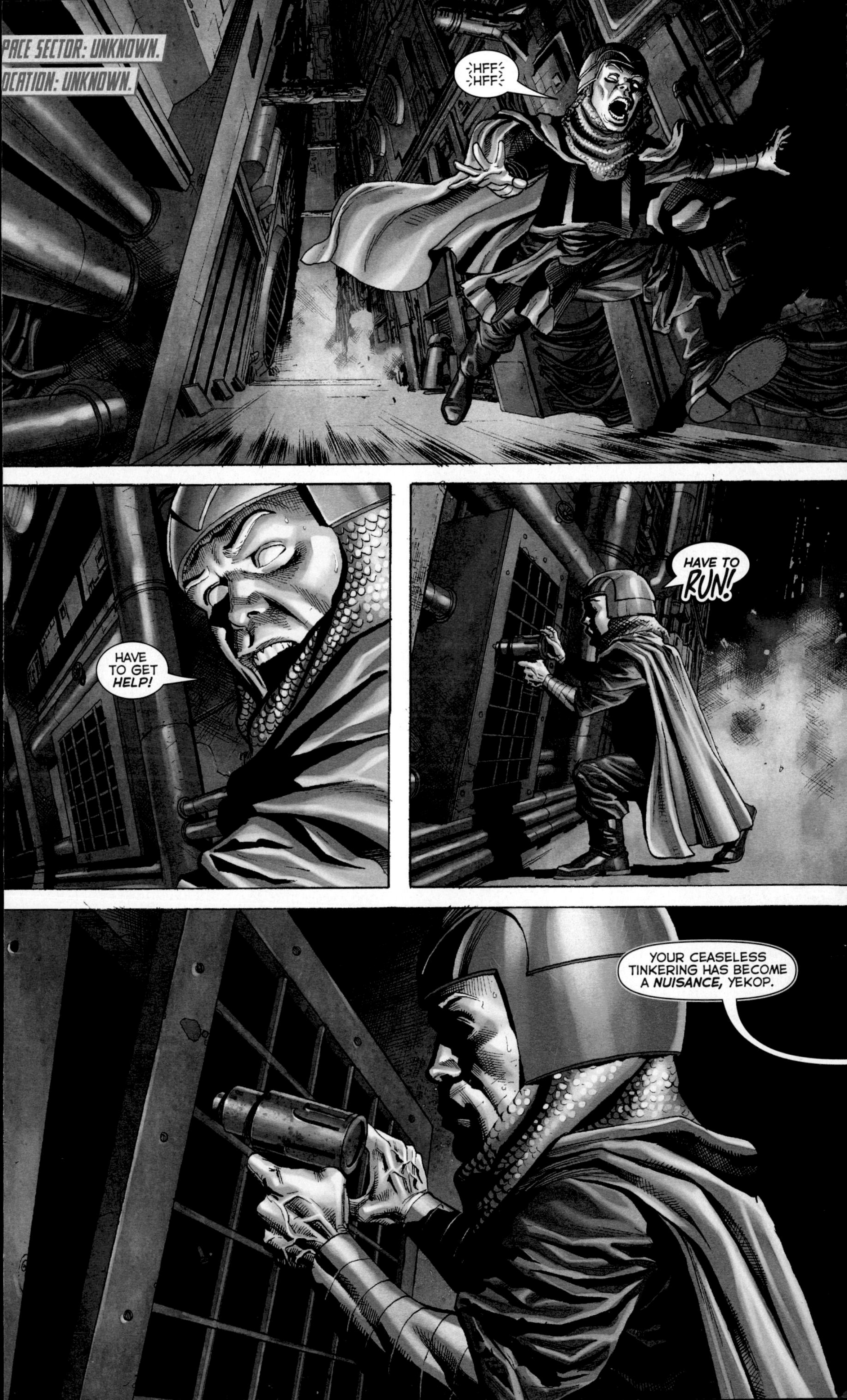
PACE SECTOR: UNKNOWN.
OCATION: UNKNOWN.
HFF HFF
HAVE TO GET HELP!
HAVE TO RUN!
YOUR CEASELESS TINKERING HAS BECOME A NUISANCE, YEKOP.

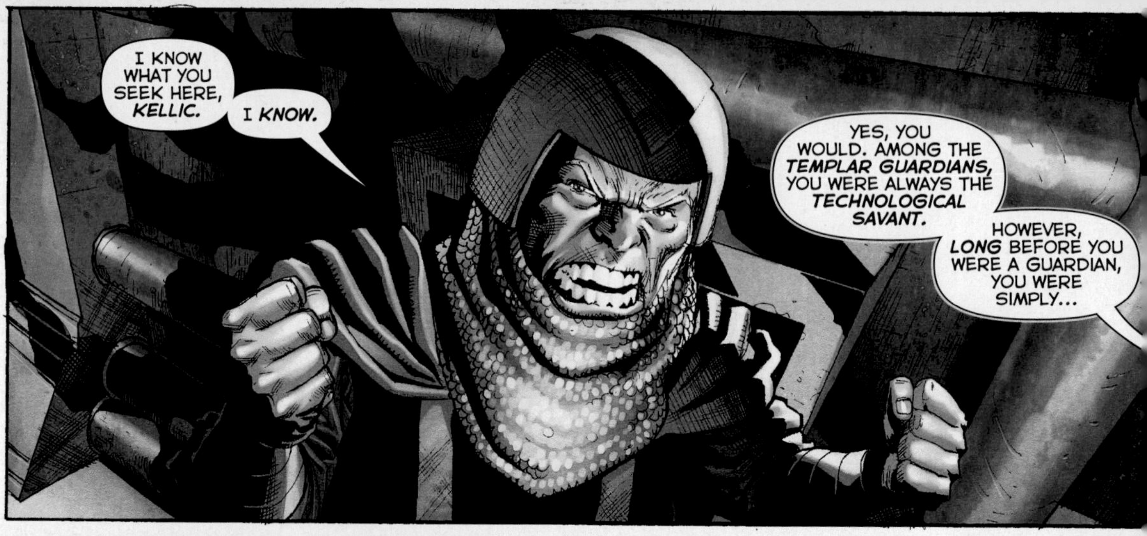
I KNOW WHAT YOU SEEK HERE, KELLIC.
I KNOW.
YES, YOU WOULD. AMONG THE TEMPLAR GUARDIANS, YOU WERE ALWAYS THE TECHNOLOGICAL SAVANT.
HOWEVER, LONG BEFORE YOU WERE A GUARDIAN, YOU WERE SIMPLY...

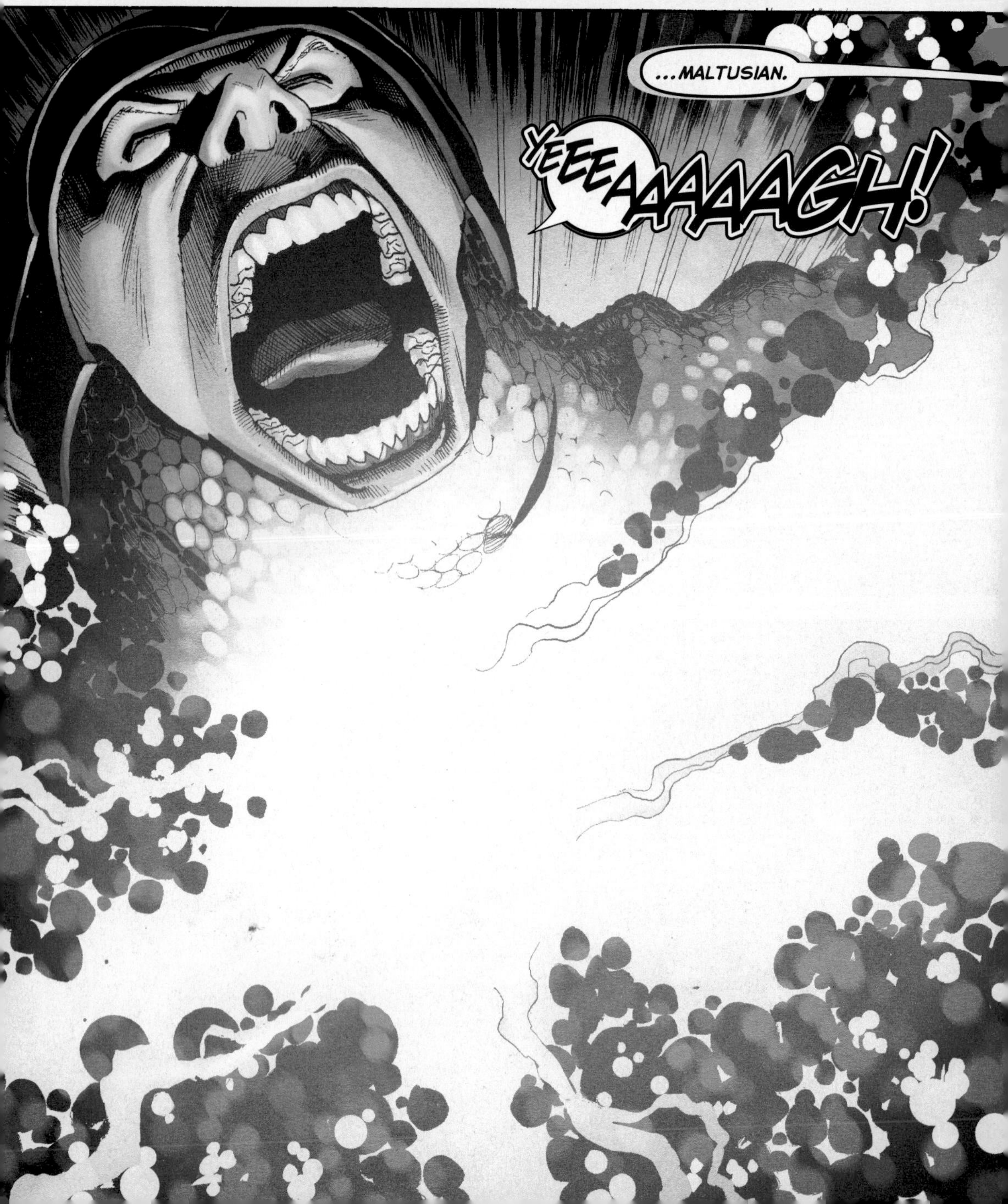
...MALTUSIAN.
YEEEAAAAAAGH!

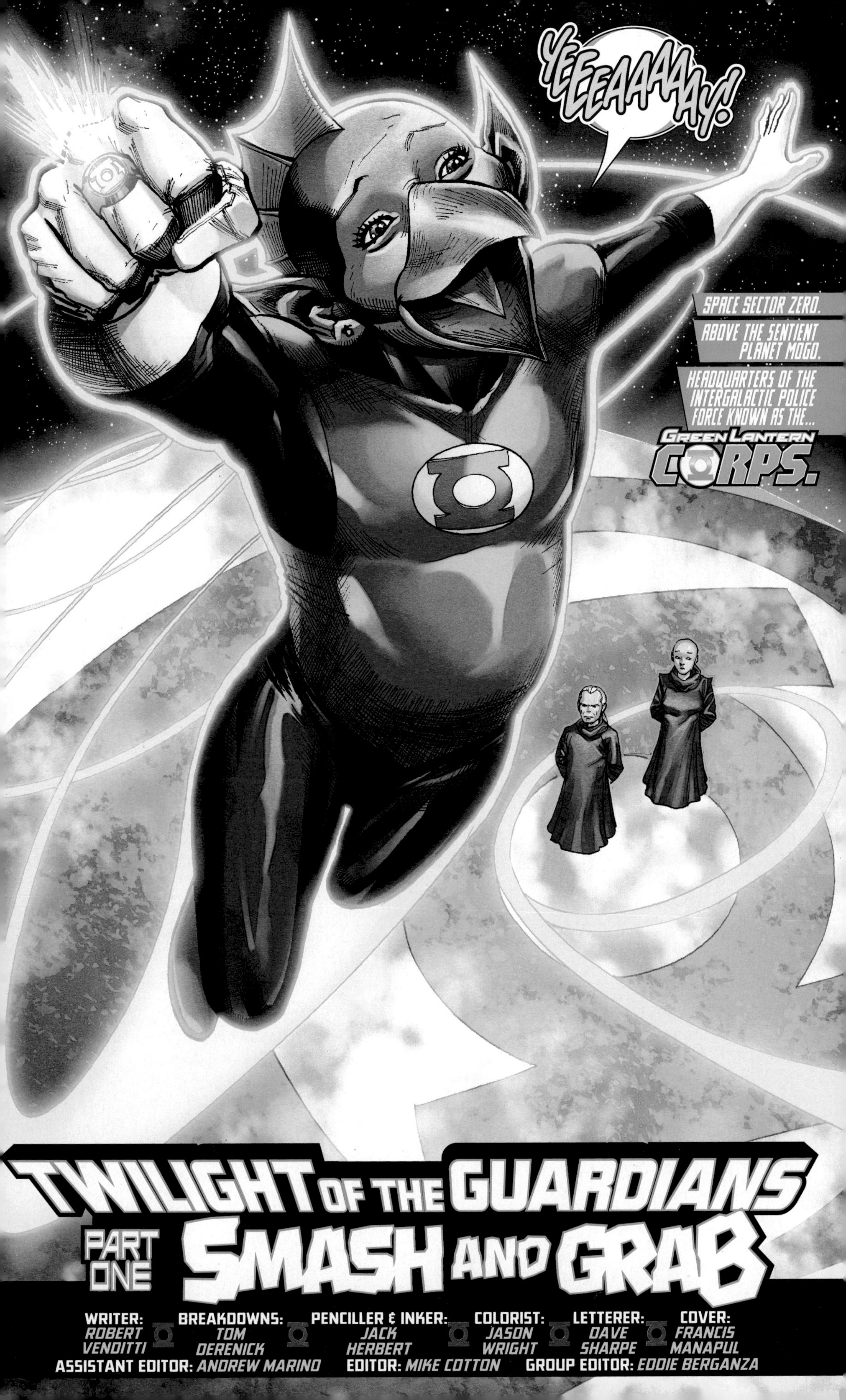
YEEEAAAAAY!
SPACE SECTOR ZERO.
ABOVE THE SENTIENT PLANET MOGO.
HEADQUARTERS OF THE INTERGALACTIC POLICE FORCE KNOWN AS THE...
GREEN LANTERN CORPS.
TWILIGHT OF THE GUARDIANS
PART ONE SMASH AND GRAB
WRITER: ROBERT VENDITTI
BREAKDOWNS: TOM DERENICK
PENCILLER & INKER: JACK HERBERT
COLORIST: JASON WRIGHT
LETTERER: DAVE SHARPE
COVER: FRANCIS MANAPUL
ASSISTANT EDITOR: ANDREW MARINO
EDITOR: MIKE COTTON
GROUP EDITOR: EDDIE BERGANZA

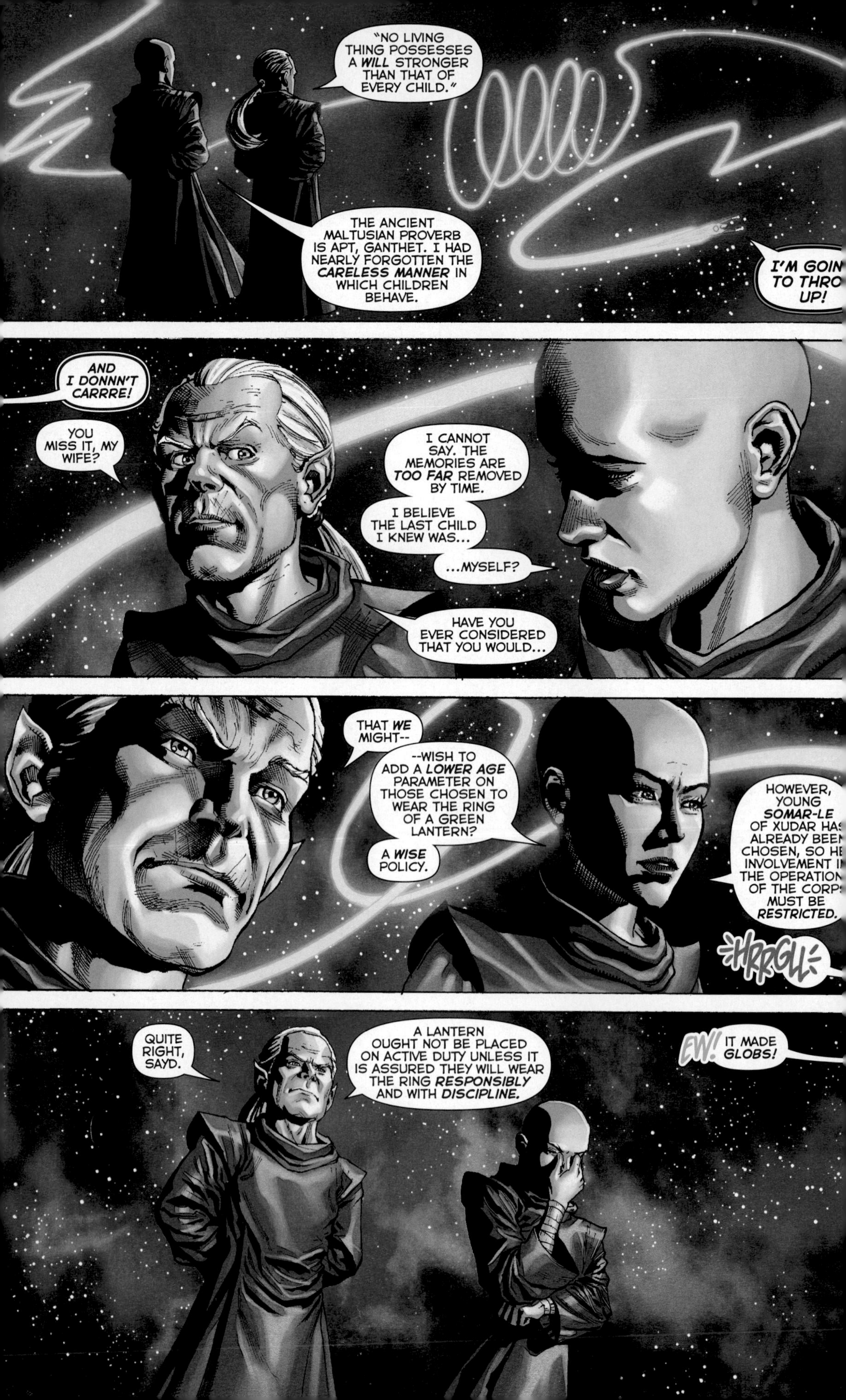
"NO LIVING THING POSSESSES A WILL STRONGER THAN THAT OF EVERY CHILD."
THE ANCIENT MALTUSIAN PROVERB IS APT, GANTHET. I HAD NEARLY FORGOTTEN THE CARELESS MANNER IN WHICH CHILDREN BEHAVE.
I'M GOIN TO THRO UP!
AND I DONNN'T CARRRE!
YOU MISS IT, MY WIFE?
I CANNOT SAY. THE MEMORIES ARE TOO FAR REMOVED BY TIME.
I BELIEVE THE LAST CHILD I KNEW WAS...
...MYSELF?
HAVE YOU EVER CONSIDERED THAT YOU WOULD...
THAT WE MIGHT--
--WISH TO ADD A LOWER AGE PARAMETER ON THOSE CHOSEN TO WEAR THE RING OF A GREEN LANTERN?
A WISE POLICY.
HOWEVER, YOUNG SOMAR-LE OF XUDAR HAS ALREADY BEEN CHOSEN, SO HE INVOLVEMENT IN THE OPERATION OF THE CORPS MUST BE RESTRICTED.
HRRGLL
QUITE RIGHT, SAYD.
A LANTERN OUGHT NOT BE PLACED ON ACTIVE DUTY UNLESS IT IS ASSURED THEY WILL WEAR THE RING RESPONSIBLY AND WITH DISCIPLINE.
EW! IT MADE GLOBS!

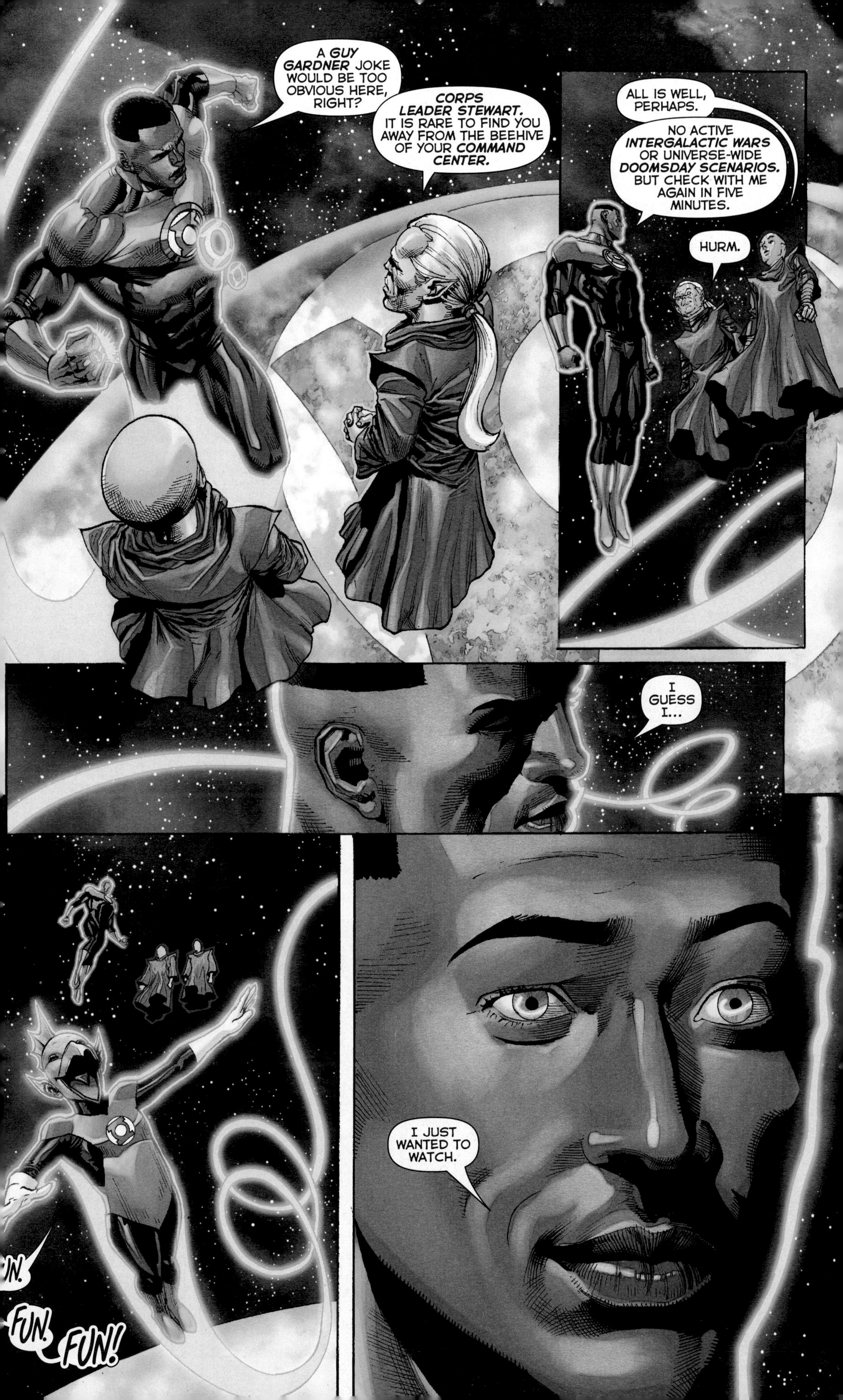
A GUY GARDNER JOKE WOULD BE TOO OBVIOUS HERE, RIGHT?
CORPS LEADER STEWART. IT IS RARE TO FIND YOU AWAY FROM THE BEEHIVE OF YOUR COMMAND CENTER.
ALL IS WELL, PERHAPS.
NO ACTIVE INTERGALACTIC WARS OR UNIVERSE-WIDE DOOMSDAY SCENARIOS. BUT CHECK WITH ME AGAIN IN FIVE MINUTES.
HURM.
I GUESS I...
FUN. FUN!
I JUST WANTED TO WATCH.

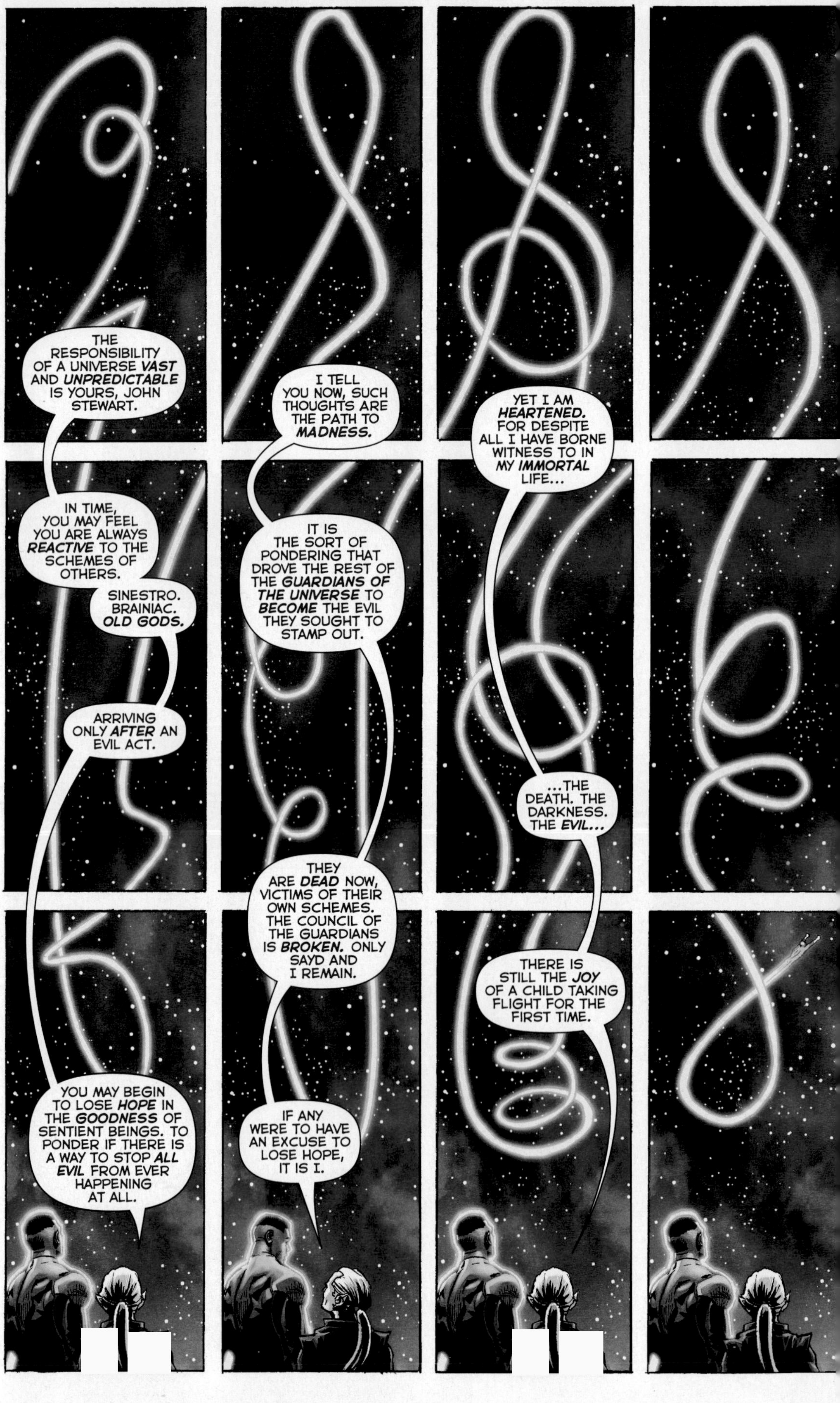

THE RESPONSIBILITY OF A UNIVERSE *VAST* AND *UNPREDICTABLE* IS YOURS, JOHN STEWART.
IN TIME, YOU MAY FEEL YOU ARE ALWAYS *REACTIVE* TO THE SCHEMES OF OTHERS.
SINESTRO. BRAINIAC. *OLD GODS.*
ARRIVING ONLY *AFTER* AN EVIL ACT.
YOU MAY BEGIN TO LOSE *HOPE* IN THE *GOODNESS* OF SENTIENT BEINGS. TO PONDER IF THERE IS A WAY TO STOP *ALL EVIL* FROM EVER HAPPENING AT ALL.
I TELL YOU NOW, SUCH THOUGHTS ARE THE PATH TO *MADNESS.*
IT IS THE SORT OF PONDERING THAT DROVE THE REST OF THE *GUARDIANS OF THE UNIVERSE* TO *BECOME* THE EVIL THEY SOUGHT TO STAMP OUT.
THEY ARE *DEAD* NOW, VICTIMS OF THEIR OWN SCHEMES. THE COUNCIL OF THE GUARDIANS IS *BROKEN.* ONLY SAYD AND I REMAIN.
IF ANY WERE TO HAVE AN EXCUSE TO LOSE HOPE, IT IS I.
YET I AM *HEARTENED.* FOR DESPITE ALL I HAVE BORNE WITNESS TO IN *MY IMMORTAL* LIFE...
...THE DEATH. THE DARKNESS. THE *EVIL...*
THERE IS STILL THE *JOY* OF A CHILD TAKING FLIGHT FOR THE FIRST TIME.

IF I'VE STEERED *CLEAR* OF YOU, GANTHET, IT'S BECAUSE PART OF ME DIDN'T WANT TO INVITE YOU AND SAYD BACK IN.

NOT AFTER EVERYTHING THE GUARDIANS DID... AND *MADE* THE CORPS DO.

AS LONG AS A BEING STILL DRAWS BREATH, IT HARBORS THE CHANCE TO *LEARN* AND BE *BETTER.*

EVEN WE IMMORTALS.

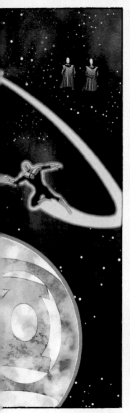

THANKS FOR THE ADVICE.

WE WILL ALWAYS BE HERE TO PROVIDE IT.

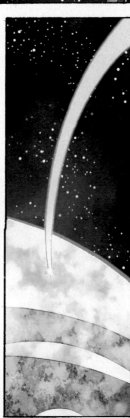

WHOOOOSH!

NOW, WHAT ARE WE TO DO WITH *THIS* ONE?

WE WILL TEACH HER THE MANY THINGS A *GREEN LANTERN RING* CAN MAKE POSSIBLE.

AND ENVY THE FORTUNE OF THOSE FOR WHOM LIFE IS STILL *NEW.*

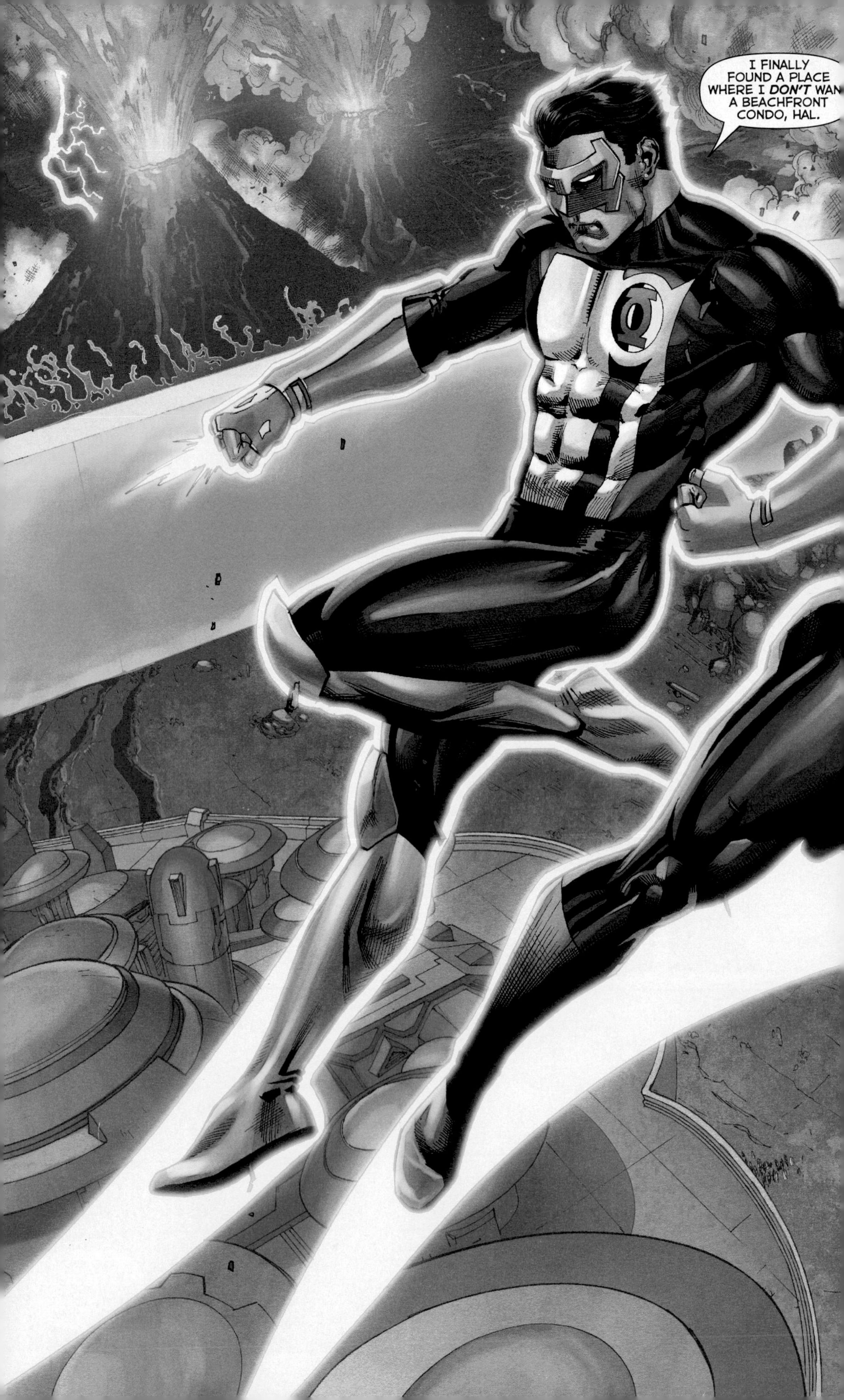
I FINALLY FOUND A PLACE WHERE I *DON'T* WAN A BEACHFRONT CONDO, HAL.

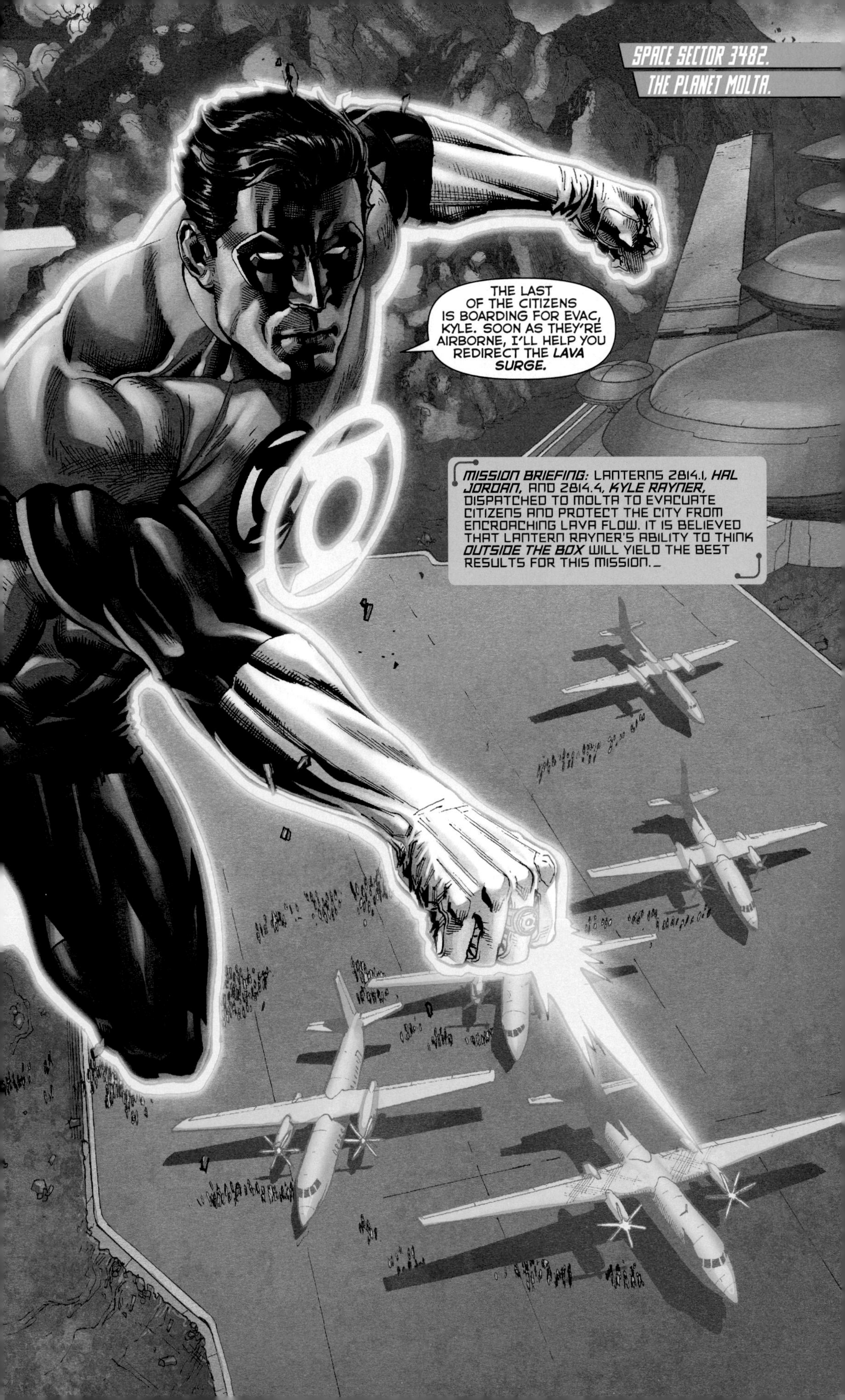
SPACE SECTOR 3482.
THE PLANET MOLTA.
THE LAST OF THE CITIZENS IS BOARDING FOR EVAC, KYLE. SOON AS THEY'RE AIRBORNE, I'LL HELP YOU REDIRECT THE LAVA SURGE.
MISSION BRIEFING: LANTERNS 2814.1, HAL JORDAN, AND 2814.4, KYLE RAYNER, DISPATCHED TO MOLTA TO EVACUATE CITIZENS AND PROTECT THE CITY FROM ENCROACHING LAVA FLOW. IT IS BELIEVED THAT LANTERN RAYNER'S ABILITY TO THINK OUTSIDE THE BOX WILL YIELD THE BEST RESULTS FOR THIS MISSION._

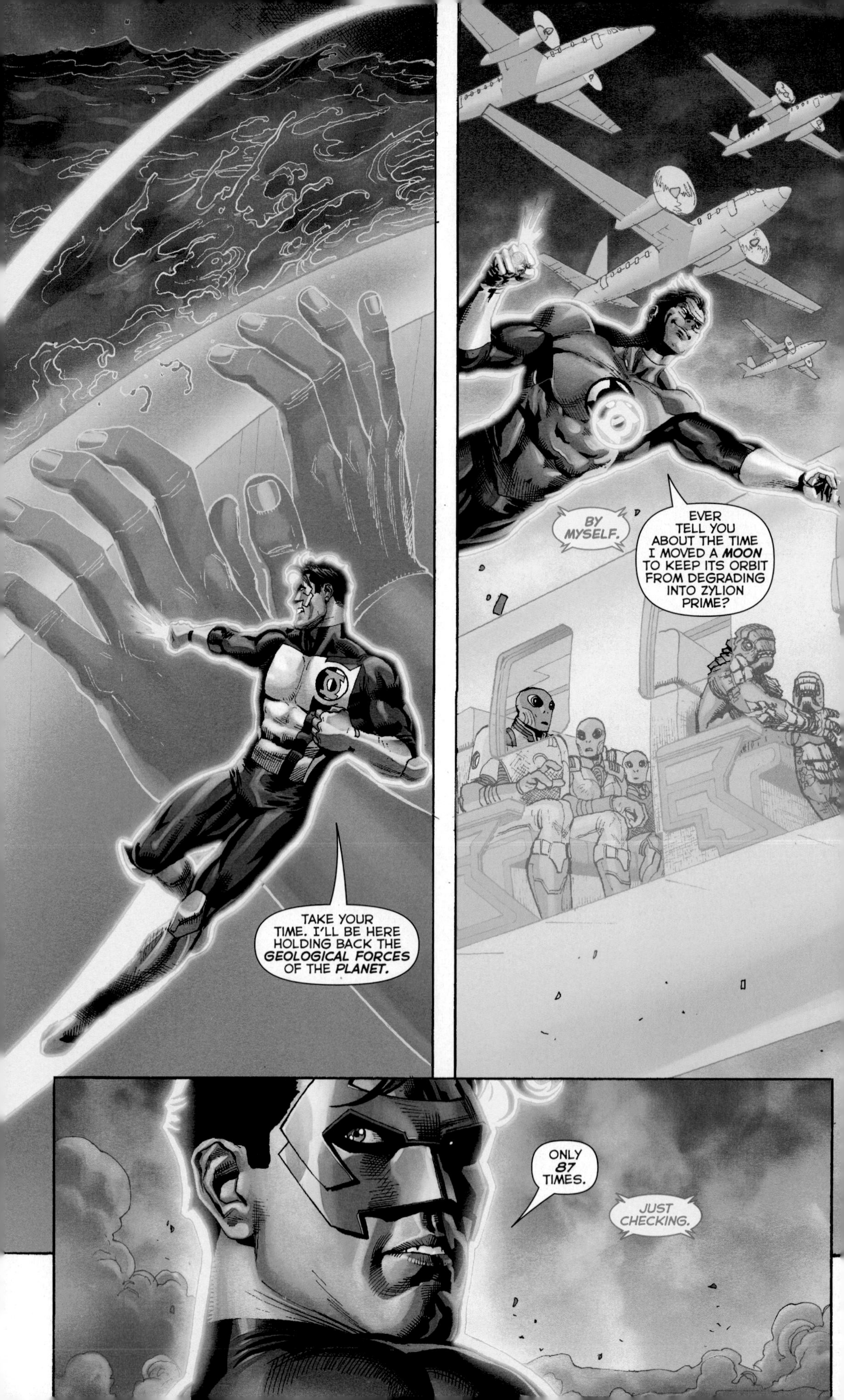
TAKE YOUR TIME. I'LL BE HERE HOLDING BACK THE **GEOLOGICAL FORCES** OF THE **PLANET.**
EVER TELL YOU ABOUT THE TIME I MOVED A **MOON** TO KEEP ITS ORBIT FROM DEGRADING INTO ZYLION PRIME?
BY MYSELF.
ONLY *87* TIMES.
JUST CHECKING.

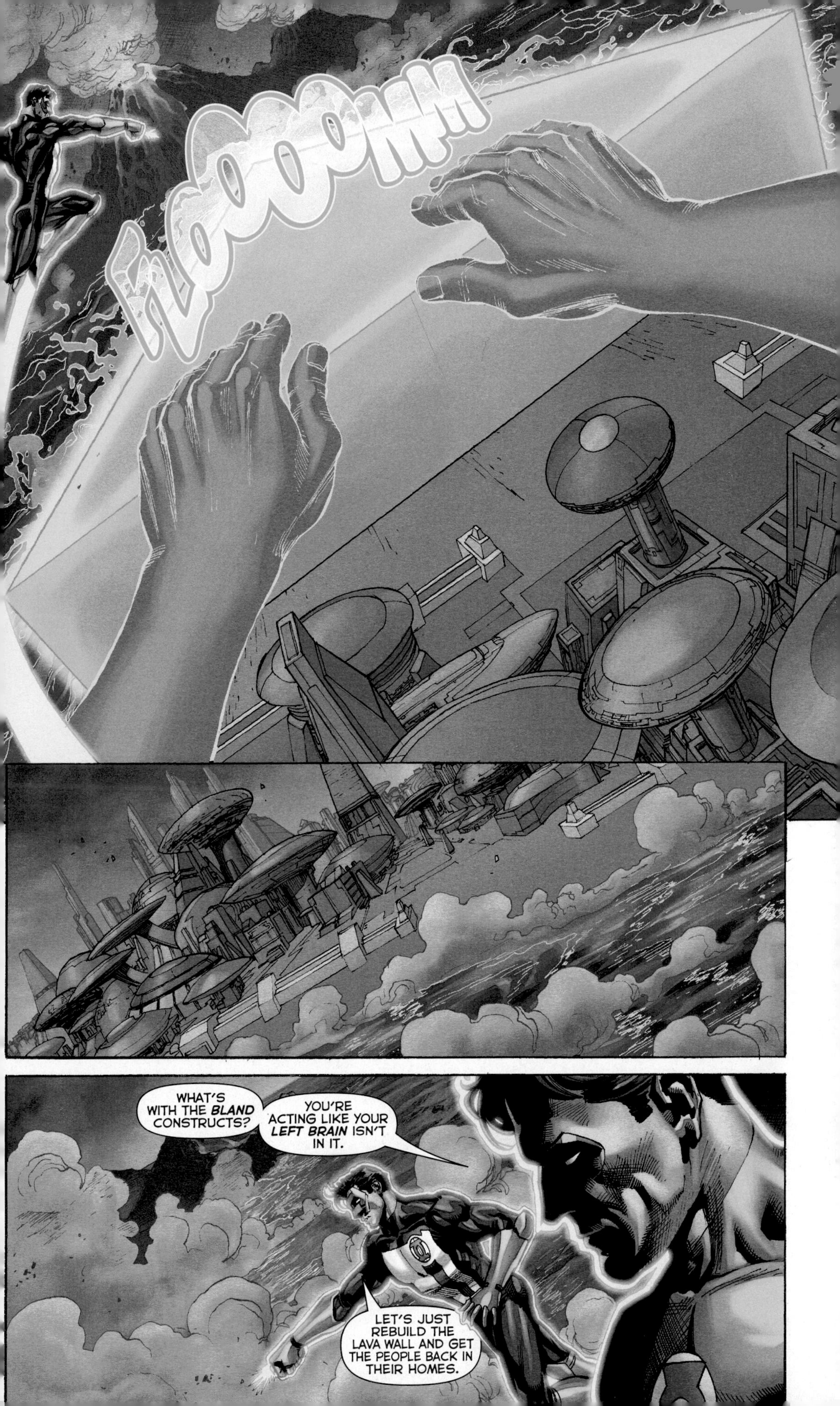
FZOOOOMM
WHAT'S WITH THE BLAND CONSTRUCTS?
YOU'RE ACTING LIKE YOUR LEFT BRAIN ISN'T IN IT.
LET'S JUST REBUILD THE LAVA WALL AND GET THE PEOPLE BACK IN THEIR HOMES.

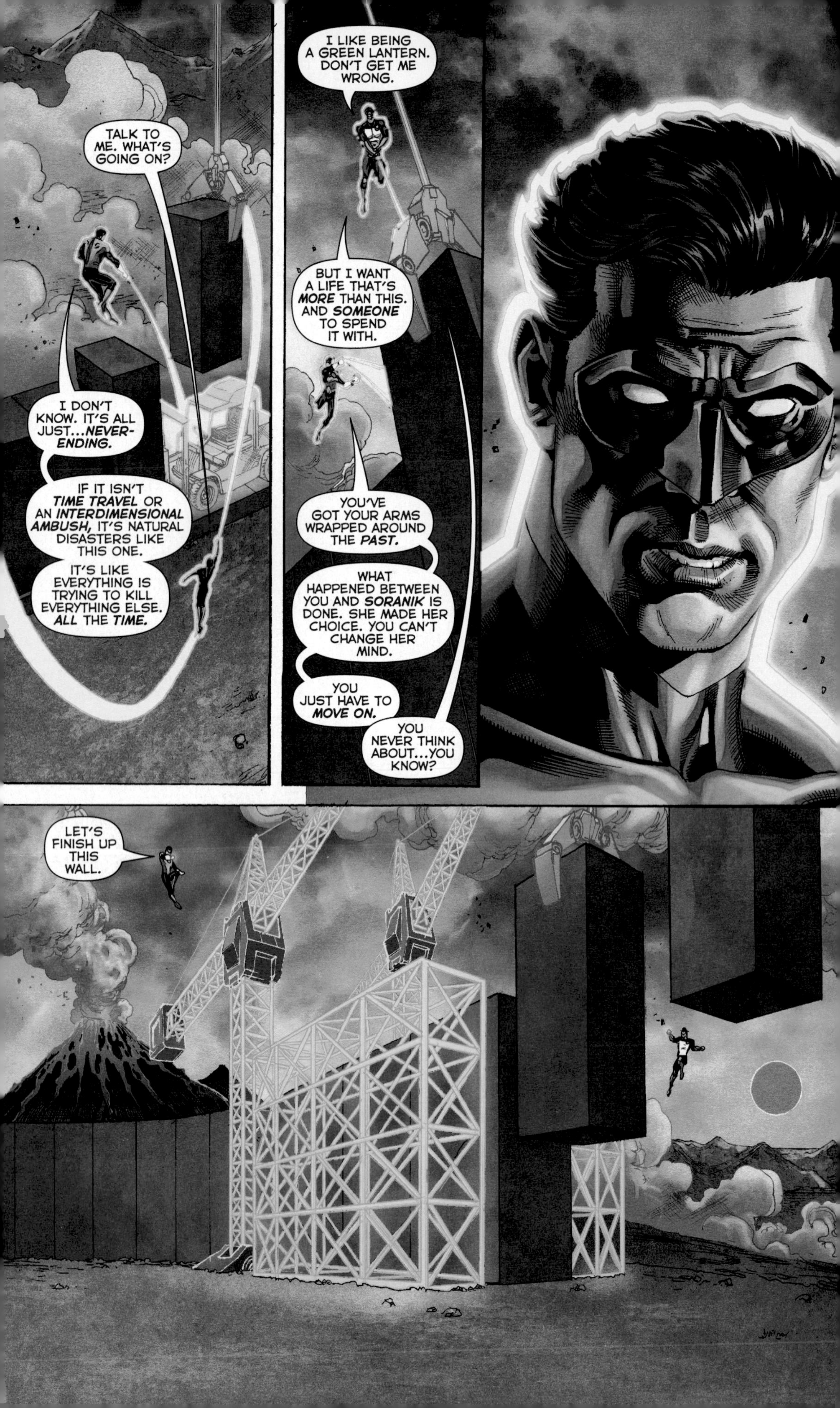
TALK TO ME. WHAT'S GOING ON?
I DON'T KNOW. IT'S ALL JUST...*NEVER-ENDING.*
IF IT ISN'T *TIME TRAVEL* OR AN *INTERDIMENSIONAL AMBUSH,* IT'S NATURAL DISASTERS LIKE THIS ONE.
IT'S LIKE EVERYTHING IS TRYING TO KILL EVERYTHING ELSE. *ALL* THE *TIME.*
I LIKE BEING A GREEN LANTERN. DON'T GET ME WRONG.
BUT I WANT A LIFE THAT'S *MORE* THAN THIS. AND *SOMEONE* TO SPEND IT WITH.
YOU'VE GOT YOUR ARMS WRAPPED AROUND THE *PAST.*
WHAT HAPPENED BETWEEN YOU AND *SORANIK* IS DONE. SHE MADE HER CHOICE. YOU CAN'T CHANGE HER MIND.
YOU JUST HAVE TO *MOVE ON.*
YOU NEVER THINK ABOUT...YOU KNOW?
LET'S FINISH UP THIS WALL.

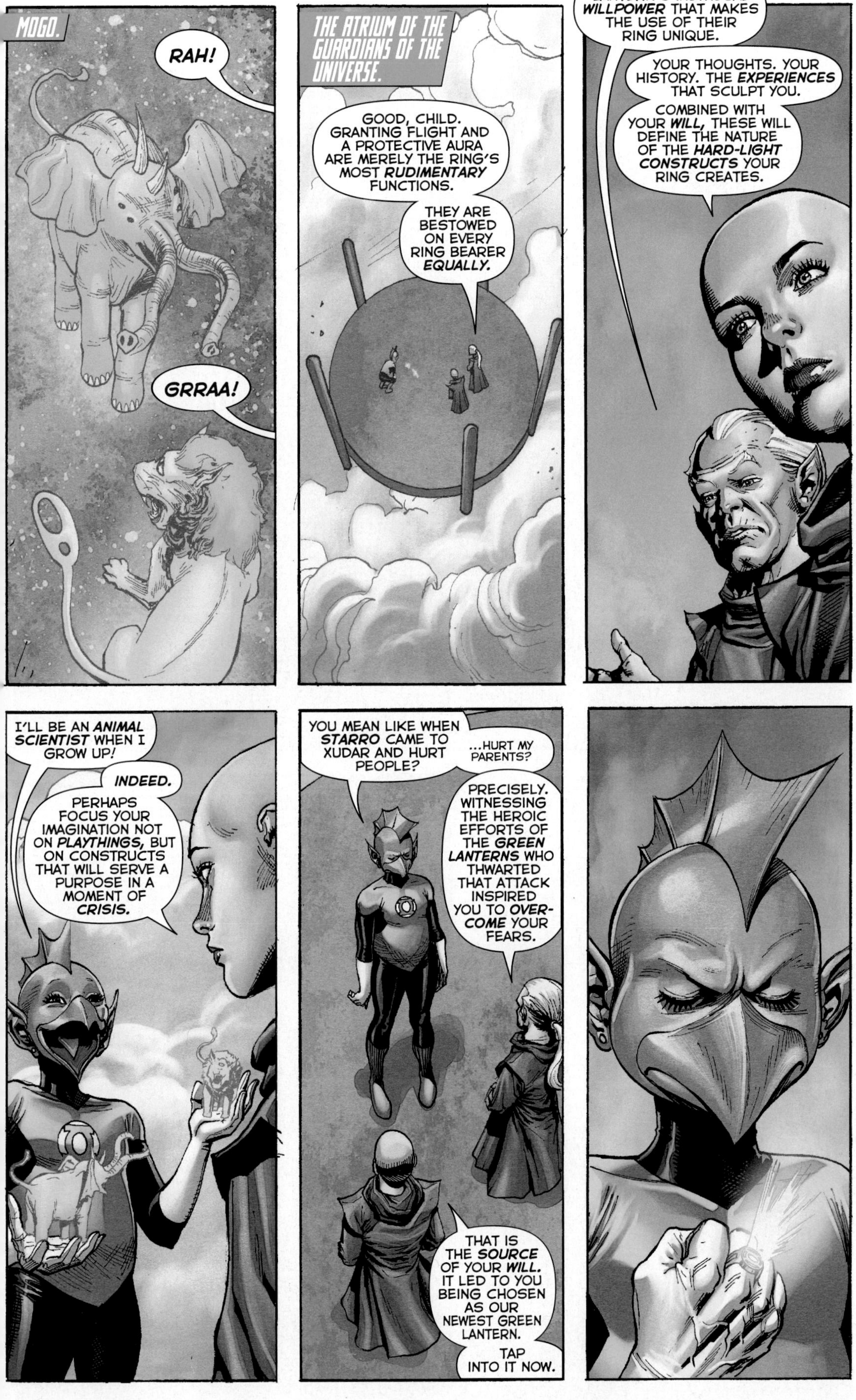
MOGO.
RAH!
GRRAA!
THE ATRIUM OF THE GUARDIANS OF THE UNIVERSE.
GOOD, CHILD. GRANTING FLIGHT AND A PROTECTIVE AURA ARE MERELY THE RING'S MOST RUDIMENTARY FUNCTIONS.
THEY ARE BESTOWED ON EVERY RING BEARER EQUALLY.
IT IS EACH LANTERN'S INDIVIDUAL WILLPOWER THAT MAKES THE USE OF THEIR RING UNIQUE.
YOUR THOUGHTS. YOUR HISTORY. THE EXPERIENCES THAT SCULPT YOU.
COMBINED WITH YOUR WILL, THESE WILL DEFINE THE NATURE OF THE HARD-LIGHT CONSTRUCTS YOUR RING CREATES.
I'LL BE AN ANIMAL SCIENTIST WHEN I GROW UP!
INDEED.
PERHAPS FOCUS YOUR IMAGINATION NOT ON PLAYTHINGS, BUT ON CONSTRUCTS THAT WILL SERVE A PURPOSE IN A MOMENT OF CRISIS.
YOU MEAN LIKE WHEN STARRO CAME TO XUDAR AND HURT PEOPLE?
...HURT MY PARENTS?
PRECISELY. WITNESSING THE HEROIC EFFORTS OF THE GREEN LANTERNS WHO THWARTED THAT ATTACK INSPIRED YOU TO OVERCOME YOUR FEARS.
THAT IS THE SOURCE OF YOUR WILL. IT LED TO YOU BEING CHOSEN AS OUR NEWEST GREEN LANTERN.
TAP INTO IT NOW.

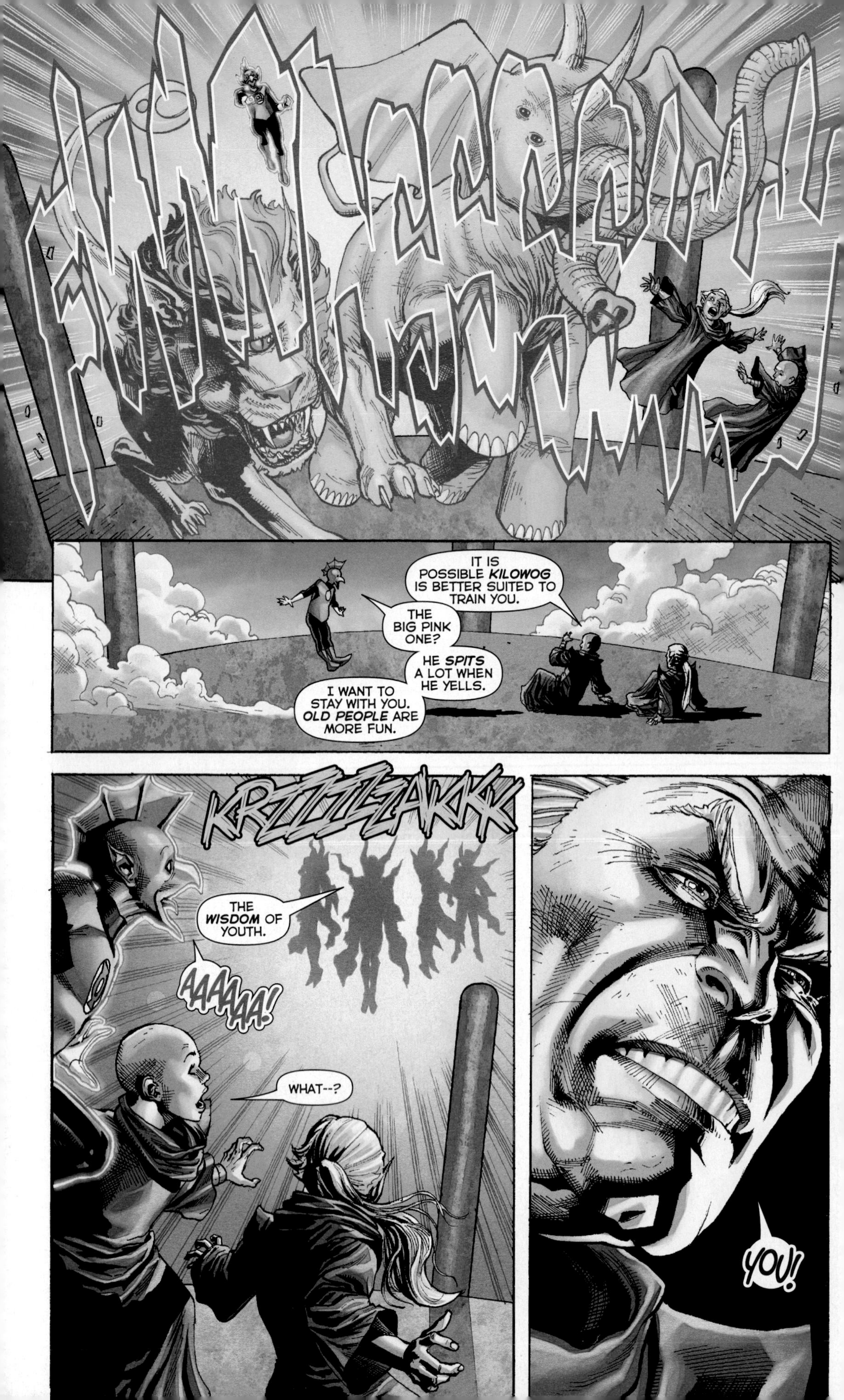
IT IS POSSIBLE KILOWOG IS BETTER SUITED TO TRAIN YOU.
THE BIG PINK ONE?
HE SPITS A LOT WHEN HE YELLS.
I WANT TO STAY WITH YOU. OLD PEOPLE ARE MORE FUN.
KRZZZZZAKKK
THE WISDOM OF YOUTH.
AAAAAA!
WHAT--?
YOU!

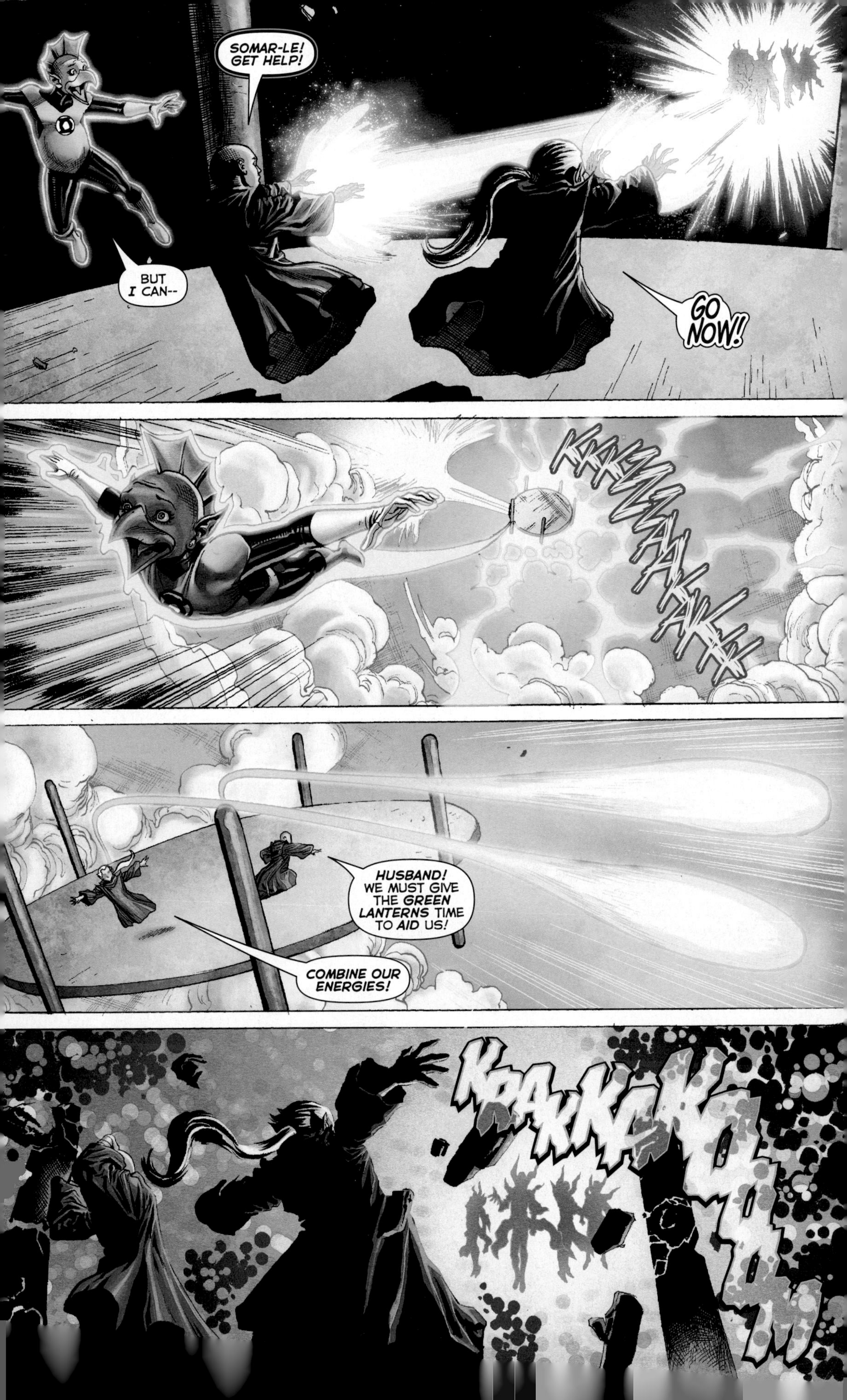

SOMAR-LE! GET HELP!
BUT I CAN--
GO NOW!
KKKKZZAAKKKKK
HUSBAND! WE MUST GIVE THE GREEN LANTERNS TIME TO AID US!
COMBINE OUR ENERGIES!

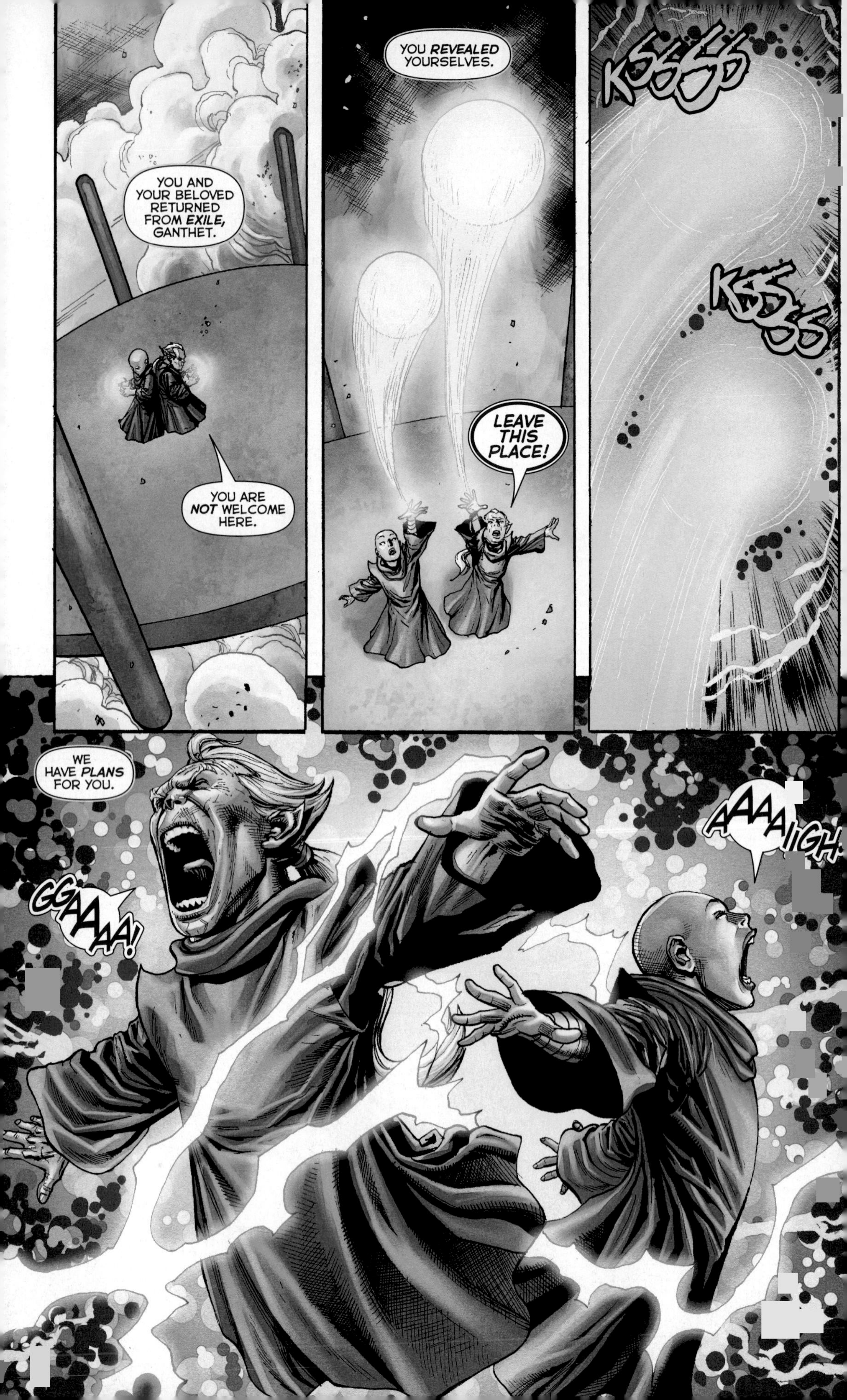

YOU AND YOUR BELOVED RETURNED FROM EXILE, GANTHET.
YOU ARE NOT WELCOME HERE.
YOU REVEALED YOURSELVES.
LEAVE THIS PLACE!
KSSSSS
KSSSSS
WE HAVE PLANS FOR YOU.
GGAAAAA!
AAAAIIGH!

STATUS REPORT, SALAAK.

EVERY ON-DUTY SECTOR TEAM HAS CHECKED IN. ALL MISSIONS ARE PROCEEDING IN AN ORDERLY FASHION.

I'VE HAD MORE EXCITING SHIFTS WRITING SPEEDING TICKETS.

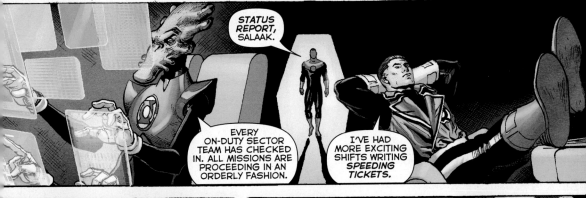

MR. JOHN! MR. JOHN!

CORPS LEADER STEWART, YOUNG MISS. YOUTH IS NO EXCUSE TO NEGLECT PROTOCOL.

IT'S ALL RIGHT, SALAAK.

WHAT'S WRONG, SOMAR-LE?

SOMEBODY DIAL UP A NANNY.

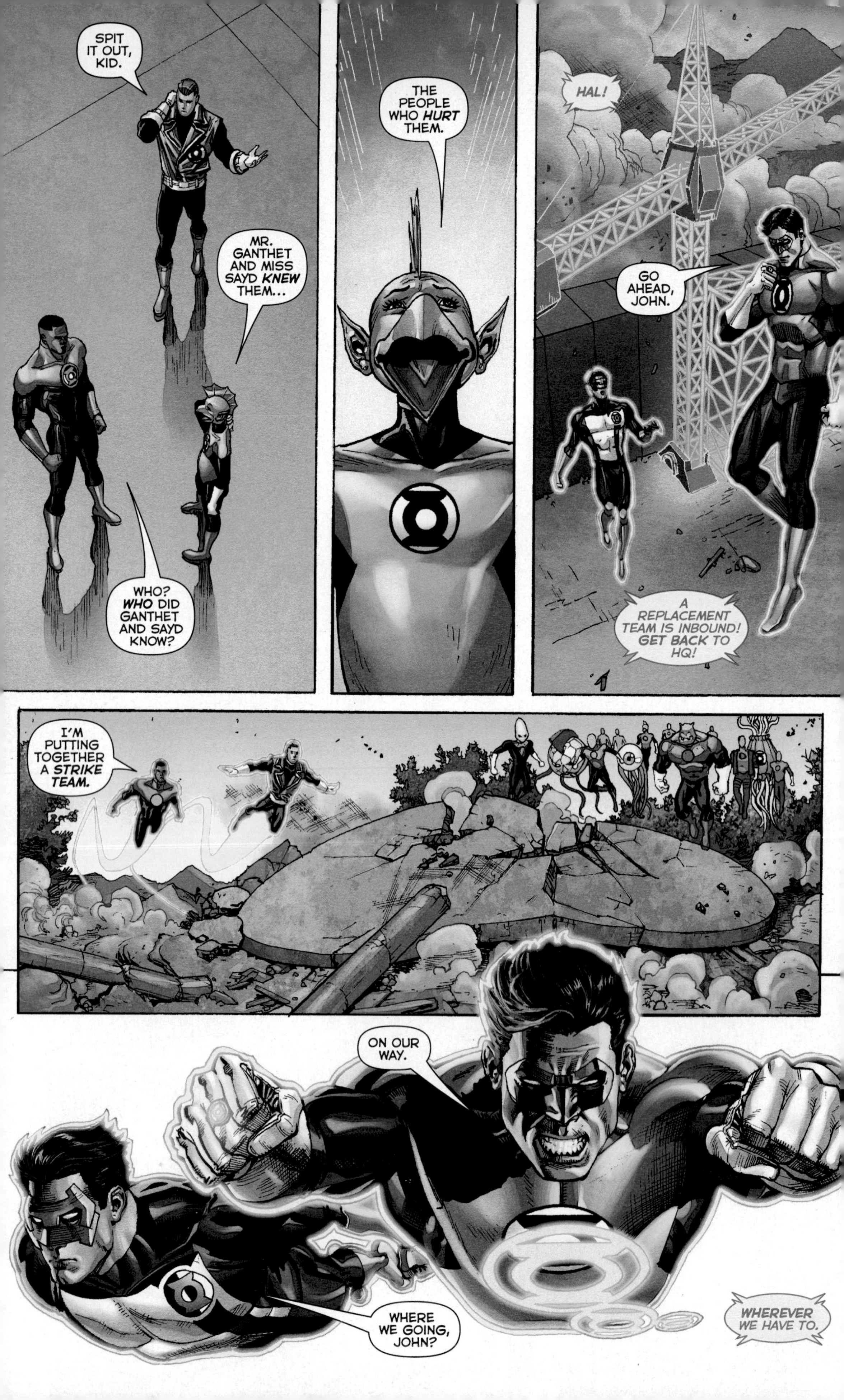
SPIT IT OUT, KID.
MR. GANTHET AND MISS SAYD KNEW THEM...
WHO? WHO DID GANTHET AND SAYD KNOW?
THE PEOPLE WHO HURT THEM.
HAL!
GO AHEAD, JOHN.
A REPLACEMENT TEAM IS INBOUND! GET BACK TO HQ!
I'M PUTTING TOGETHER A STRIKE TEAM.
ON OUR WAY.
WHERE WE GOING, JOHN?
WHEREVER WE HAVE TO.

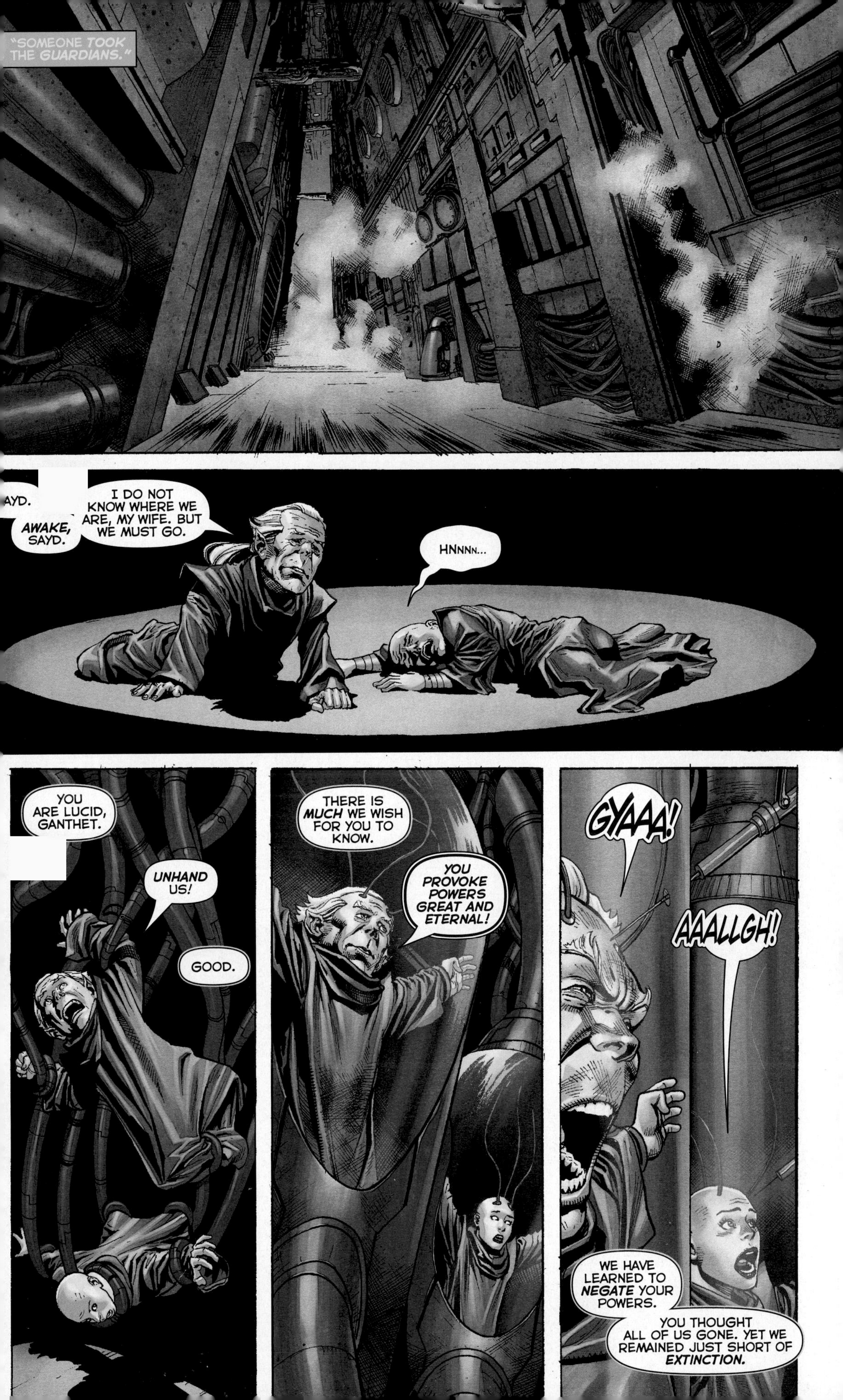
"SOMEONE TOOK THE GUARDIANS."
AYD.
AWAKE, SAYD.
I DO NOT KNOW WHERE WE ARE, MY WIFE. BUT WE MUST GO.
HNNNN...
YOU ARE LUCID, GANTHET.
UNHAND US!
GOOD.
THERE IS MUCH WE WISH FOR YOU TO KNOW.
YOU PROVOKE POWERS GREAT AND ETERNAL!
GYAAA!
AAALLGH!
WE HAVE LEARNED TO NEGATE YOUR POWERS.
YOU THOUGHT ALL OF US GONE. YET WE REMAINED JUST SHORT OF EXTINCTION.

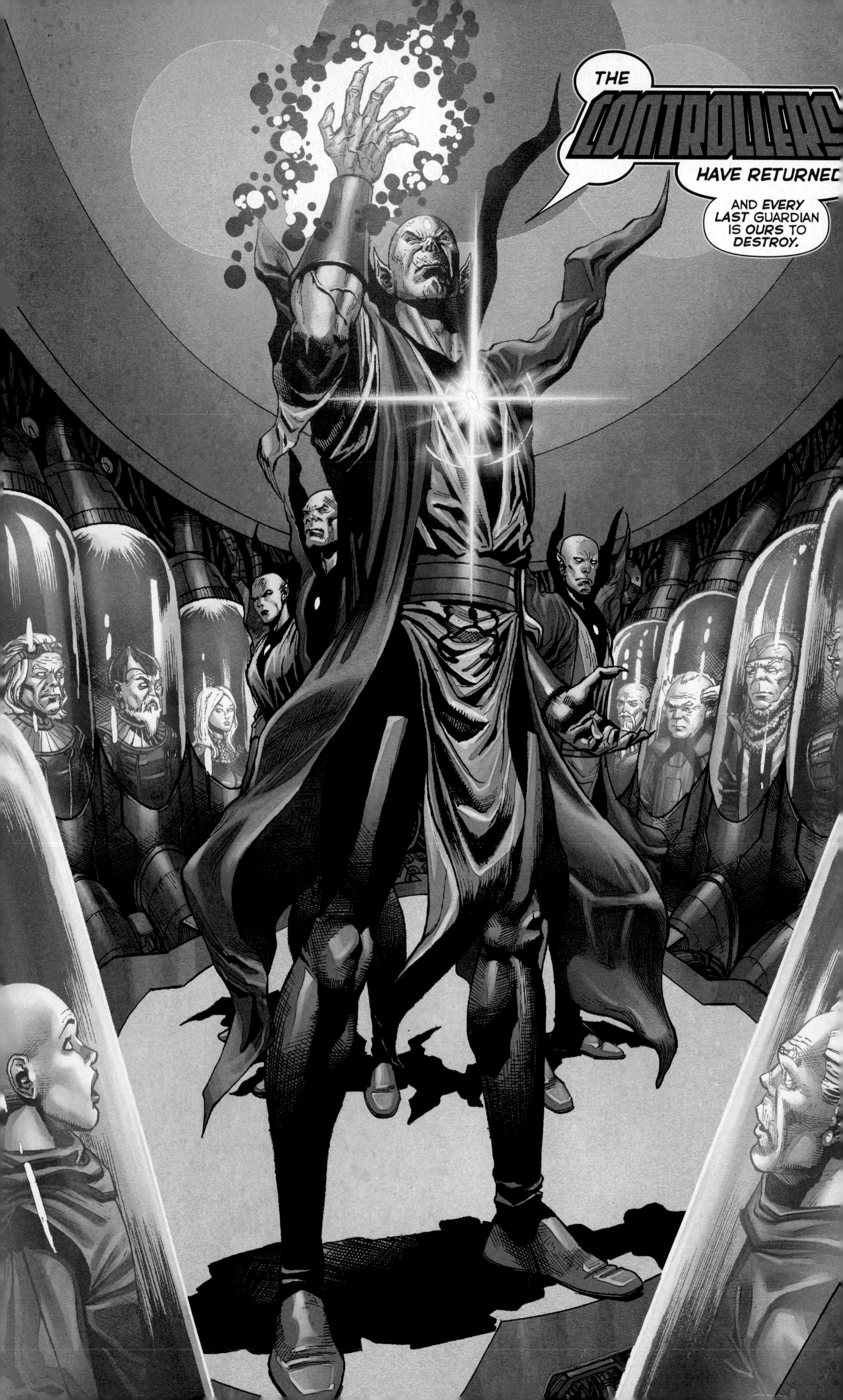
THE CONTROLLERS HAVE RETURNED
AND EVERY LAST GUARDIAN IS OURS TO DESTROY.

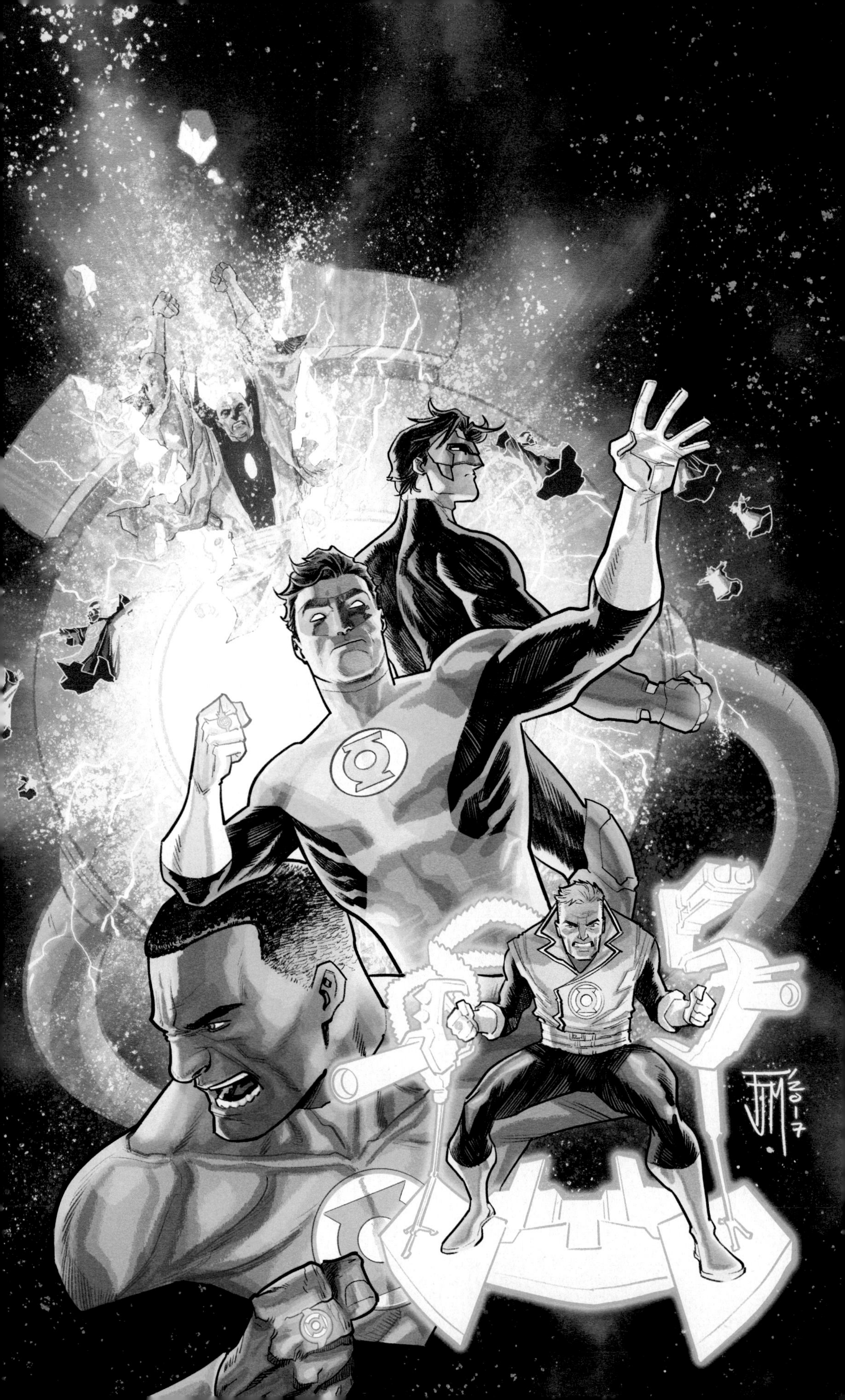

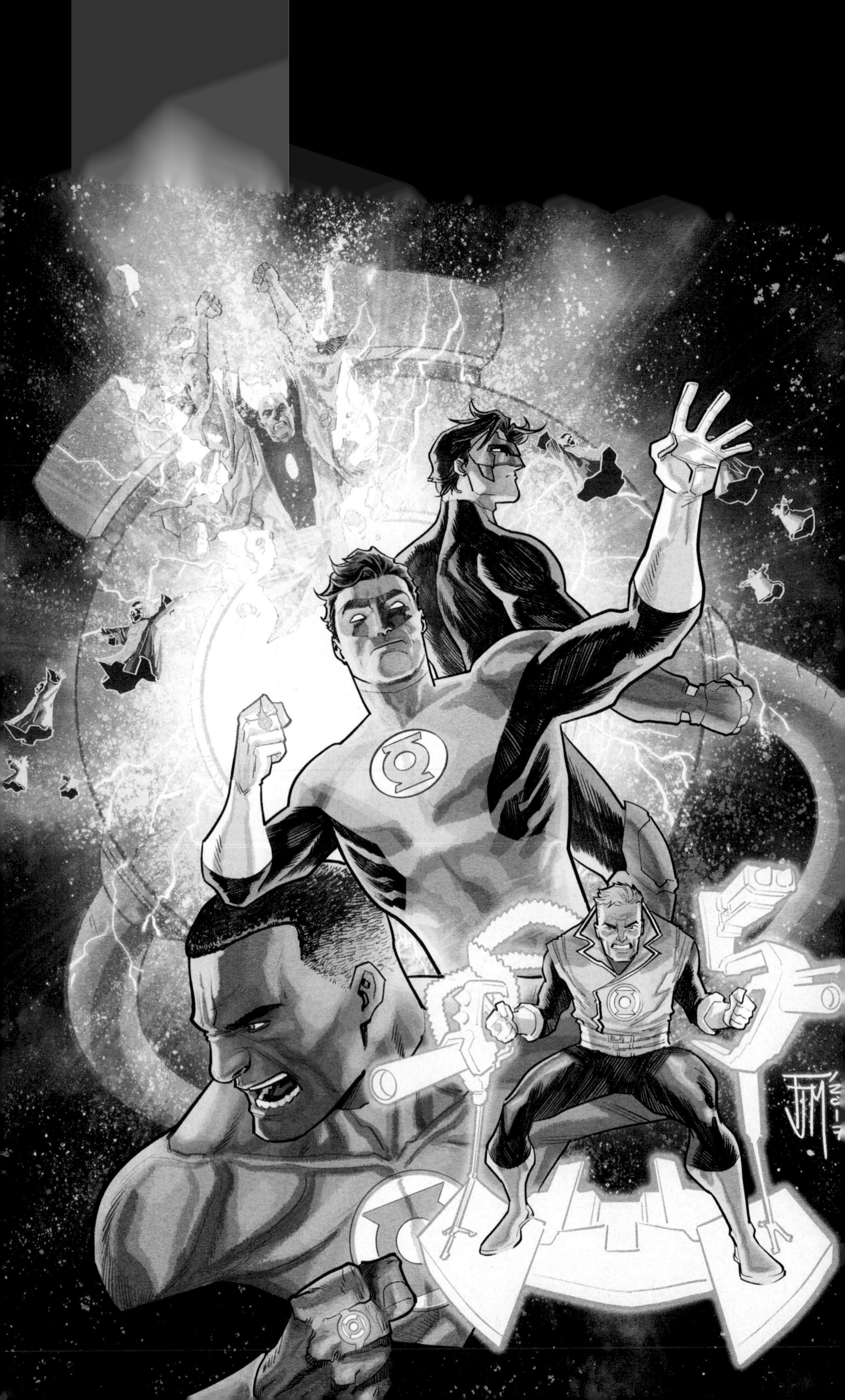

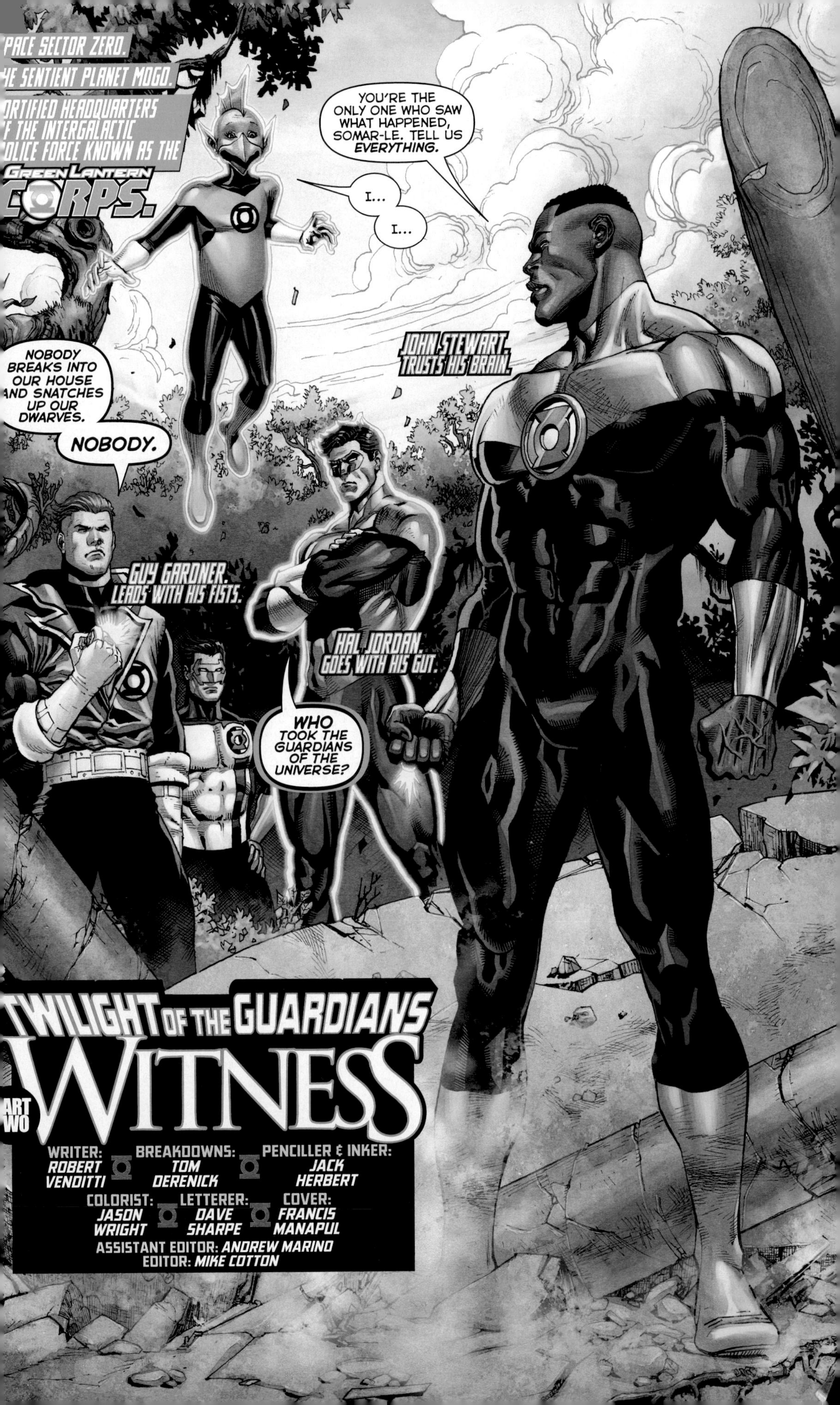
PACE SECTOR ZERO.
HE SENTIENT PLANET MOGO.
ORTIFIED HEADQUARTERS F THE INTERGALACTIC OLICE FORCE KNOWN AS THE
GREEN LANTERN CORPS.
YOU'RE THE ONLY ONE WHO SAW WHAT HAPPENED, SOMAR-LE. TELL US EVERYTHING.
I...
I...
JOHN STEWART. TRUSTS HIS BRAIN.
NOBODY BREAKS INTO OUR HOUSE AND SNATCHES UP OUR DWARVES.
NOBODY.
GUY GARDNER. LEADS WITH HIS FISTS.
HAL JORDAN. GOES WITH HIS GUT.
WHO TOOK THE GUARDIANS OF THE UNIVERSE?
TWILIGHT OF THE GUARDIANS
ART WO
WITNESS
WRITER: ROBERT VENDITTI
BREAKDOWNS: TOM DERENICK
PENCILLER & INKER: JACK HERBERT
COLORIST: JASON WRIGHT
LETTERER: DAVE SHARPE
COVER: FRANCIS MANAPUL
ASSISTANT EDITOR: ANDREW MARINO
EDITOR: MIKE COTTON

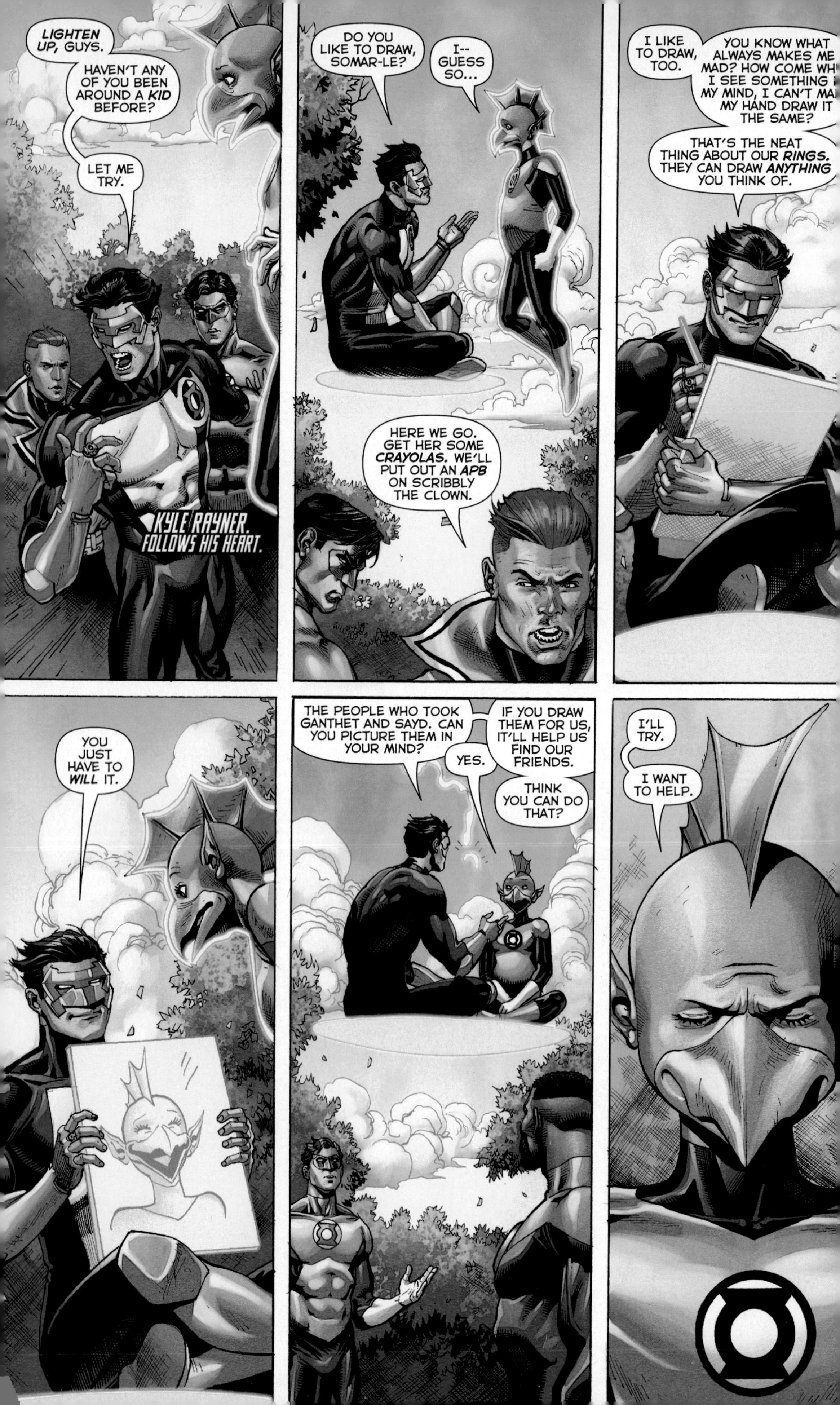

LIGHTEN UP, GUYS.
HAVEN'T ANY OF YOU BEEN AROUND A KID BEFORE?
LET ME TRY.
KYLE RAYNER. FOLLOWS HIS HEART.
DO YOU LIKE TO DRAW, SOMAR-LE?
I-- GUESS SO...
HERE WE GO. GET HER SOME CRAYOLAS. WE'LL PUT OUT AN APB ON SCRIBBLY THE CLOWN.
I LIKE TO DRAW, TOO.
YOU KNOW WHAT ALWAYS MAKES ME MAD? HOW COME WH I SEE SOMETHING MY MIND, I CAN'T MA MY HAND DRAW IT THE SAME?
THAT'S THE NEAT THING ABOUT OUR RINGS. THEY CAN DRAW ANYTHING YOU THINK OF.
YOU JUST HAVE TO WILL IT.
THE PEOPLE WHO TOOK GANTHET AND SAYD. CAN YOU PICTURE THEM IN YOUR MIND?
YES.
IF YOU DRAW THEM FOR US, IT'LL HELP US FIND OUR FRIENDS.
THINK YOU CAN DO THAT?
I'LL TRY.
I WANT TO HELP.

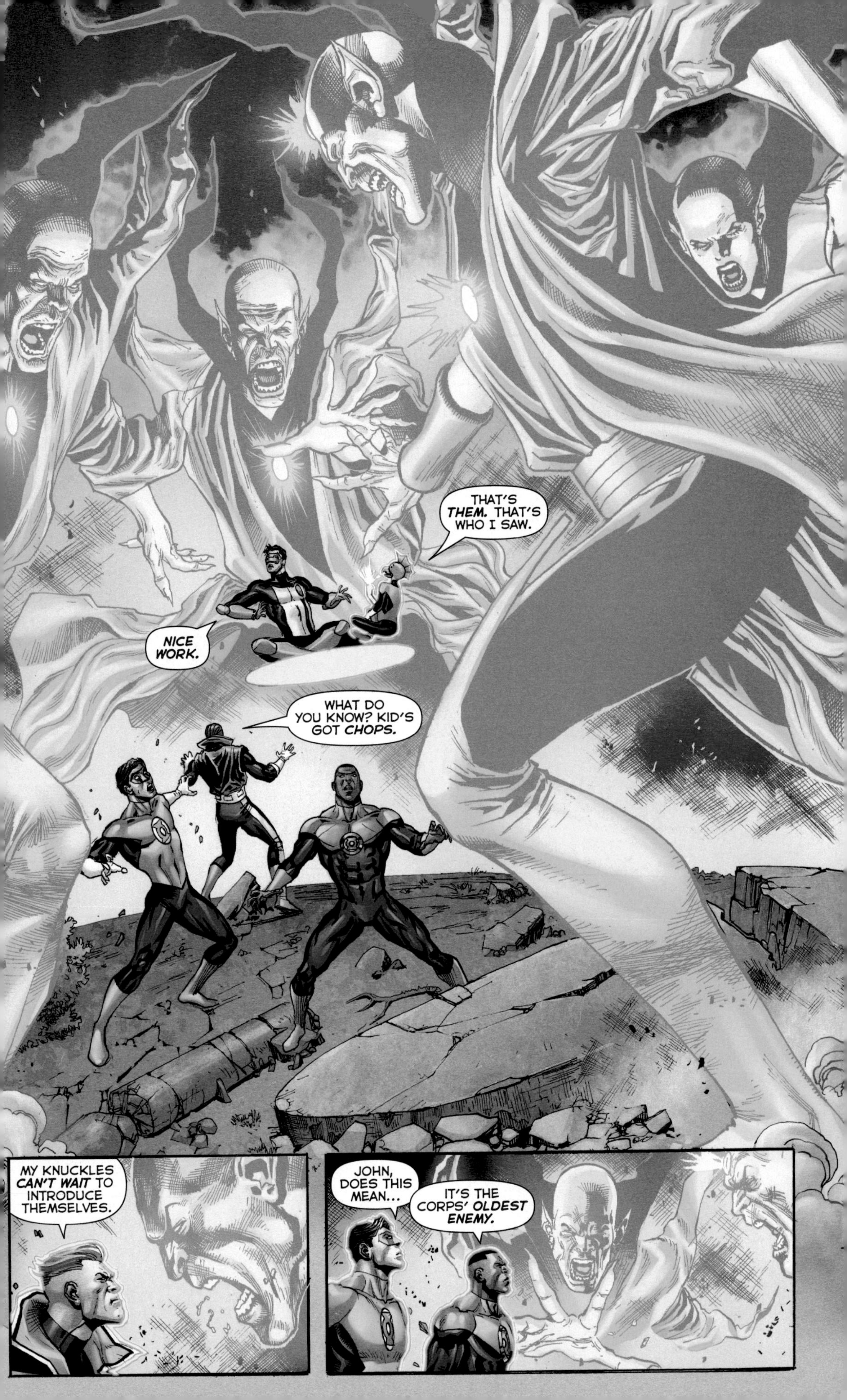

THAT'S *THEM.* THAT'S WHO I SAW.
NICE WORK.
WHAT DO YOU KNOW? KID'S GOT *CHOPS.*
MY KNUCKLES *CAN'T WAIT* TO INTRODUCE THEMSELVES.
JOHN, DOES THIS MEAN...
IT'S THE CORPS' *OLDEST ENEMY.*

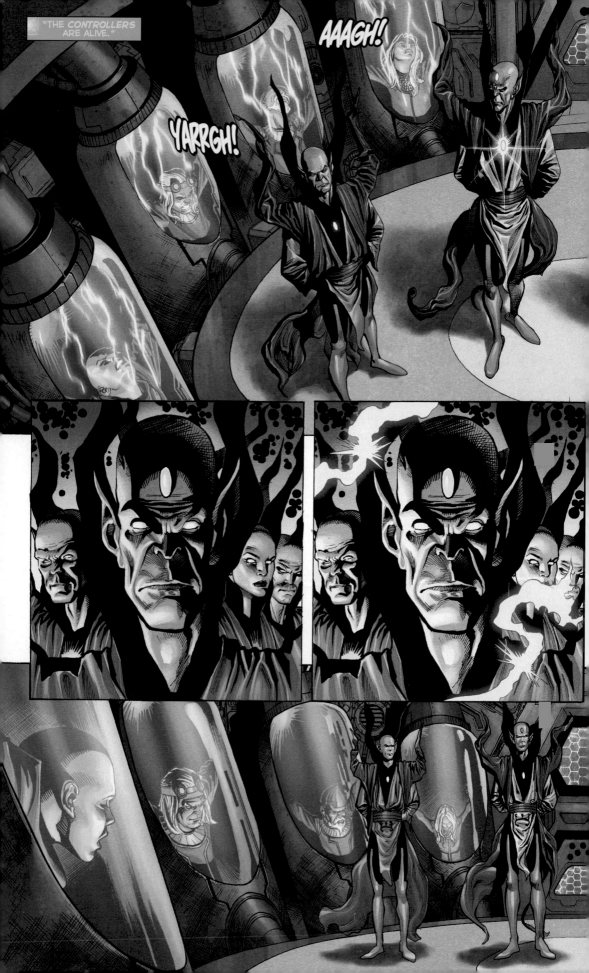

"THE CONTROLLERS ARE ALIVE."

AAAGH!

YARRGH!

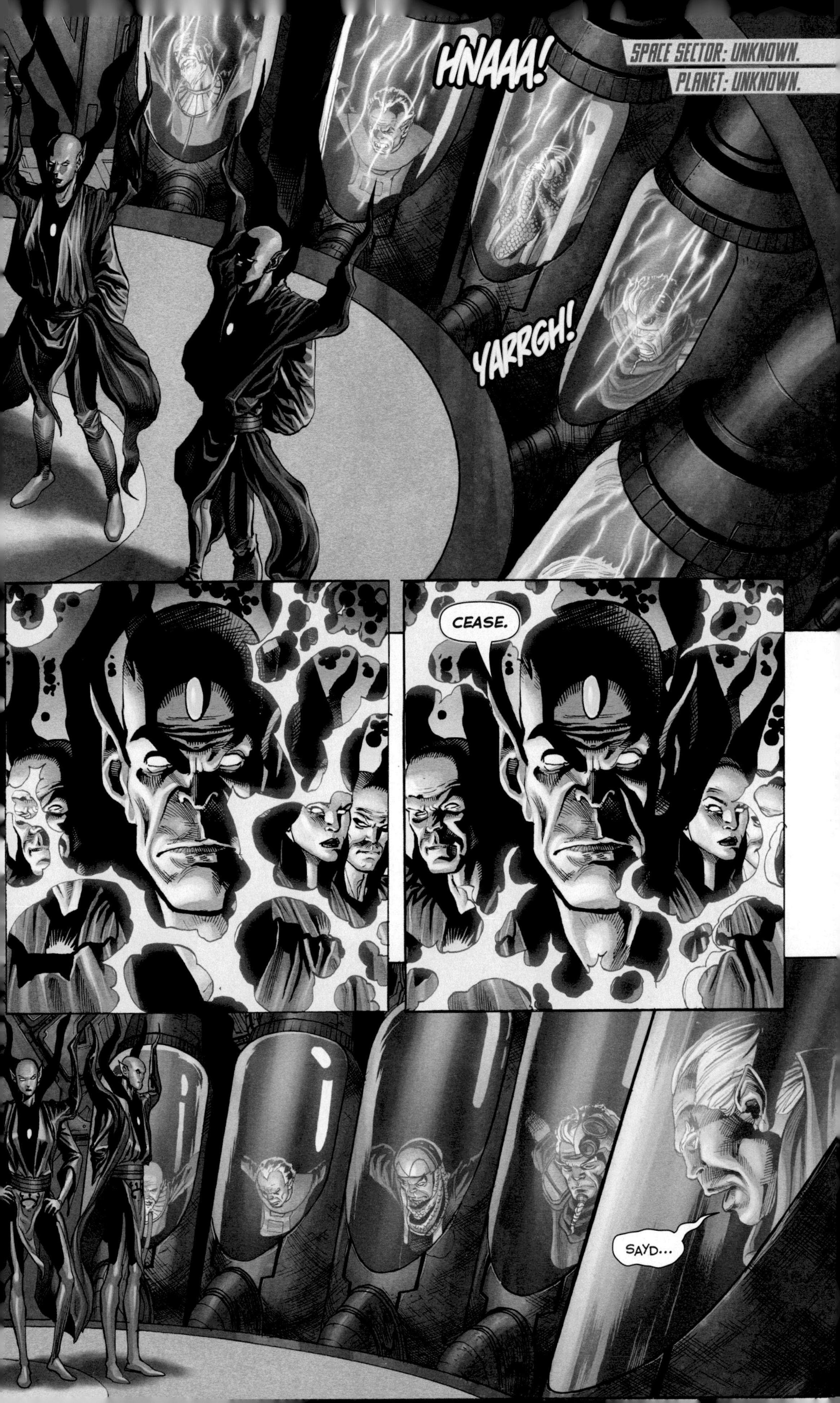
SPACE SECTOR: UNKNOWN.
PLANET: UNKNOWN.
HNAAA!
YARRGH!
CEASE.
SAYD...

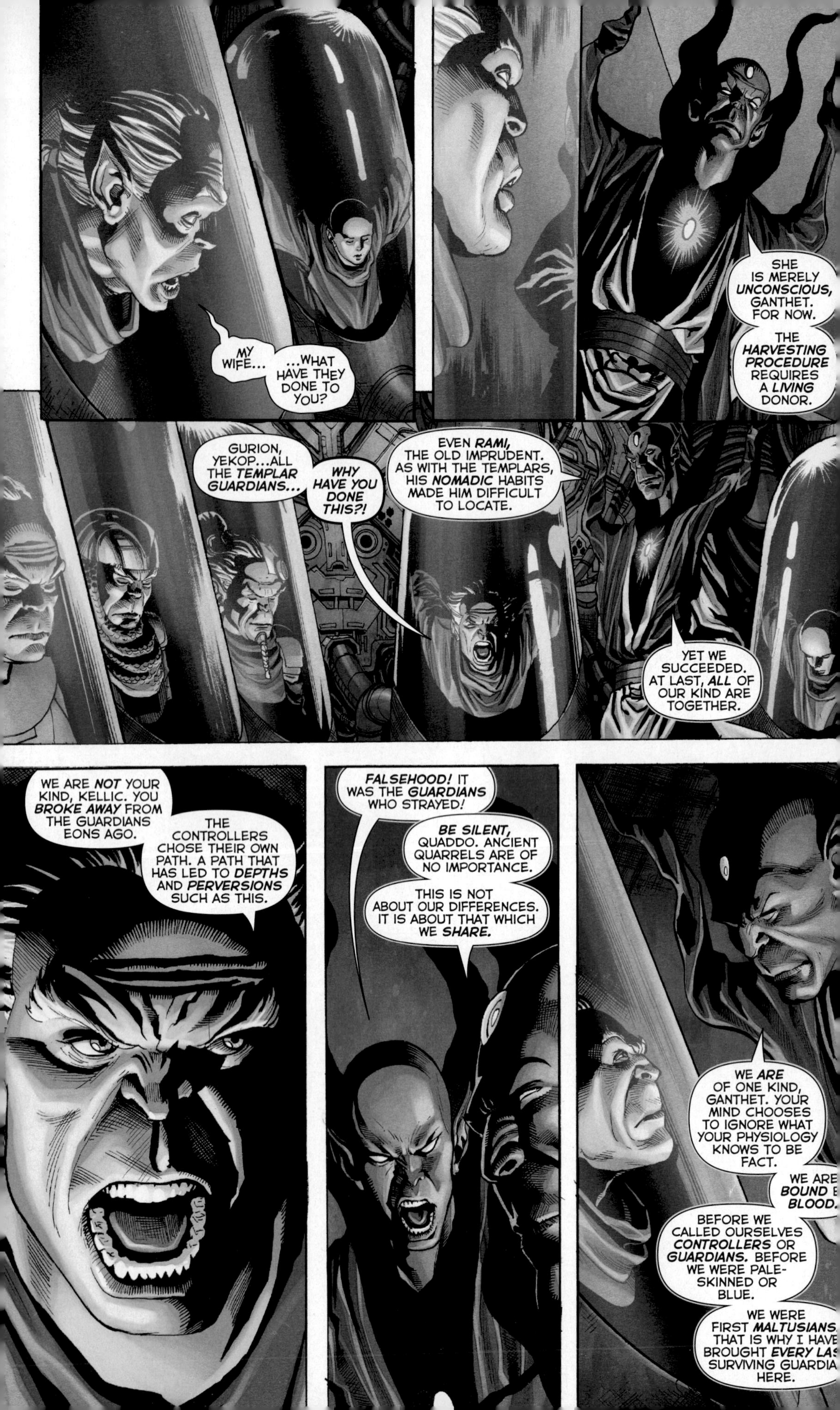

MY WIFE...
...WHAT HAVE THEY DONE TO YOU?
SHE IS MERELY UNCONSCIOUS, GANTHET. FOR NOW.
THE HARVESTING PROCEDURE REQUIRES A LIVING DONOR.
GURION, YEKOP...ALL THE TEMPLAR GUARDIANS...
WHY HAVE YOU DONE THIS?!
EVEN RAMI, THE OLD IMPRUDENT. AS WITH THE TEMPLARS, HIS NOMADIC HABITS MADE HIM DIFFICULT TO LOCATE.
YET WE SUCCEEDED. AT LAST, ALL OF OUR KIND ARE TOGETHER.
WE ARE NOT YOUR KIND, KELLIC. YOU BROKE AWAY FROM THE GUARDIANS EONS AGO.
THE CONTROLLERS CHOSE THEIR OWN PATH. A PATH THAT HAS LED TO DEPTHS AND PERVERSIONS SUCH AS THIS.
FALSEHOOD! IT WAS THE GUARDIANS WHO STRAYED!
BE SILENT, QUADDO. ANCIENT QUARRELS ARE OF NO IMPORTANCE.
THIS IS NOT ABOUT OUR DIFFERENCES. IT IS ABOUT THAT WHICH WE SHARE.
WE ARE OF ONE KIND, GANTHET. YOUR MIND CHOOSES TO IGNORE WHAT YOUR PHYSIOLOGY KNOWS TO BE FACT.
WE ARE BOUND BLOOD.
BEFORE WE CALLED OURSELVES CONTROLLERS OR GUARDIANS. BEFORE WE WERE PALE-SKINNED OR BLUE.
WE WERE FIRST MALTUSIANS. THAT IS WHY I HAVE BROUGHT EVERY LAS SURVIVING GUARDIA HERE.

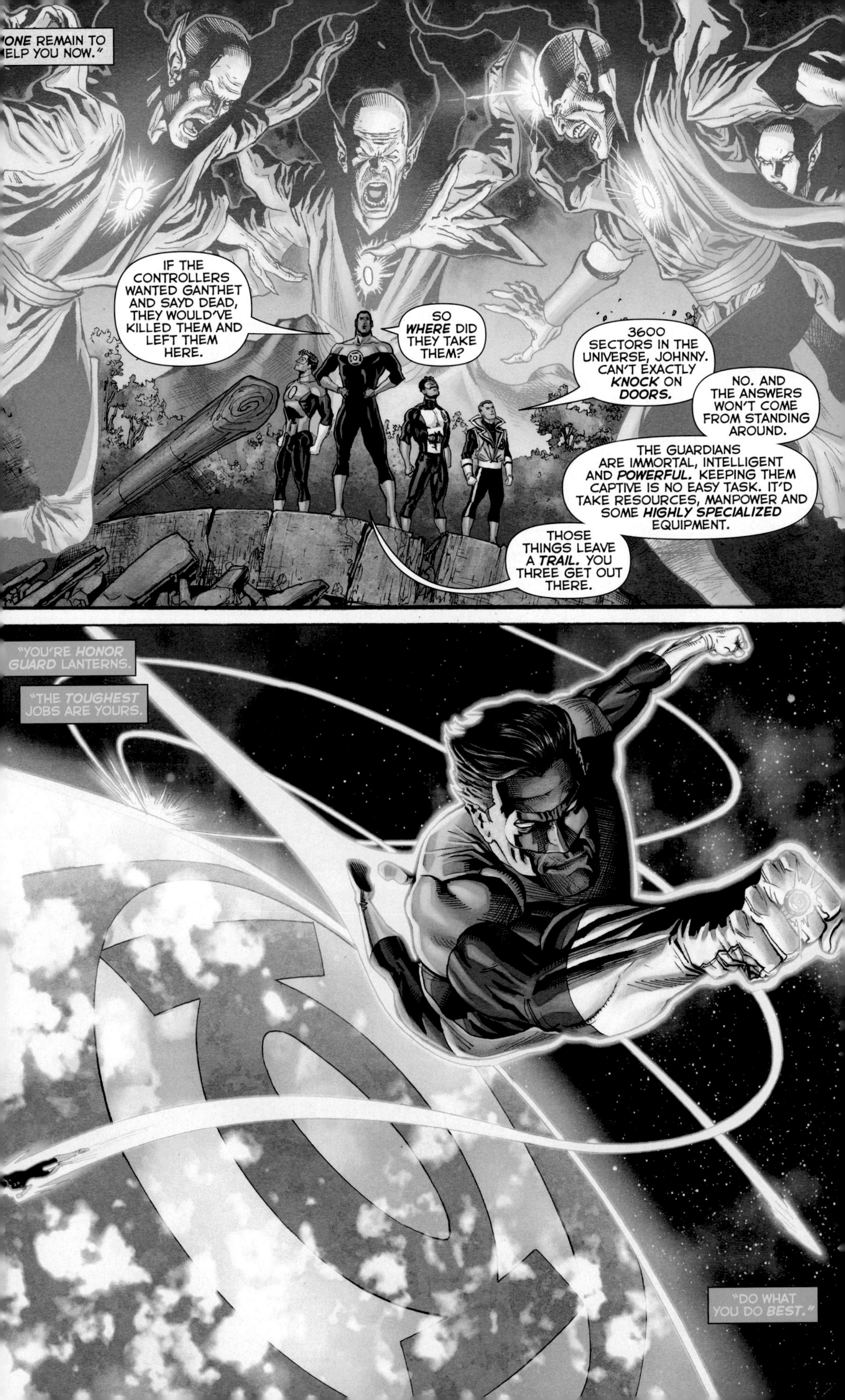
"ONE REMAIN TO
ELP YOU NOW."
IF THE CONTROLLERS WANTED GANTHET AND SAYD DEAD, THEY WOULD'VE KILLED THEM AND LEFT THEM HERE.
SO WHERE DID THEY TAKE THEM?
3600 SECTORS IN THE UNIVERSE, JOHNNY. CAN'T EXACTLY KNOCK ON DOORS.
NO. AND THE ANSWERS WON'T COME FROM STANDING AROUND.
THE GUARDIANS ARE IMMORTAL, INTELLIGENT AND POWERFUL. KEEPING THEM CAPTIVE IS NO EASY TASK. IT'D TAKE RESOURCES, MANPOWER AND SOME HIGHLY SPECIALIZED EQUIPMENT.
THOSE THINGS LEAVE A TRAIL. YOU THREE GET OUT THERE.
"YOU'RE HONOR GUARD LANTERNS.
"THE TOUGHEST JOBS ARE YOURS.
"DO WHAT YOU DO BEST."

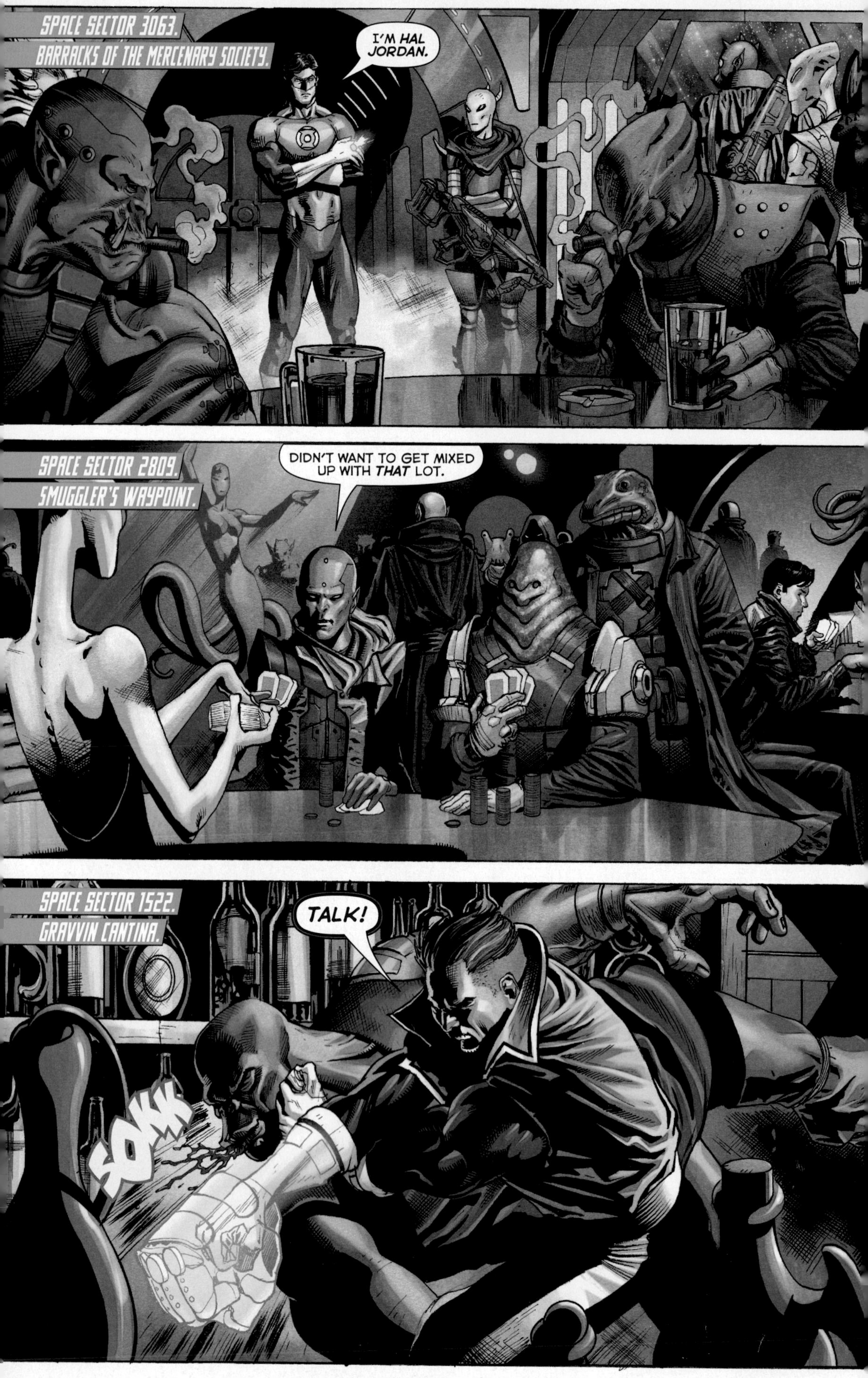
SPACE SECTOR 3063.
BARRACKS OF THE MERCENARY SOCIETY.
I'M HAL JORDAN.
SPACE SECTOR 2809.
SMUGGLER'S WAYPOINT.
DIDN'T WANT TO GET MIXED UP WITH THAT LOT.
SPACE SECTOR 1522.
GRAVVIN CANTINA.
TALK!
SOKK

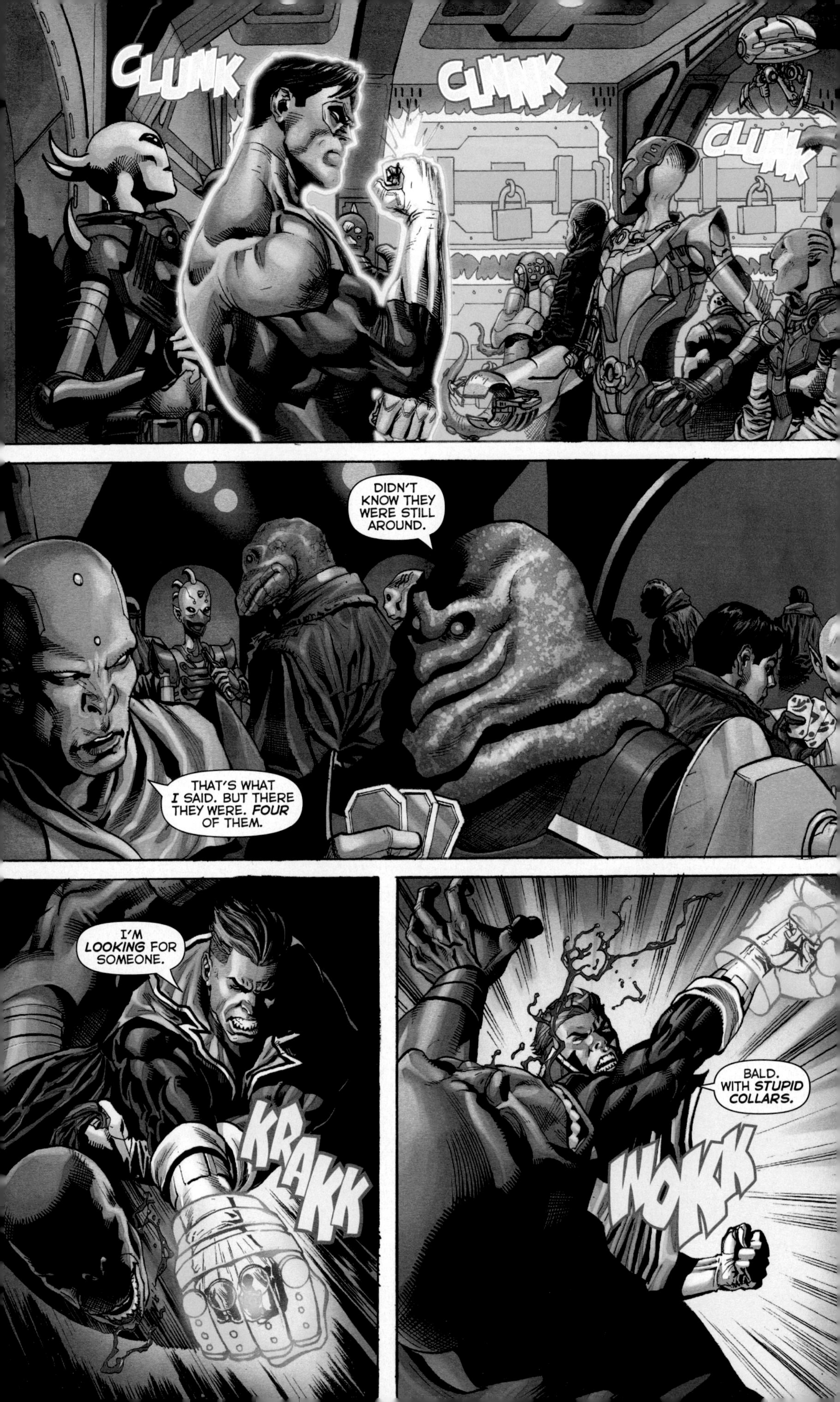
CLUNK
CLUNK
CLUNK
DIDN'T KNOW THEY WERE STILL AROUND.
THAT'S WHAT I SAID. BUT THERE THEY WERE. FOUR OF THEM.
I'M LOOKING FOR SOMEONE.
KRAKK
BALD. WITH STUPID COLLARS.
WOKK

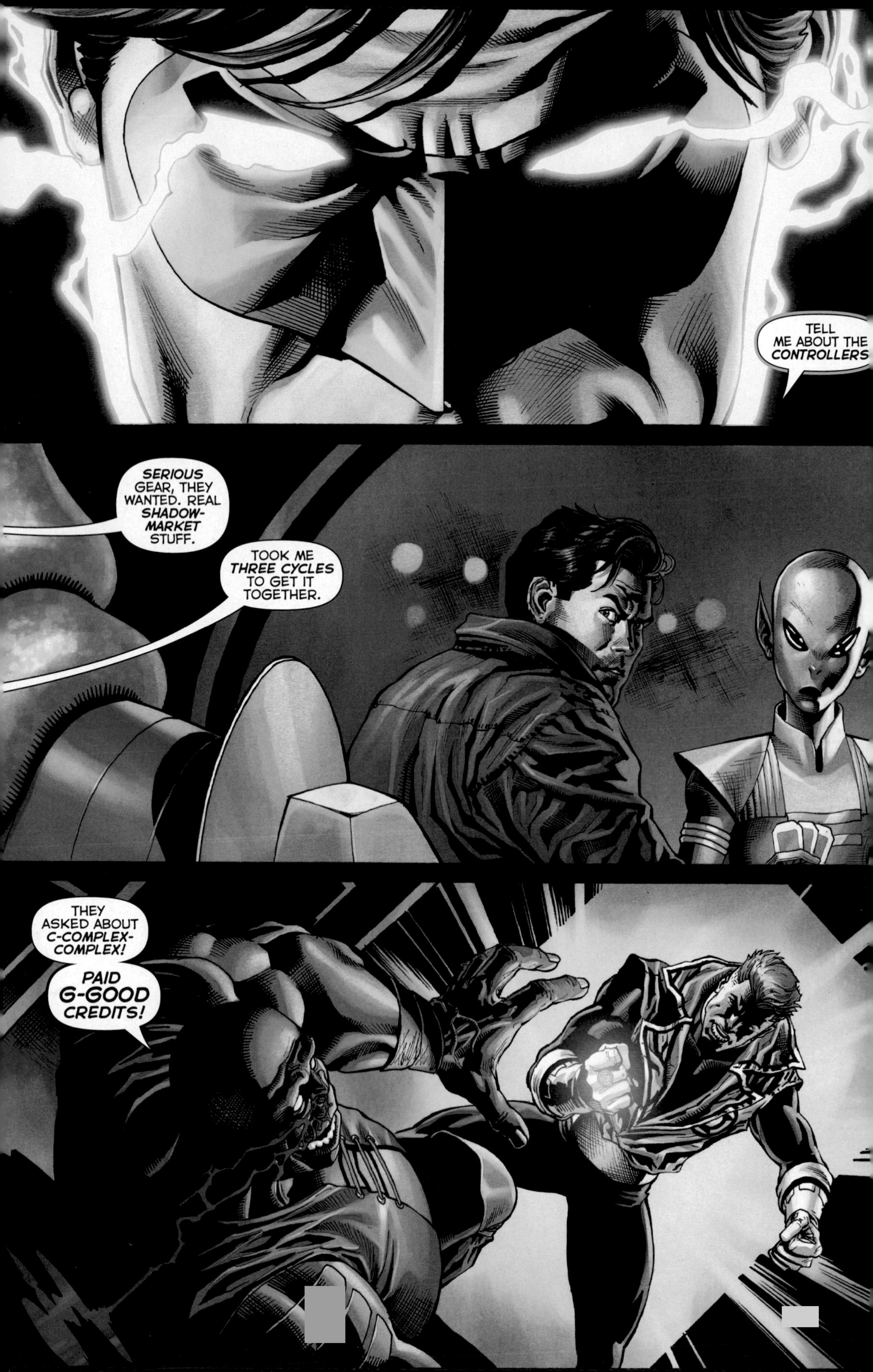
TELL ME ABOUT THE CONTROLLERS
SERIOUS GEAR, THEY WANTED. REAL SHADOW-MARKET STUFF.
TOOK ME THREE CYCLES TO GET IT TOGETHER.
THEY ASKED ABOUT C-COMPLEX-COMPLEX!
PAID G-GOOD CREDITS!

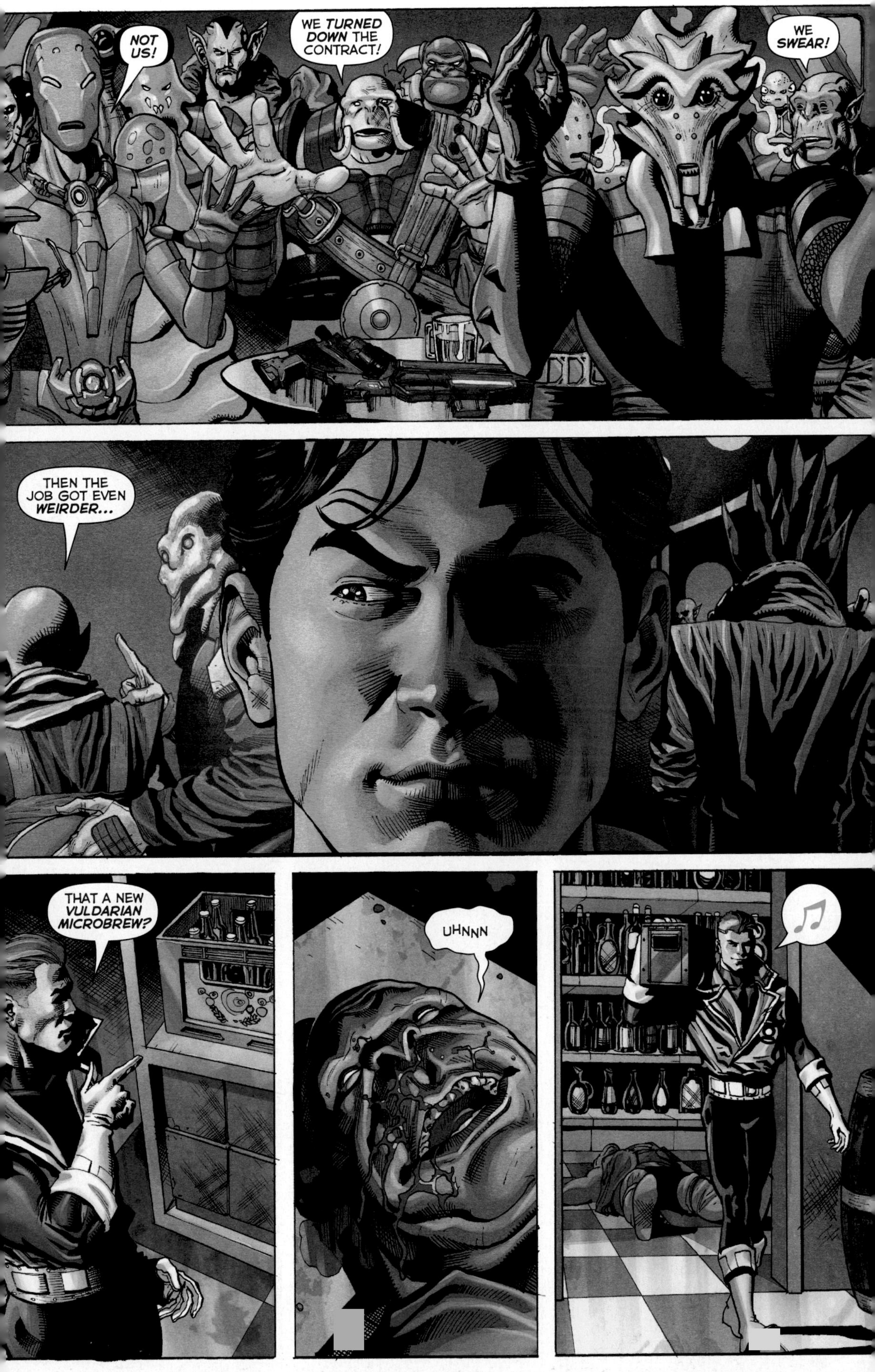
NOT US!
WE TURNED DOWN THE CONTRACT!
WE SWEAR!
THEN THE JOB GOT EVEN WEIRDER...
THAT A NEW VULDARIAN MICROBREW?
UHNNN
♫

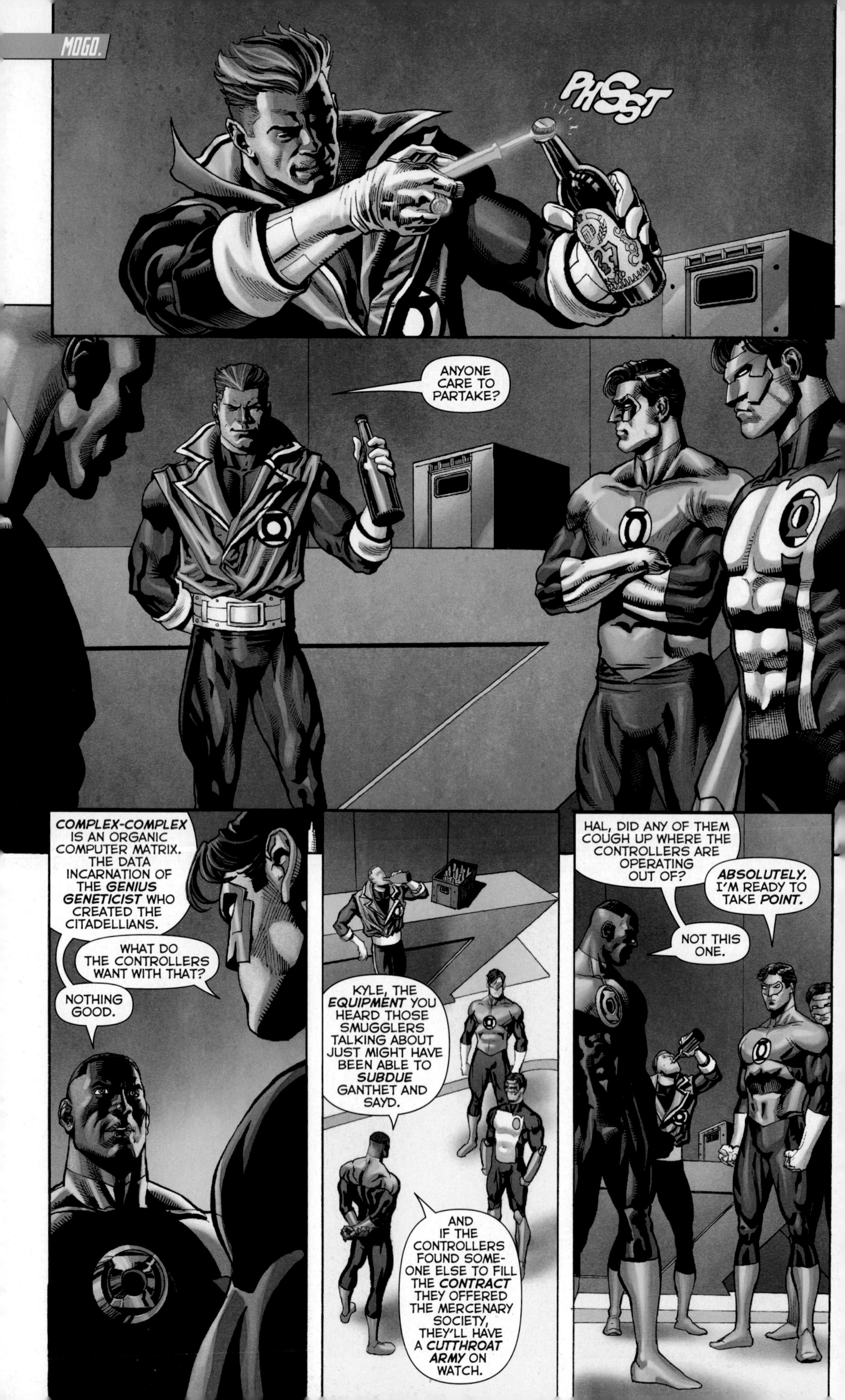
MOGO.
PHSST
ANYONE CARE TO PARTAKE?
COMPLEX-COMPLEX IS AN ORGANIC COMPUTER MATRIX. THE DATA INCARNATION OF THE GENIUS GENETICIST WHO CREATED THE CITADELLIANS.
WHAT DO THE CONTROLLERS WANT WITH THAT?
NOTHING GOOD.
KYLE, THE EQUIPMENT YOU HEARD THOSE SMUGGLERS TALKING ABOUT JUST MIGHT HAVE BEEN ABLE TO SUBDUE GANTHET AND SAYD.
AND IF THE CONTROLLERS FOUND SOME-ONE ELSE TO FILL THE CONTRACT THEY OFFERED THE MERCENARY SOCIETY, THEY'LL HAVE A CUTTHROAT ARMY ON WATCH.
HAL, DID ANY OF THEM COUGH UP WHERE THE CONTROLLERS ARE OPERATING OUT OF?
NOT THIS ONE.
ABSOLUTELY. I'M READY TO TAKE POINT.

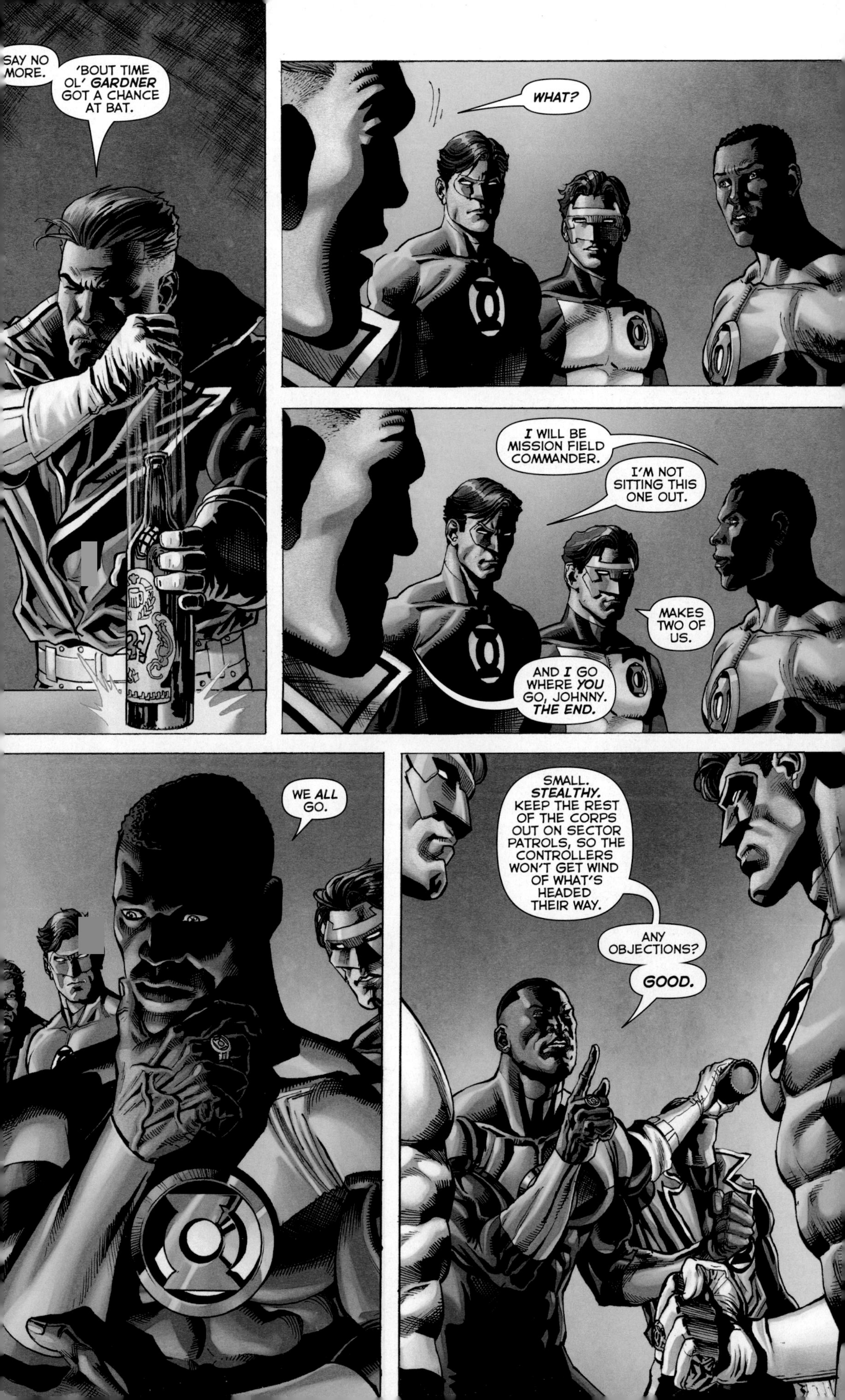
SAY NO MORE.
'BOUT TIME OL' GARDNER GOT A CHANCE AT BAT.
WHAT?
I WILL BE MISSION FIELD COMMANDER.
I'M NOT SITTING THIS ONE OUT.
MAKES TWO OF US.
AND I GO WHERE YOU GO, JOHNNY. THE END.
WE ALL GO.
SMALL. STEALTHY. KEEP THE REST OF THE CORPS OUT ON SECTOR PATROLS, SO THE CONTROLLERS WON'T GET WIND OF WHAT'S HEADED THEIR WAY.
ANY OBJECTIONS?
GOOD.

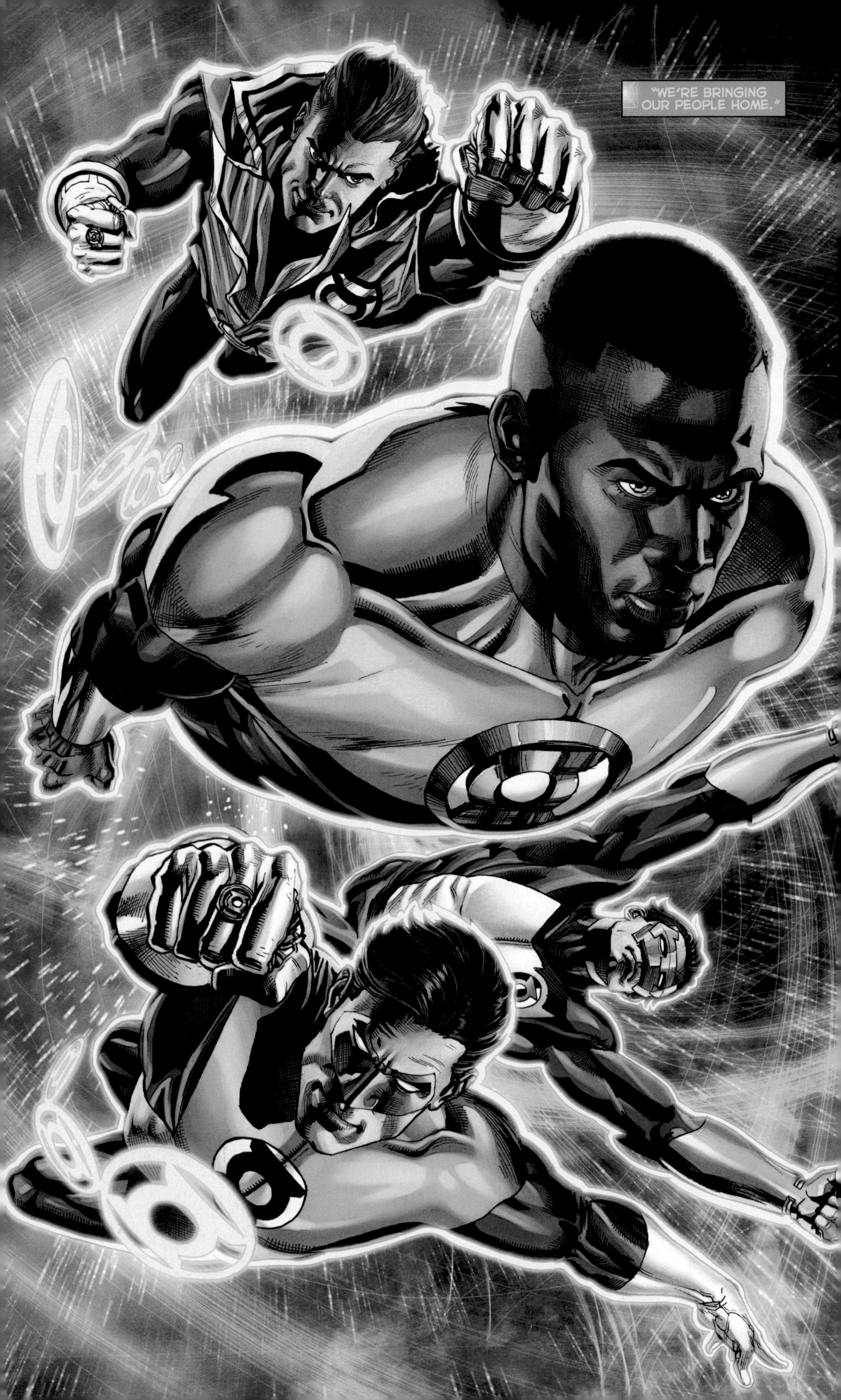
"WE'RE BRINGING OUR PEOPLE HOME."

DO YOU REMEMBER, GANTHET? DO YOU REMEMBER *MALTUS*?

I REMEMBER.

WE WERE A *MULTITUDE* THEN.

"A PLANET TEEMING WITH DIVERSITY. AND AT THE *APEX* STOOD OURSELVES.

"ART. PHILOSOPHY. SCIENCE.

"OUR DISCOVERIES WERE AS *PLENTIFUL* AS THE STARS.

"WE SHARED OUR KNOWLEDGE WITH THE UNIVERSE, AND THE UNIVERSE KNEW OUR NAME.

"WE WERE *ESTEEMED. REVERED.*"

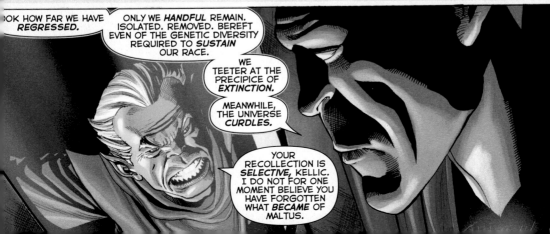

[LO]OK HOW FAR WE HAVE *REGRESSED.*

ONLY WE *HANDFUL* REMAIN. ISOLATED. REMOVED. BEREFT EVEN OF THE GENETIC DIVERSITY REQUIRED TO *SUSTAIN* OUR RACE.

WE TEETER AT THE PRECIPICE OF *EXTINCTION.*

MEANWHILE, THE UNIVERSE *CURDLES.*

YOUR RECOLLECTION IS *SELECTIVE,* KELLIC. I DO NOT FOR ONE MOMENT BELIEVE YOU HAVE FORGOTTEN WHAT *BECAME* OF MALTUS.

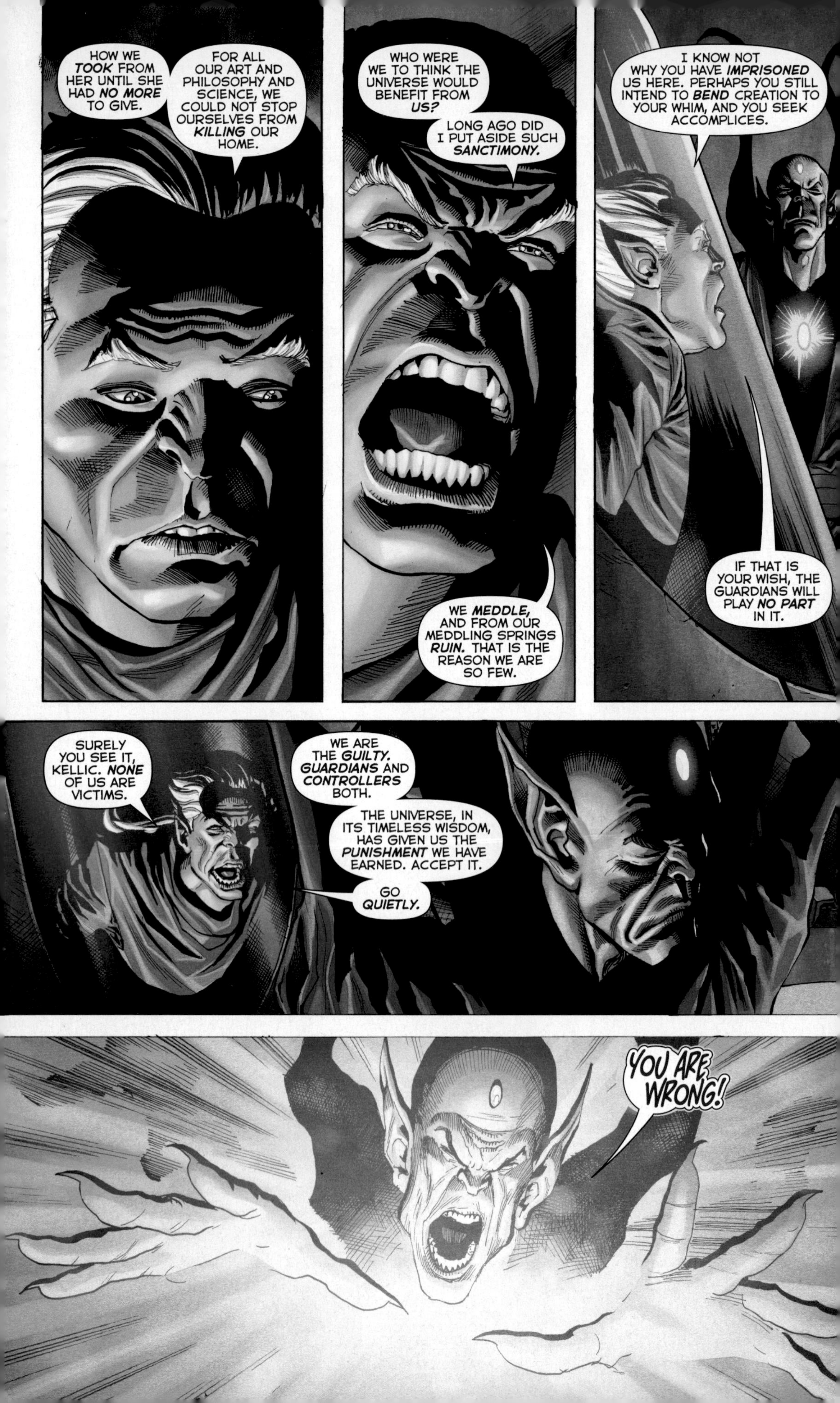
HOW WE TOOK FROM HER UNTIL SHE HAD NO MORE TO GIVE.
FOR ALL OUR ART AND PHILOSOPHY AND SCIENCE, WE COULD NOT STOP OURSELVES FROM KILLING OUR HOME.
WHO WERE WE TO THINK THE UNIVERSE WOULD BENEFIT FROM US?
LONG AGO DID I PUT ASIDE SUCH SANCTIMONY.
WE MEDDLE, AND FROM OUR MEDDLING SPRINGS RUIN. THAT IS THE REASON WE ARE SO FEW.
I KNOW NOT WHY YOU HAVE IMPRISONED US HERE. PERHAPS YOU STILL INTEND TO BEND CREATION TO YOUR WHIM, AND YOU SEEK ACCOMPLICES.
IF THAT IS YOUR WISH, THE GUARDIANS WILL PLAY NO PART IN IT.
SURELY YOU SEE IT, KELLIC. NONE OF US ARE VICTIMS.
WE ARE THE GUILTY. GUARDIANS AND CONTROLLERS BOTH.
THE UNIVERSE, IN ITS TIMELESS WISDOM, HAS GIVEN US THE PUNISHMENT WE HAVE EARNED. ACCEPT IT.
GO QUIETLY.
YOU ARE WRONG!

GNNYAAAGH!

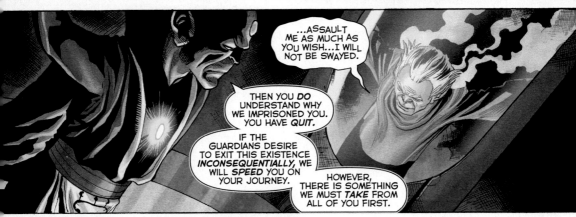

...ASSAULT ME AS MUCH AS YOU WISH...I WILL NOT BE SWAYED.

THEN YOU *DO* UNDERSTAND WHY WE IMPRISONED YOU. YOU HAVE *QUIT*.

IF THE GUARDIANS DESIRE TO EXIT THIS EXISTENCE *INCONSEQUENTIALLY*, WE WILL *SPEED* YOU ON YOUR JOURNEY.

HOWEVER, THERE IS SOMETHING WE MUST *TAKE* FROM ALL OF YOU FIRST.

THE HARVESTER IS READY FOR THIS ONE.

LEAVE HIM BE!

...BROTHER?

BEGIN.

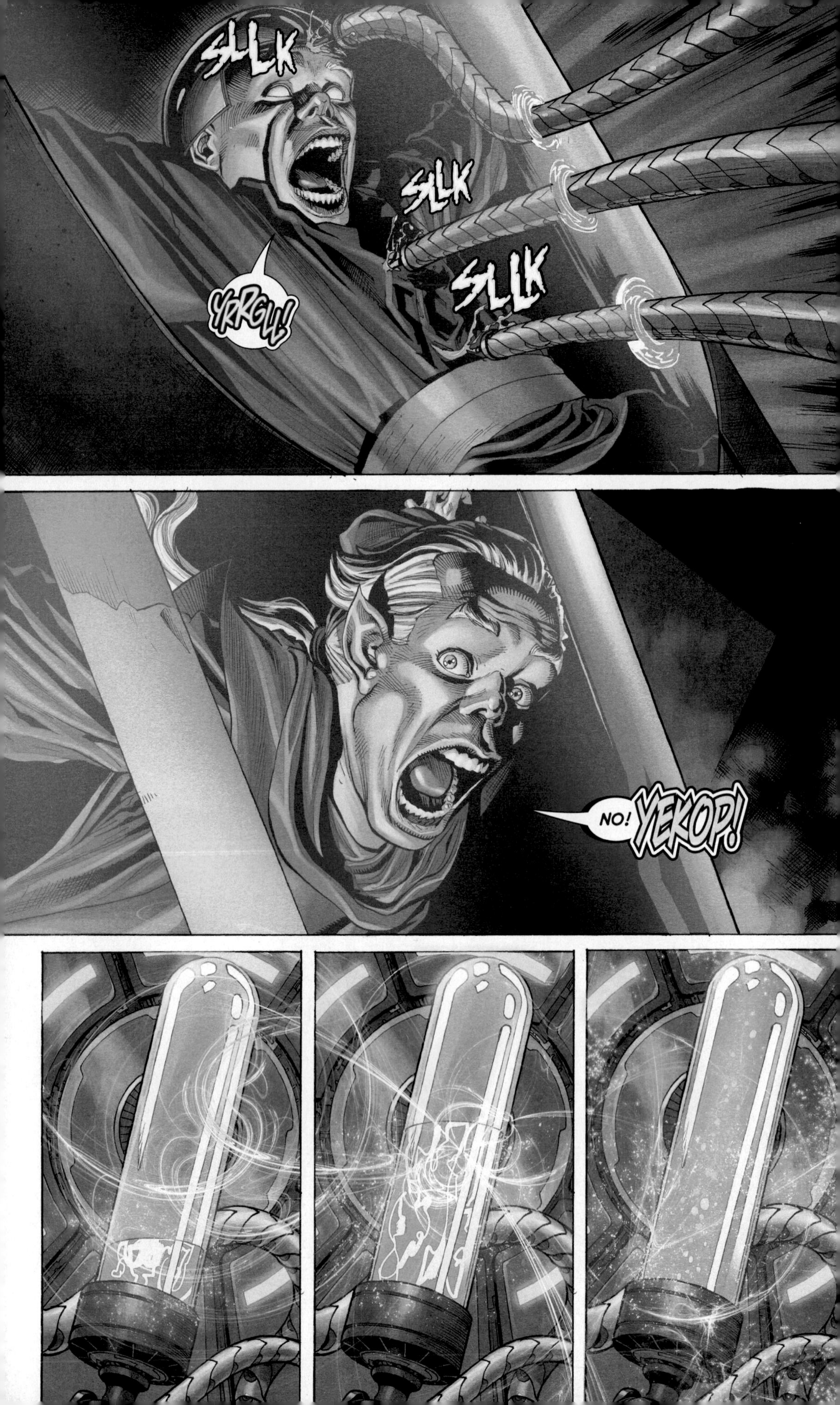
SLLK
SLLK
SLLK
YRRGLL!
NO! YEKOP!

KELLIC... WHAT HAVE YOU DONE?

THE CONTROLLERS AND THE GUARDIANS HAVE QUARRELED ACROSS THE EONS. WE HAVE *WARRED.*

BUT DEEP DOWN IN OUR *MOLECULES,* WE REMAIN THE SAME.

WE CARRY THE PRECIOUS GIFT OF *MALTUS* WITHIN US.

IT WILL BE *HARVESTED* FROM EACH OF YOU.

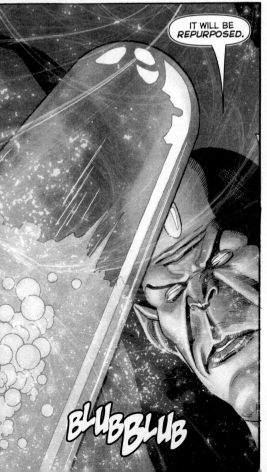

IT WILL BE *REPURPOSED.*

BLUB BLUB

AND FROM THE *BOUNTY...*

KZZZN

KZZAKK

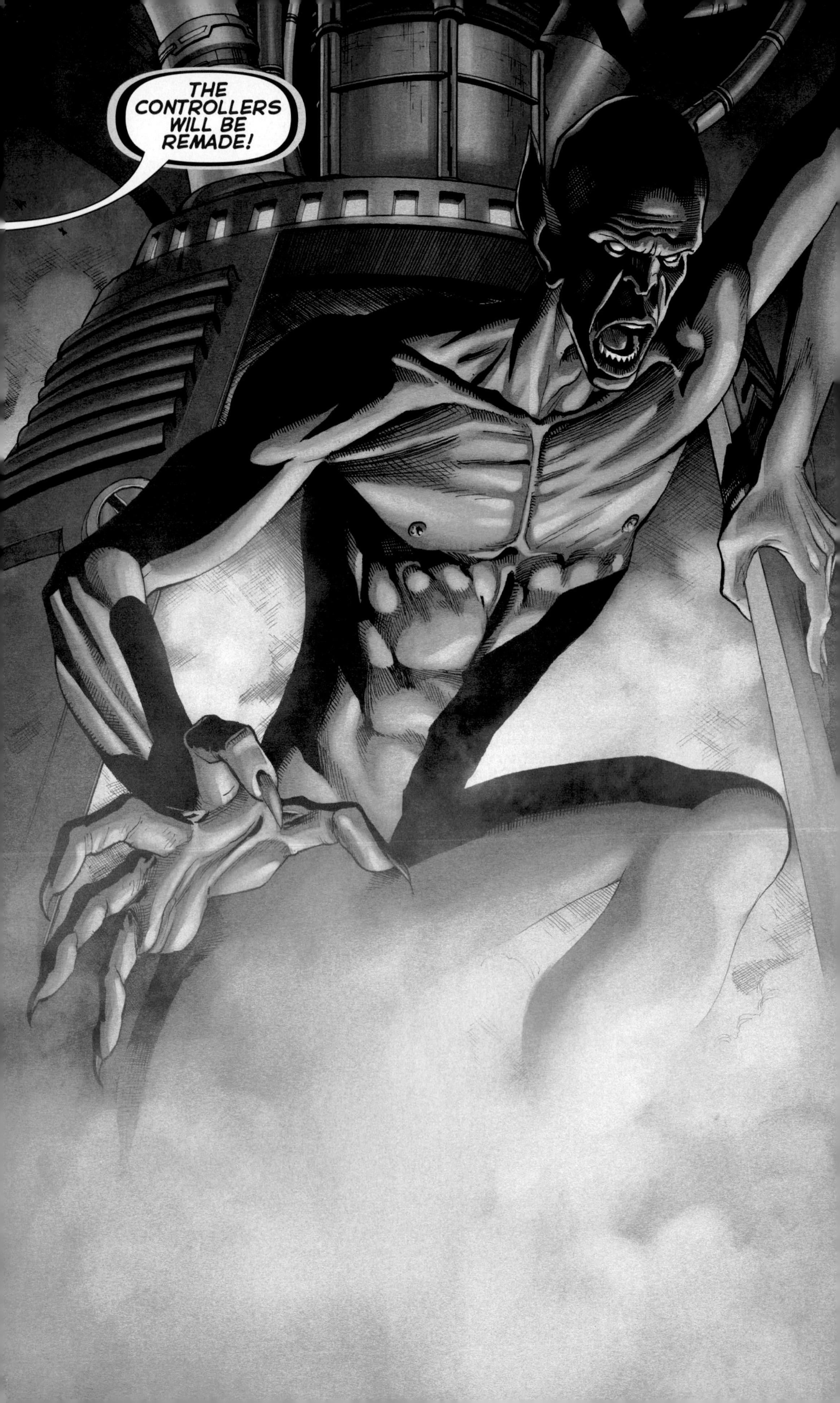
THE CONTROLLERS WILL BE REMADE!

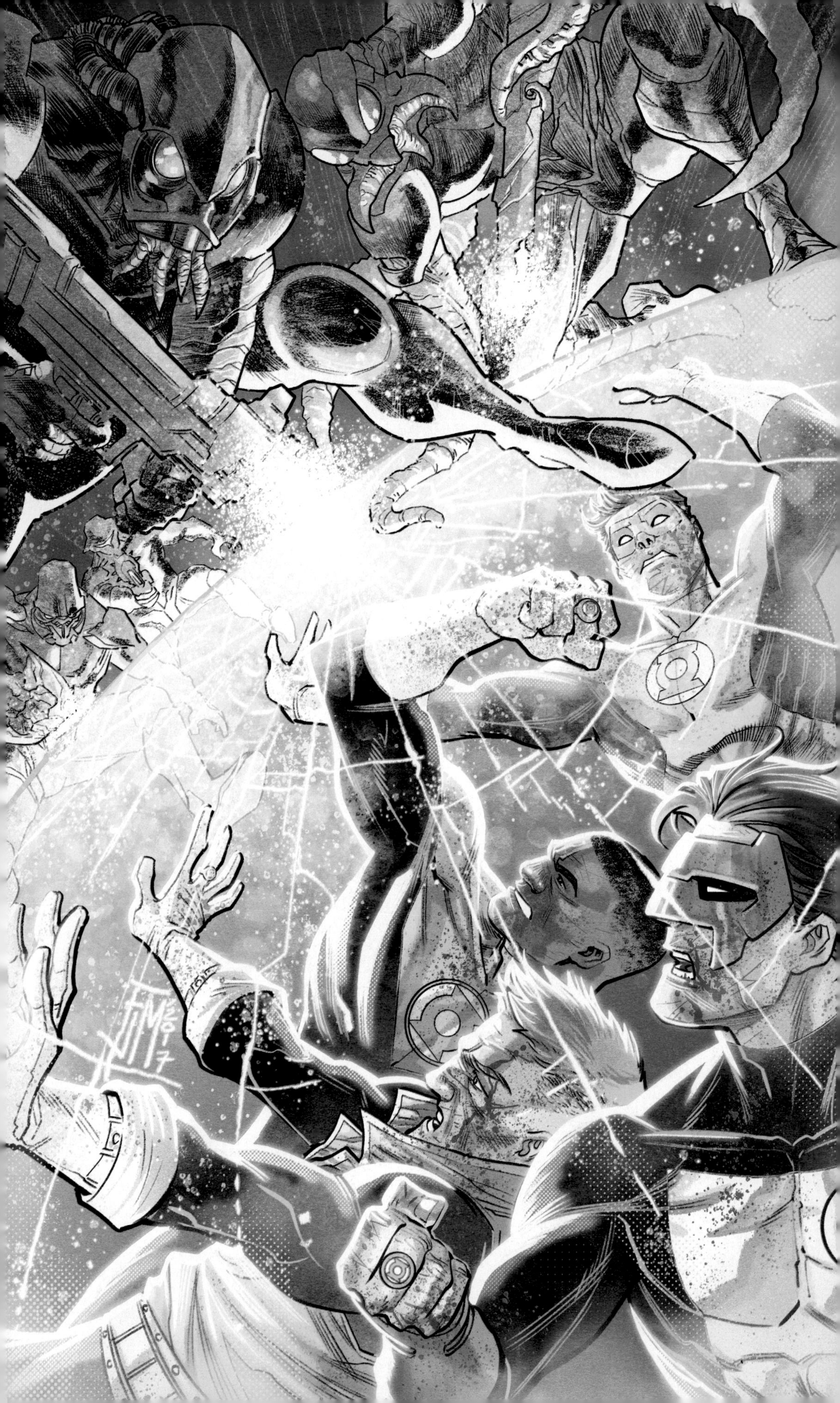

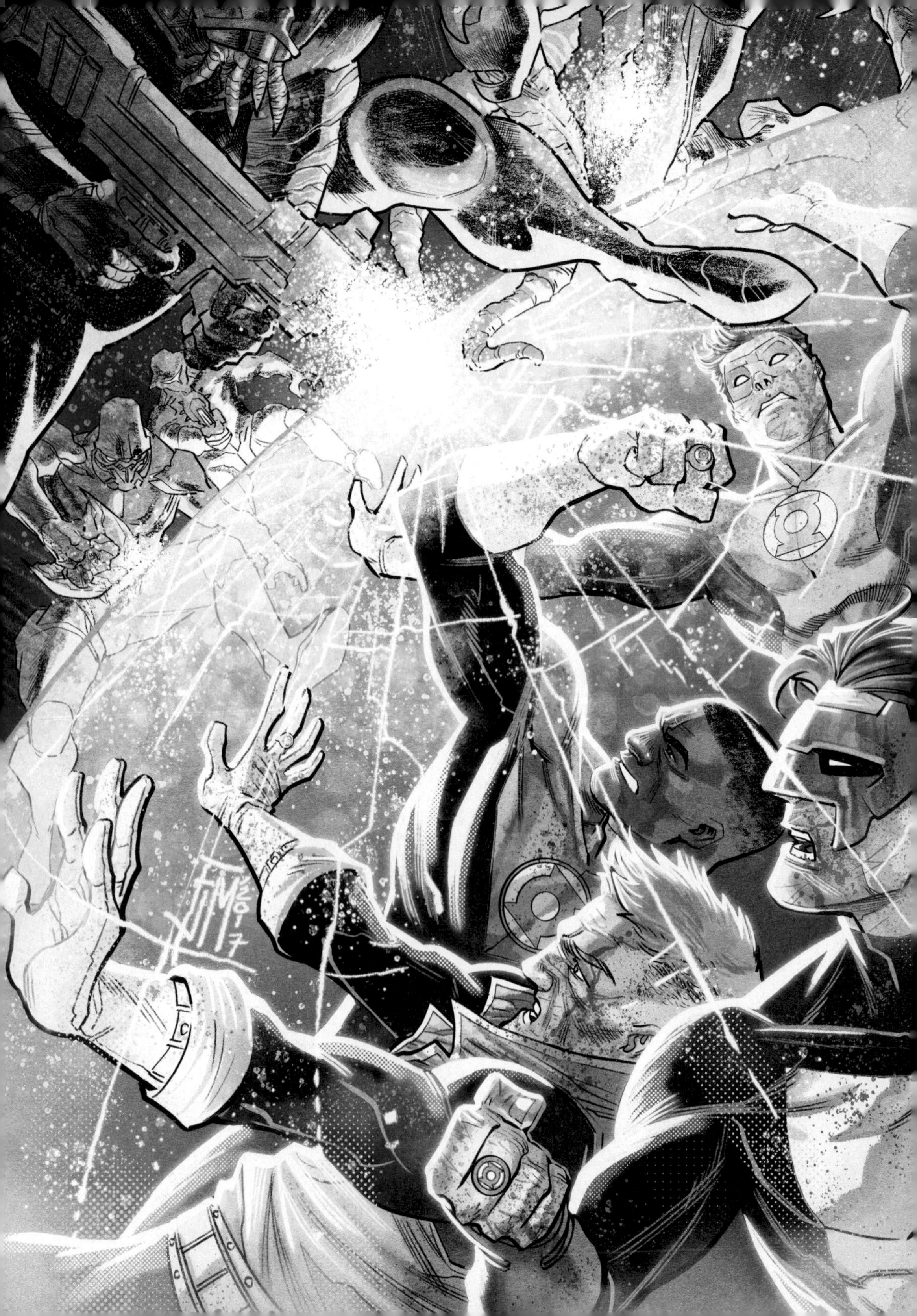

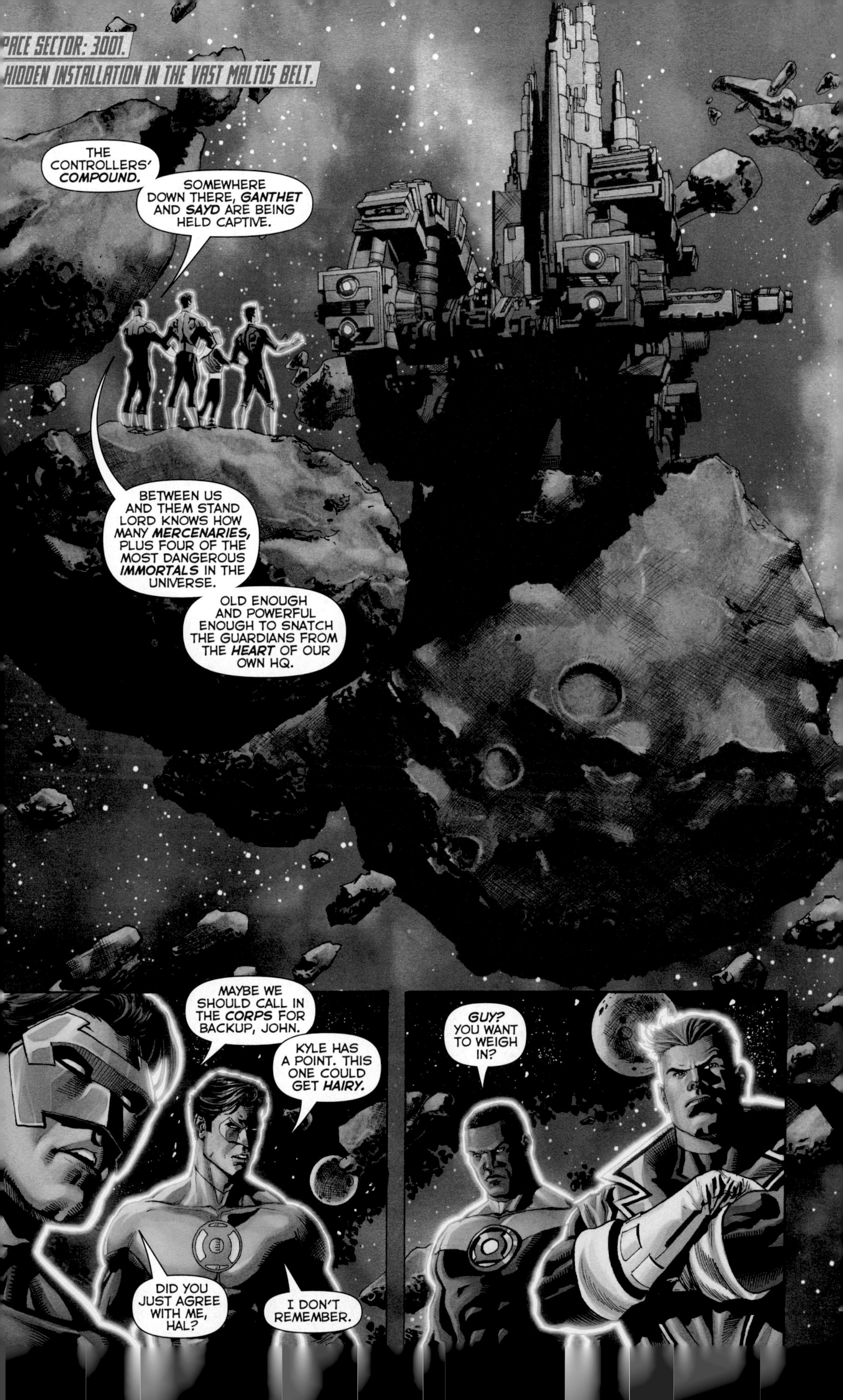
PACE SECTOR: 3001.
HIDDEN INSTALLATION IN THE VAST MALTUS BELT.
THE CONTROLLERS' COMPOUND.
SOMEWHERE DOWN THERE, GANTHET AND SAYD ARE BEING HELD CAPTIVE.
BETWEEN US AND THEM STAND LORD KNOWS HOW MANY MERCENARIES, PLUS FOUR OF THE MOST DANGEROUS IMMORTALS IN THE UNIVERSE.
OLD ENOUGH AND POWERFUL ENOUGH TO SNATCH THE GUARDIANS FROM THE HEART OF OUR OWN HQ.
MAYBE WE SHOULD CALL IN THE CORPS FOR BACKUP, JOHN.
KYLE HAS A POINT. THIS ONE COULD GET HAIRY.
DID YOU JUST AGREE WITH ME, HAL?
I DON'T REMEMBER.
GUY? YOU WANT TO WEIGH IN?

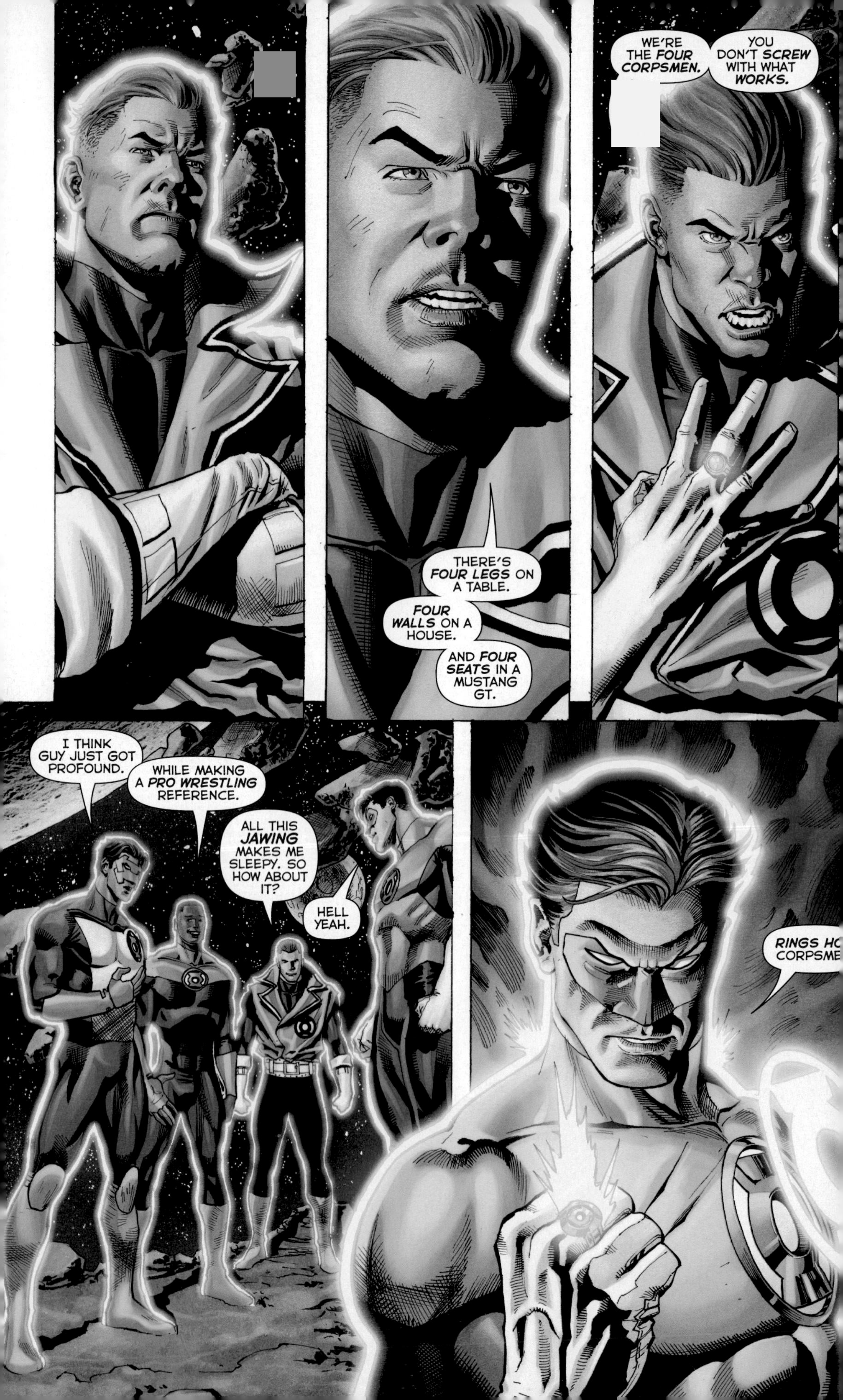
THERE'S FOUR LEGS ON A TABLE.
FOUR WALLS ON A HOUSE.
AND FOUR SEATS IN A MUSTANG GT.
WE'RE THE FOUR CORPSMEN.
YOU DON'T SCREW WITH WHAT WORKS.
I THINK GUY JUST GOT PROFOUND.
WHILE MAKING A PRO WRESTLING REFERENCE.
ALL THIS JAWING MAKES ME SLEEPY. SO HOW ABOUT IT?
HELL YEAH.

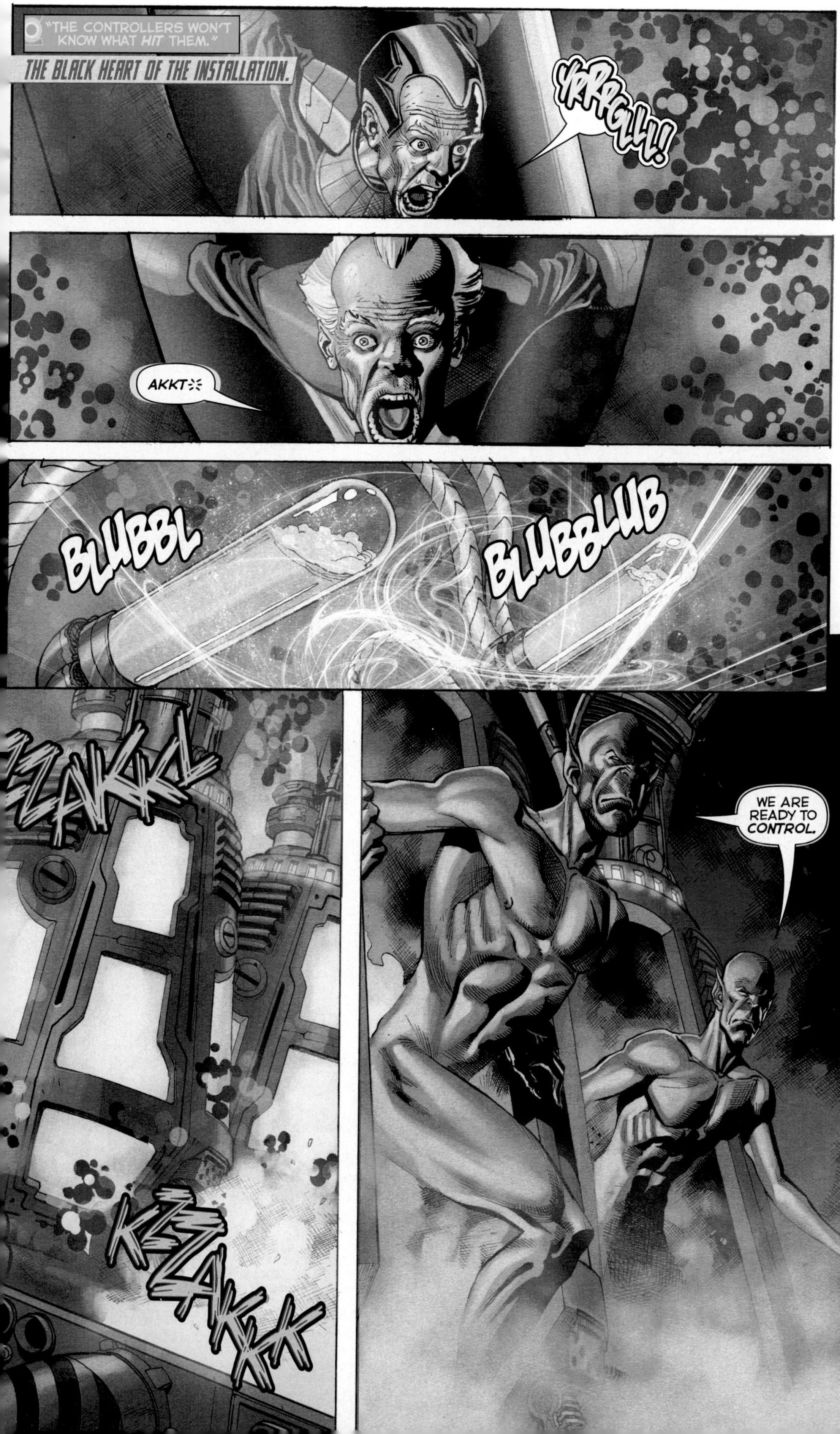
"THE CONTROLLERS WON'T KNOW WHAT HIT THEM."
THE BLACK HEART OF THE INSTALLATION.
YRRAGLLL!
AKKT
BLUBBL
BLUBBLUB
KZAKKL
KZZAKKK
WE ARE READY TO CONTROL.

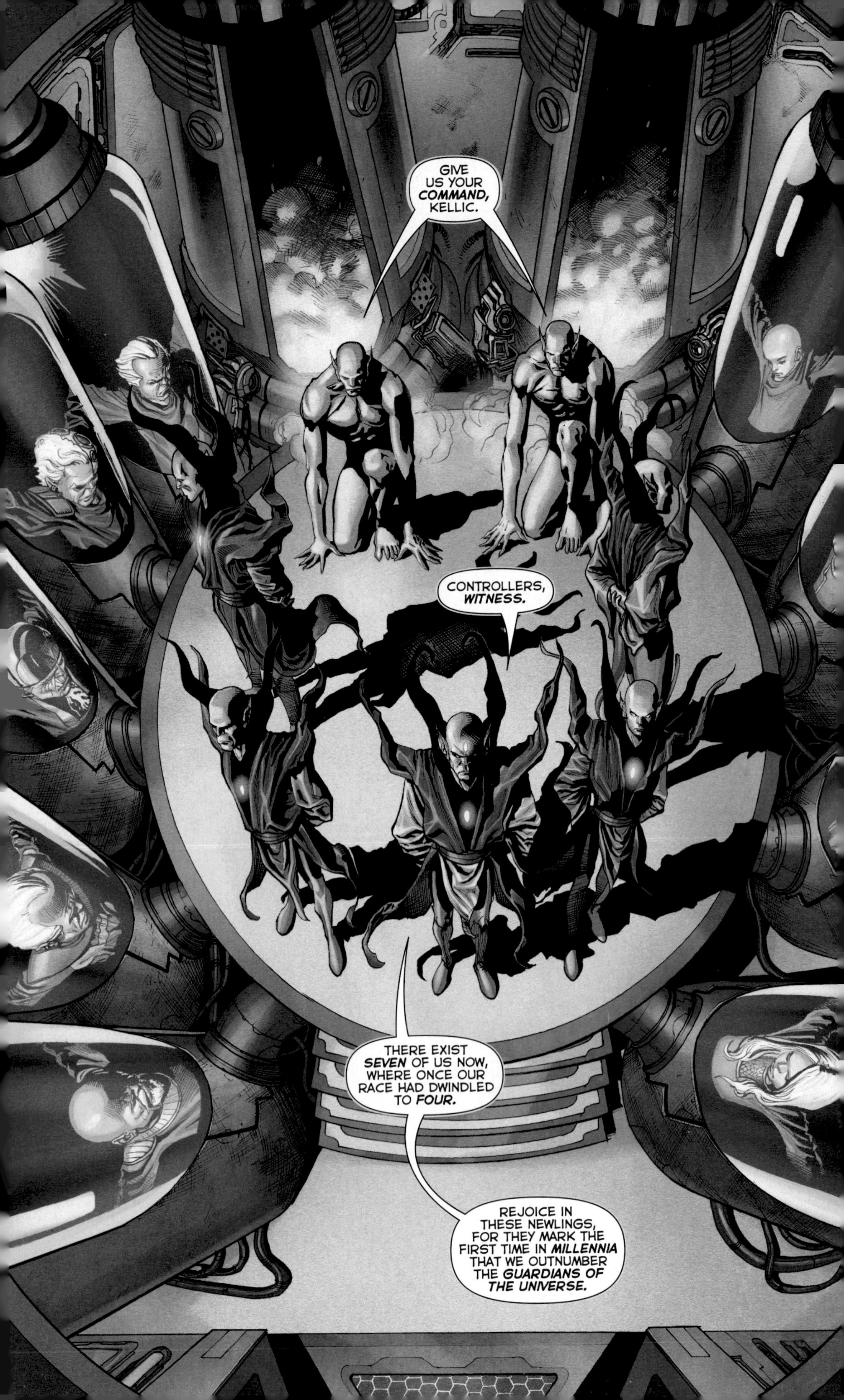

GIVE US YOUR *COMMAND,* KELLIC.
CONTROLLERS, *WITNESS.*
THERE EXIST *SEVEN* OF US NOW, WHERE ONCE OUR RACE HAD DWINDLED TO *FOUR.*
REJOICE IN THESE NEWLINGS, FOR THEY MARK THE FIRST TIME IN *MILLENNIA* THAT WE OUTNUMBER THE *GUARDIANS OF THE UNIVERSE.*

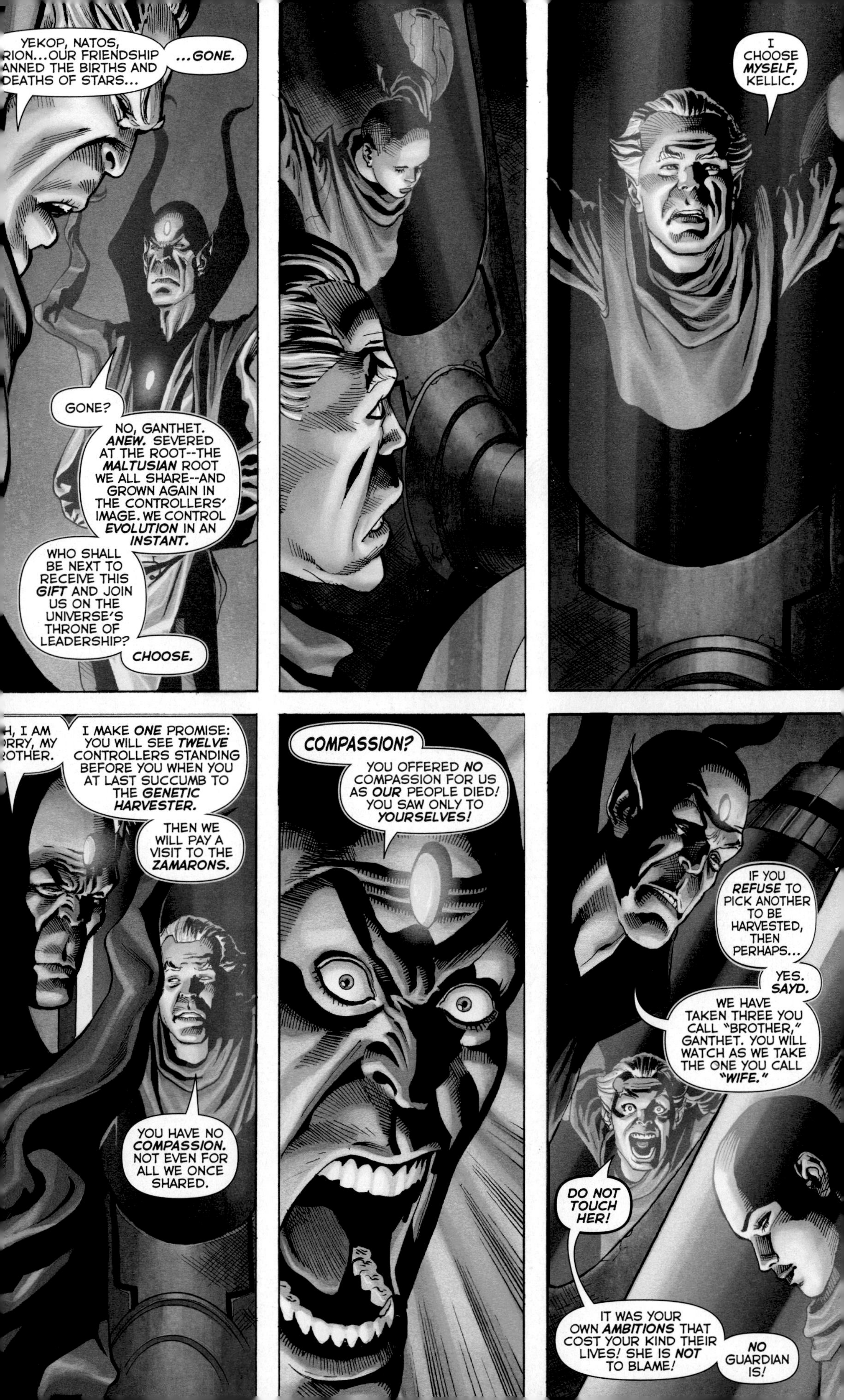
YEKOP, NATOS, RION...OUR FRIENDSHIP ANNED THE BIRTHS AND DEATHS OF STARS...
...GONE.
GONE?
NO, GANTHET. ANEW. SEVERED AT THE ROOT--THE MALTUSIAN ROOT WE ALL SHARE--AND GROWN AGAIN IN THE CONTROLLERS' IMAGE. WE CONTROL EVOLUTION IN AN INSTANT.
WHO SHALL BE NEXT TO RECEIVE THIS GIFT AND JOIN US ON THE UNIVERSE'S THRONE OF LEADERSHIP?
CHOOSE.
I CHOOSE MYSELF, KELLIC.
H, I AM RRY, MY ROTHER.
I MAKE ONE PROMISE: YOU WILL SEE TWELVE CONTROLLERS STANDING BEFORE YOU WHEN YOU AT LAST SUCCUMB TO THE GENETIC HARVESTER.
THEN WE WILL PAY A VISIT TO THE ZAMARONS.
YOU HAVE NO COMPASSION. NOT EVEN FOR ALL WE ONCE SHARED.
COMPASSION?
YOU OFFERED NO COMPASSION FOR US AS OUR PEOPLE DIED! YOU SAW ONLY TO YOURSELVES!
IF YOU REFUSE TO PICK ANOTHER TO BE HARVESTED, THEN PERHAPS...
YES. SAYD.
WE HAVE TAKEN THREE YOU CALL "BROTHER," GANTHET. YOU WILL WATCH AS WE TAKE THE ONE YOU CALL "WIFE."
DO NOT TOUCH HER!
IT WAS YOUR OWN AMBITIONS THAT COST YOUR KIND THEIR LIVES! SHE IS NOT TO BLAME!
NO GUARDIAN IS!

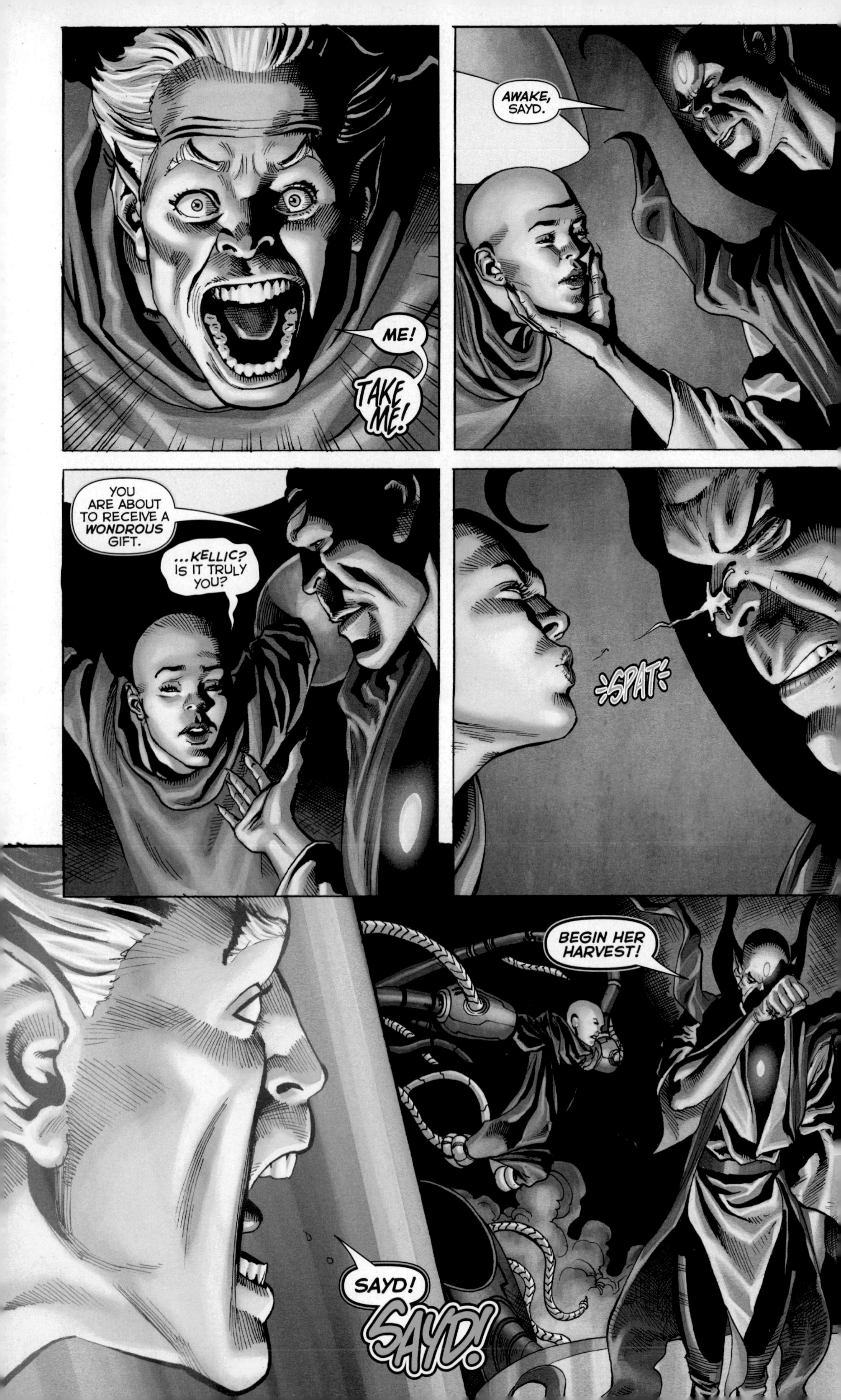

ME!
TAKE ME!
AWAKE, SAYD.
YOU ARE ABOUT TO RECEIVE A WONDROUS GIFT.
...KELLIC? IS IT TRULY YOU?
SPAT
BEGIN HER HARVEST!
SAYD!
SAYD!

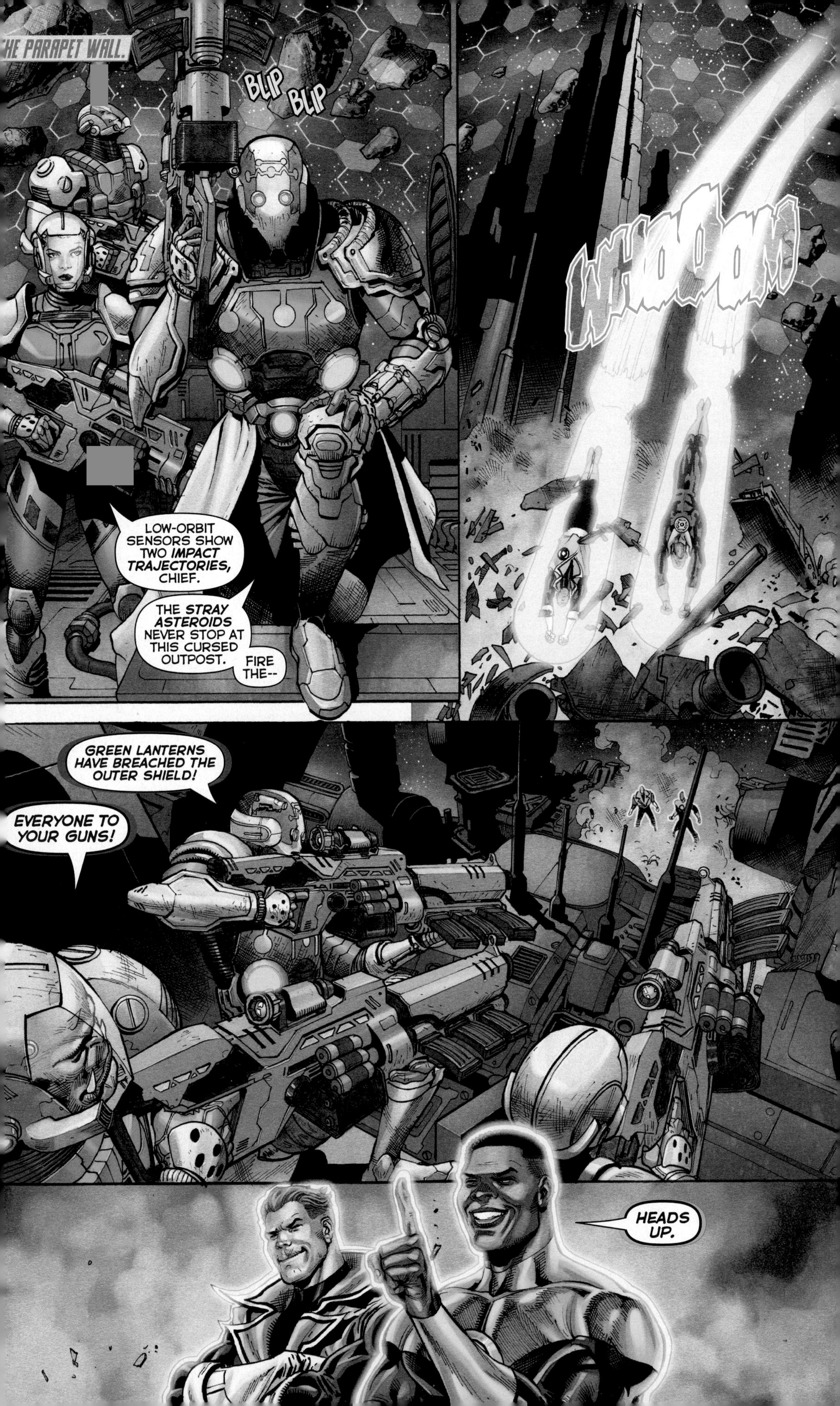
HE PARAPET WALL.
BLIP
BLIP
LOW-ORBIT SENSORS SHOW TWO IMPACT TRAJECTORIES, CHIEF.
THE STRAY ASTEROIDS NEVER STOP AT THIS CURSED OUTPOST.
FIRE THE--
WHOOOM
GREEN LANTERNS HAVE BREACHED THE OUTER SHIELD!
EVERYONE TO YOUR GUNS!
HEADS UP.

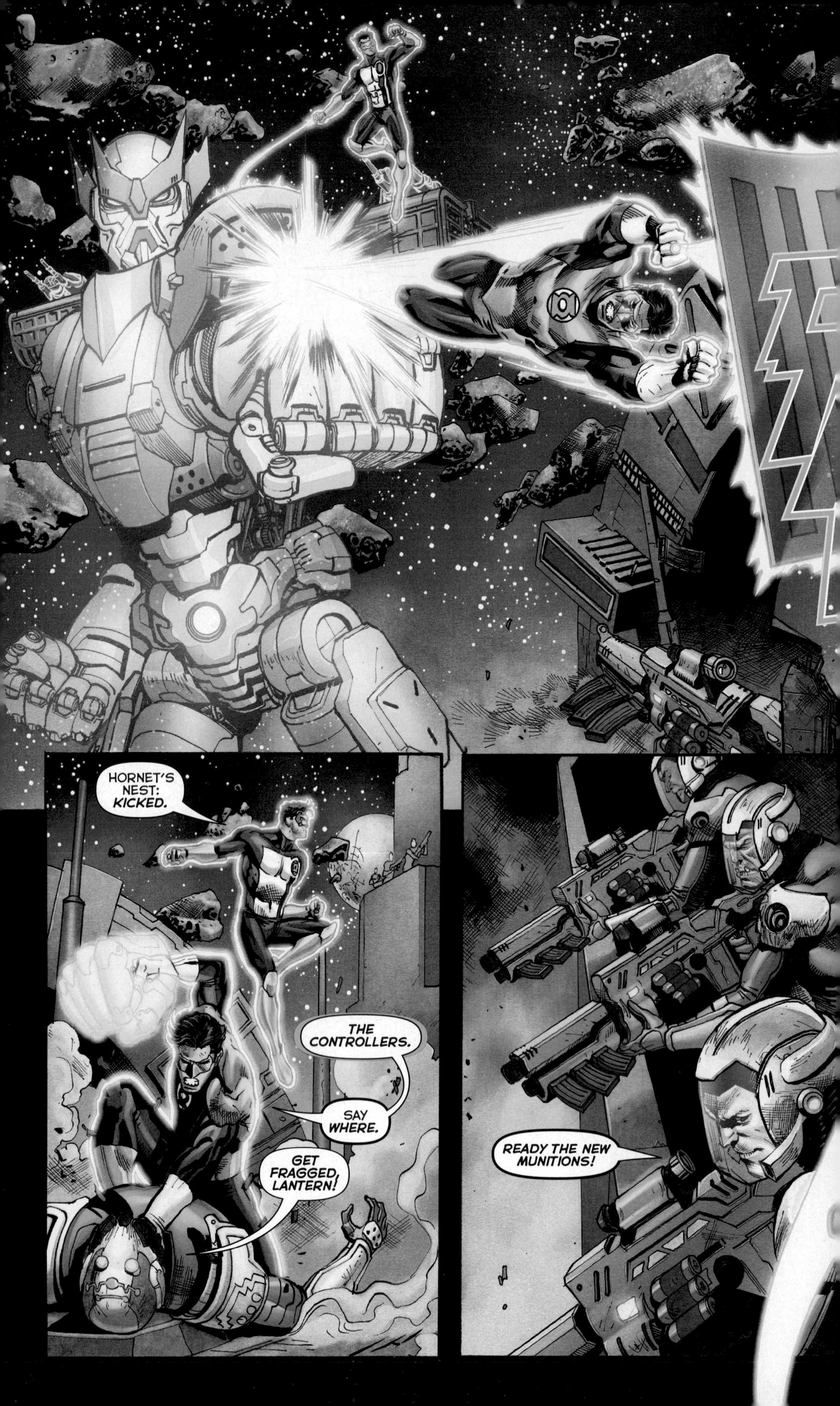
HORNET'S NEST: KICKED.
THE CONTROLLERS.
SAY WHERE.
GET FRAGGED, LANTERN!
READY THE NEW MUNITIONS!

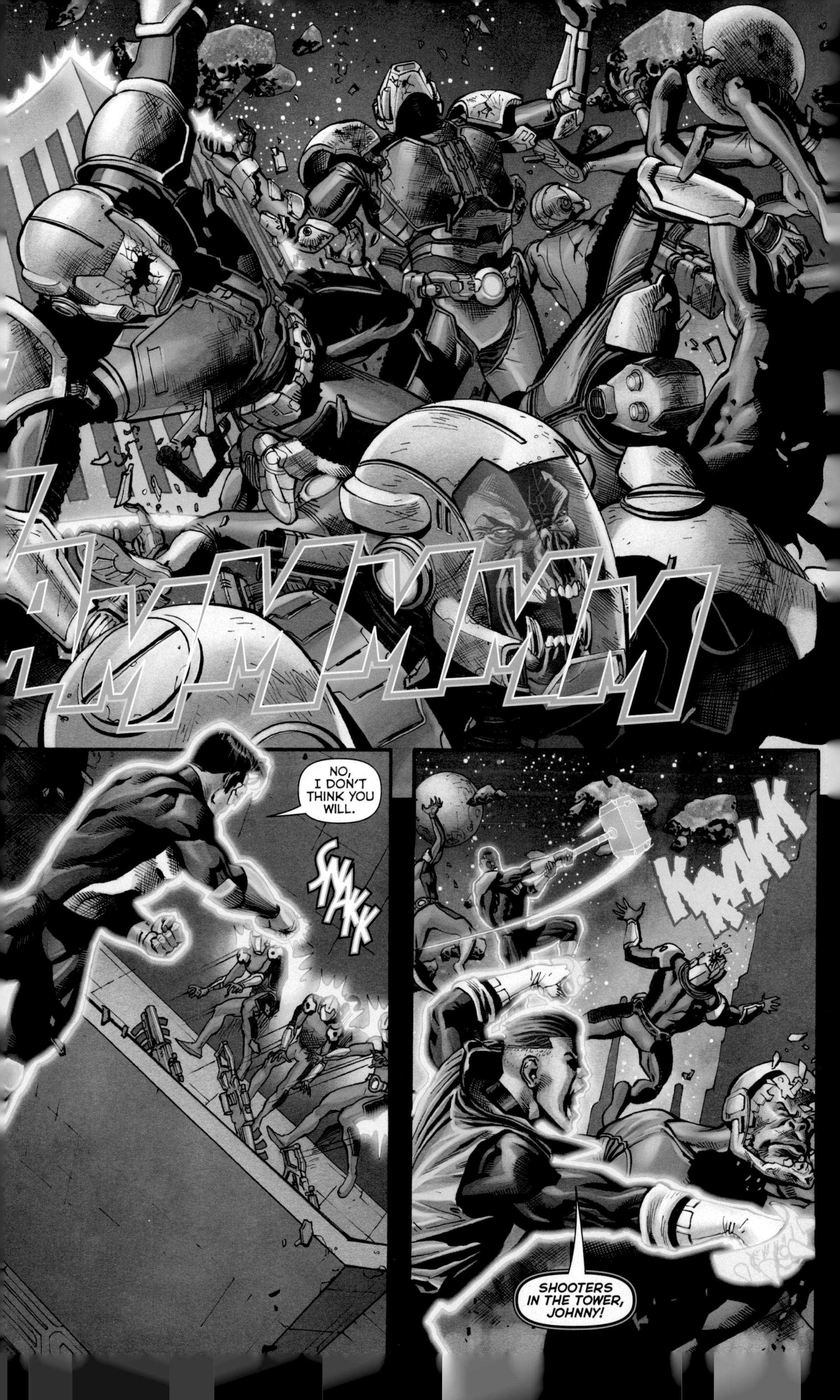
ZMMMMM
NO, I DON'T THINK YOU WILL.
SNAKK
KRAKK
SHOOTERS IN THE TOWER, JOHNNY!

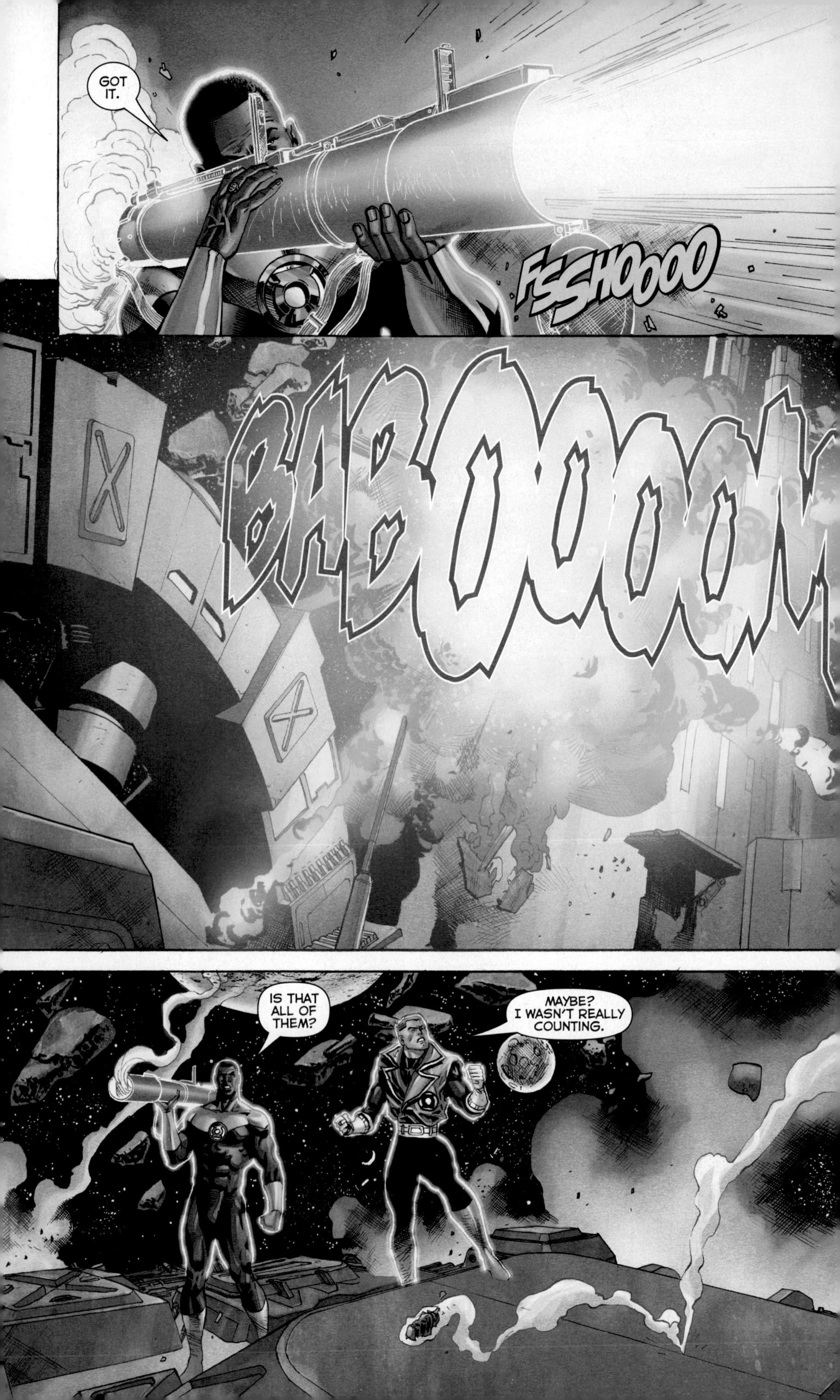
GOT IT.
FSSHOOOO
BABOOOOM
IS THAT ALL OF THEM?
MAYBE? I WASN'T REALLY COUNTING.

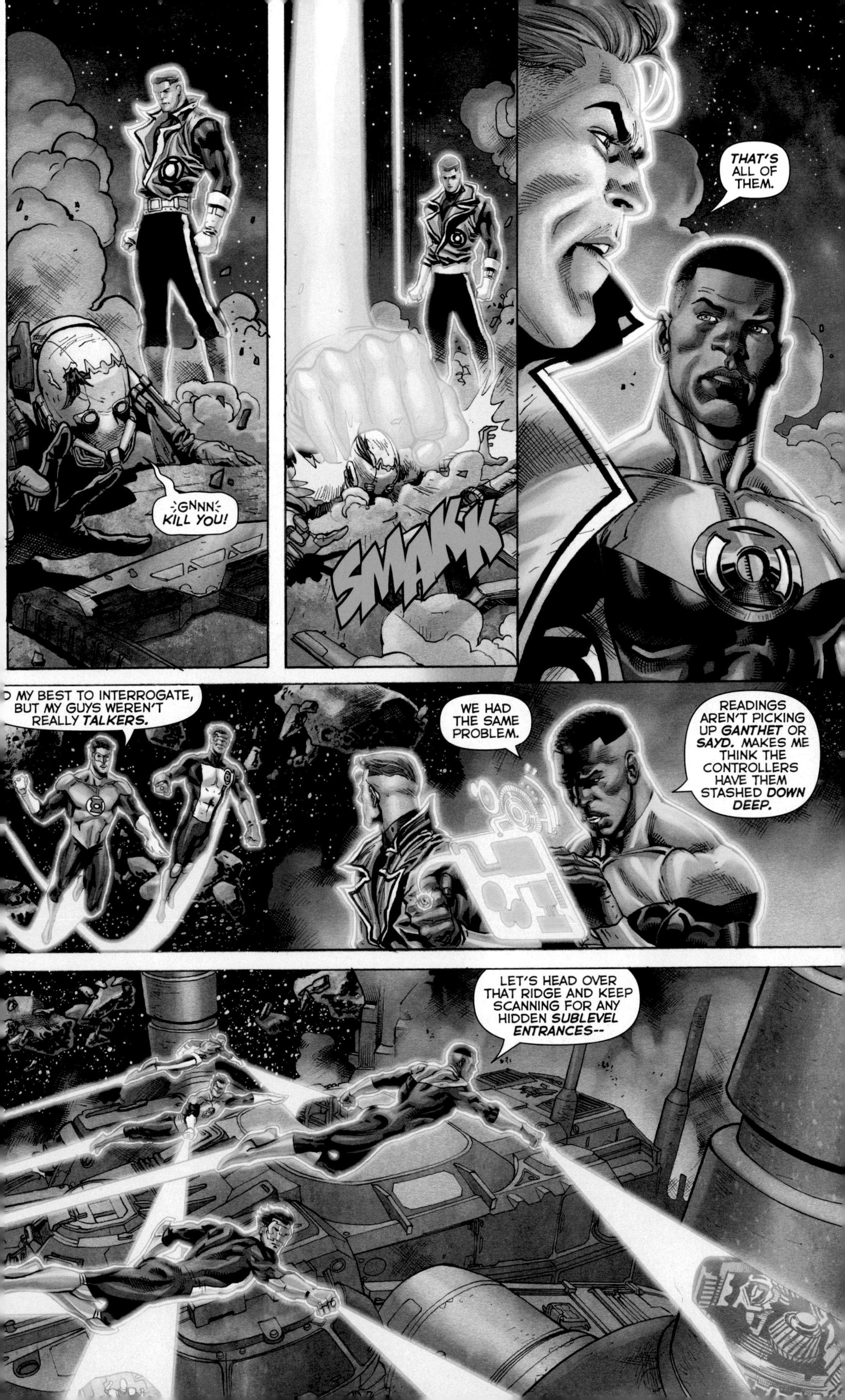

-GNNN- KILL YOU!
SMAKK
THAT'S ALL OF THEM.
D MY BEST TO INTERROGATE, BUT MY GUYS WEREN'T REALLY TALKERS.
WE HAD THE SAME PROBLEM.
READINGS AREN'T PICKING UP GANTHET OR SAYD. MAKES ME THINK THE CONTROLLERS HAVE THEM STASHED DOWN DEEP.
LET'S HEAD OVER THAT RIDGE AND KEEP SCANNING FOR ANY HIDDEN SUBLEVEL ENTRANCES--

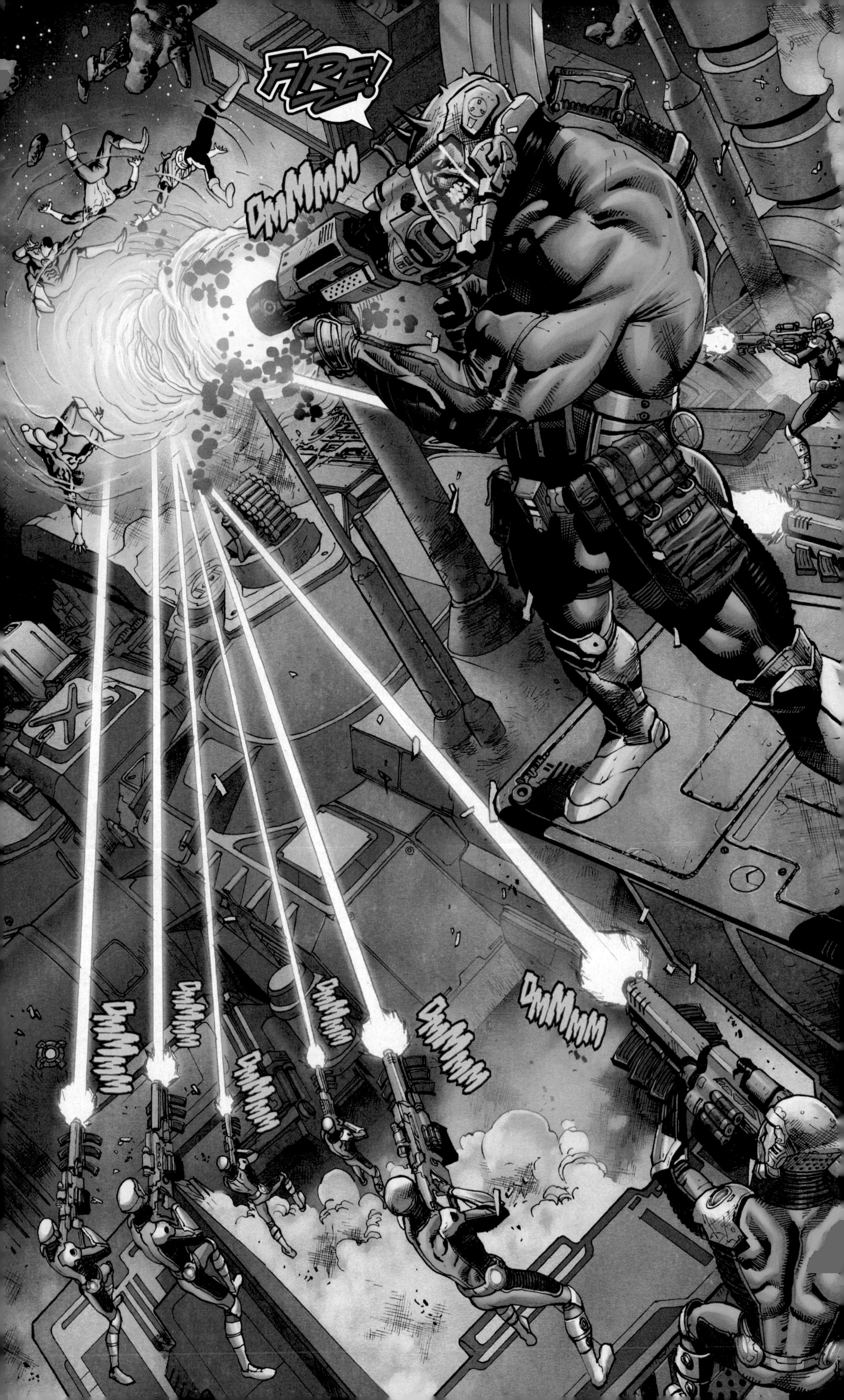
FIRE!
DMMMM
DMMMM
DMMMM
DMMMM
DMMMM
DMMMM
DMMMM
DMMMM

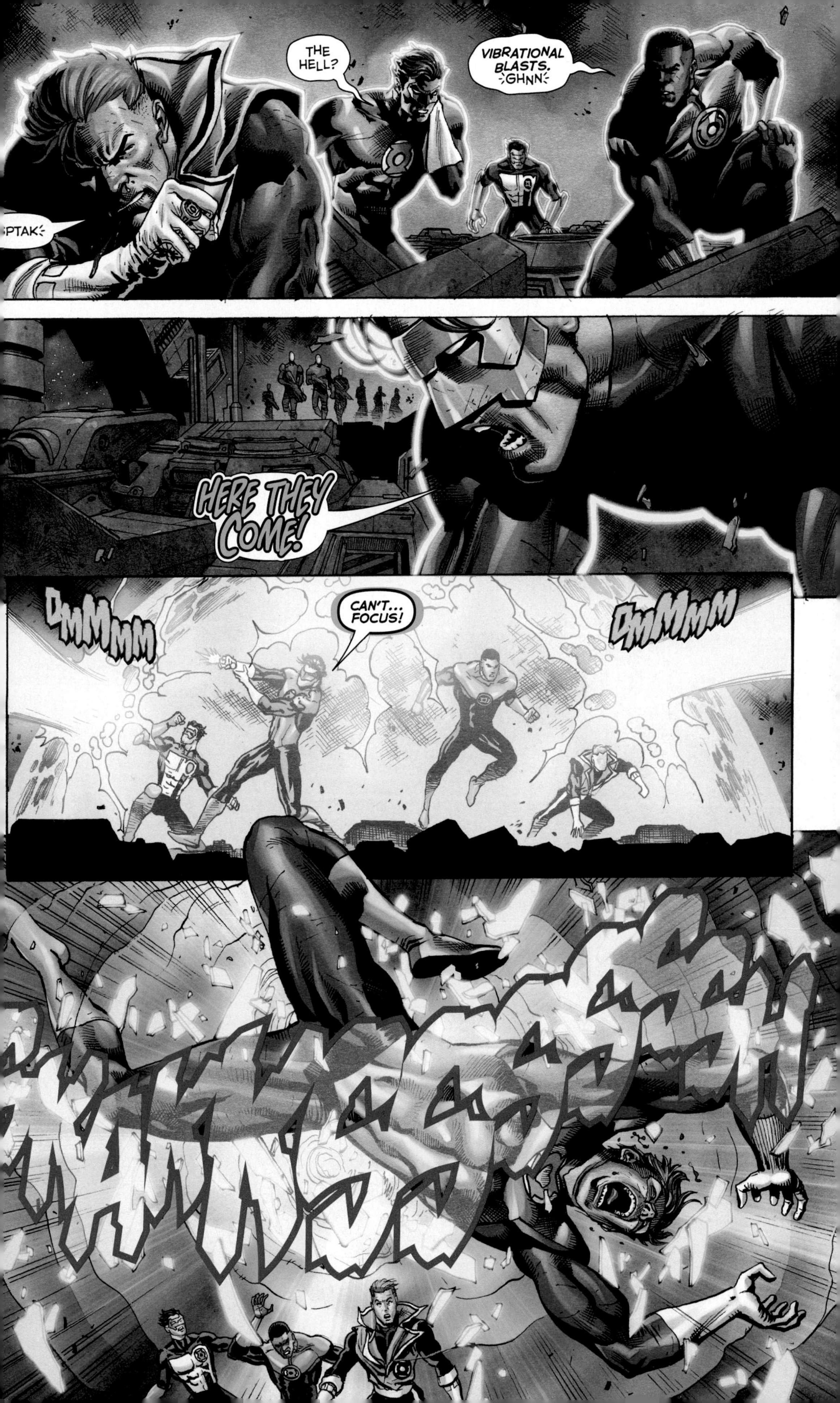
SPTAK
THE HELL?
VIBRATIONAL BLASTS. GHNN
HERE THEY COME!
DMMMM
CAN'T... FOCUS!
DMMMM

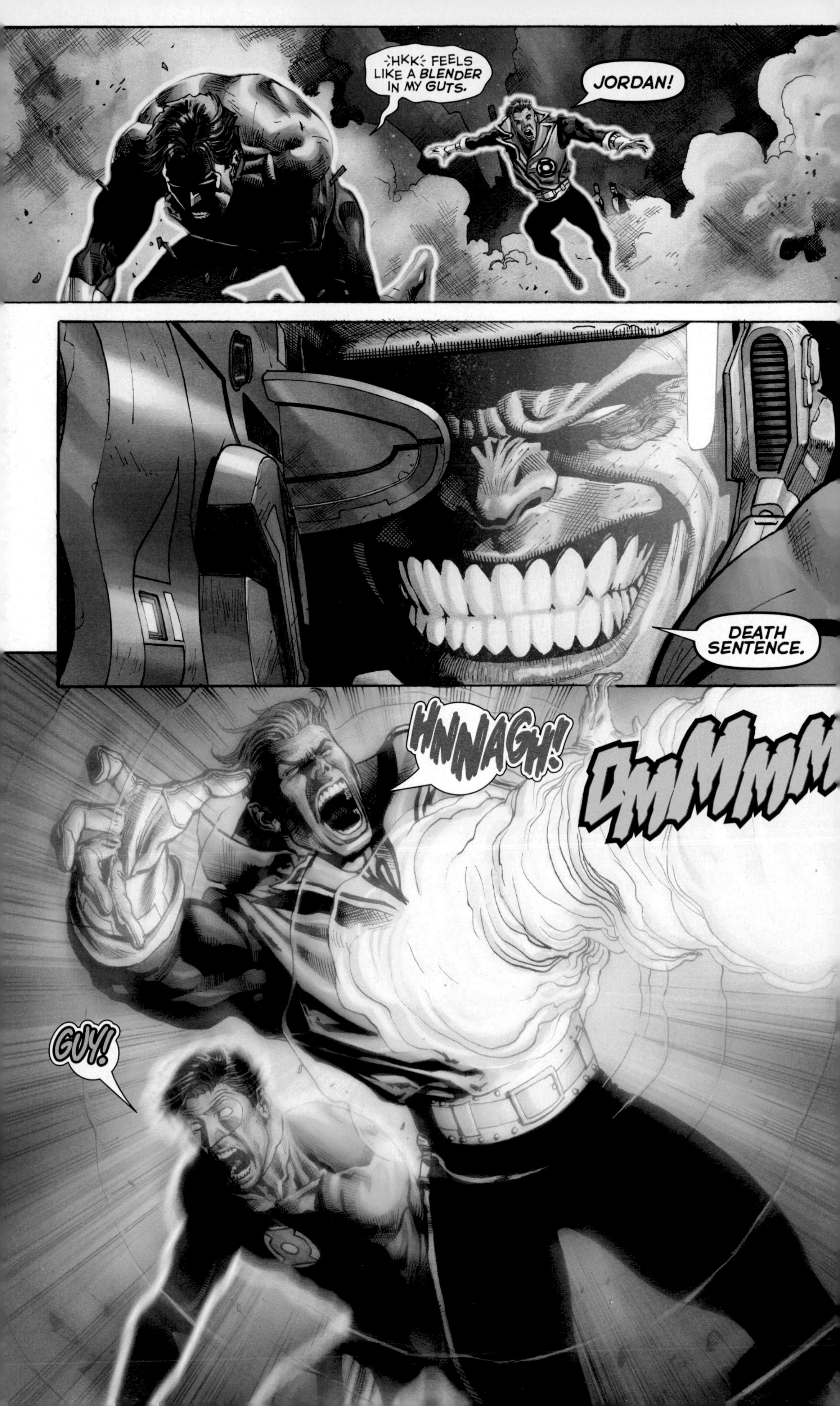

-HKK- FEELS LIKE A BLENDER IN MY GUTS.
JORDAN!
DEATH SENTENCE.
HNNAGH!
DMMMM
GUY!

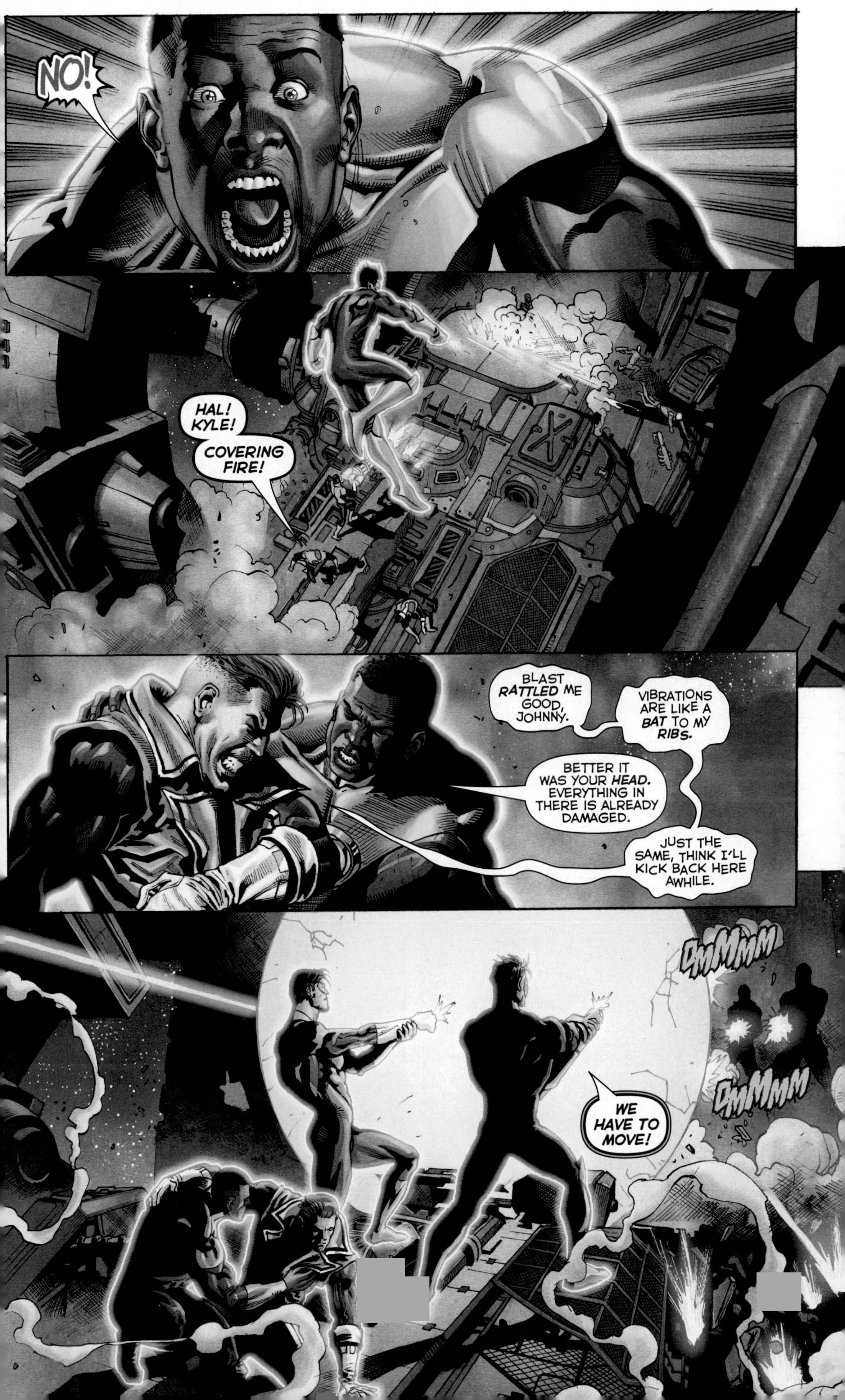
NO!
HAL! KYLE!
COVERING FIRE!
BLAST RATTLED ME GOOD, JOHNNY.
VIBRATIONS ARE LIKE A BAT TO MY RIBS.
BETTER IT WAS YOUR HEAD. EVERYTHING IN THERE IS ALREADY DAMAGED.
JUST THE SAME, THINK I'LL KICK BACK HERE AWHILE.
OMMMM
OMMMM
WE HAVE TO MOVE!

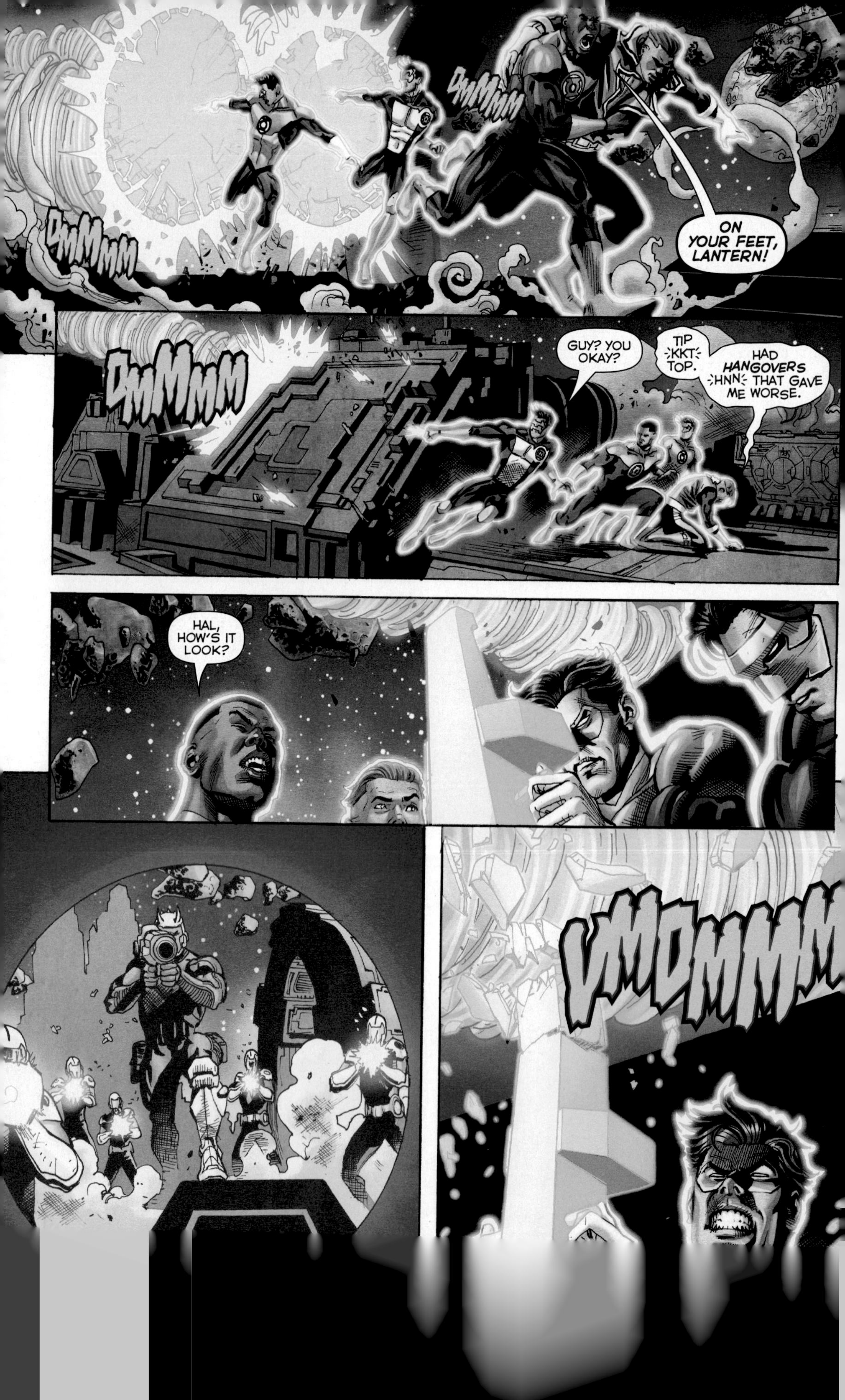
DMMMM
DMMMM
ON YOUR FEET, LANTERN!
DMMMM
GUY? YOU OKAY?
TIP -KKT- TOP.
HAD HANGOVERS -HNN- THAT GAVE ME WORSE.
HAL, HOW'S IT LOOK?
VMDMMM

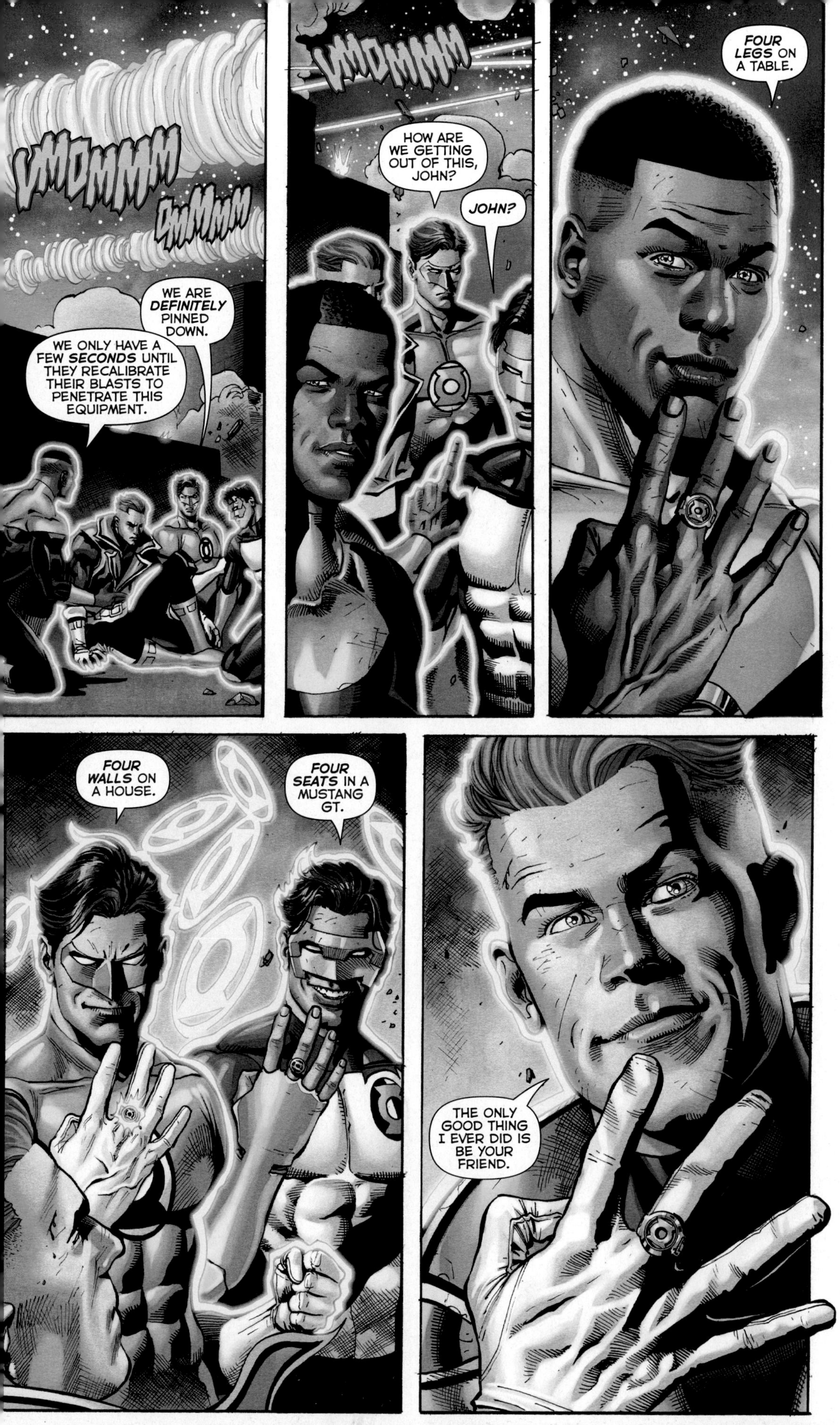
VMMMMM
DMMMM
WE ARE *DEFINITELY* PINNED DOWN.
WE ONLY HAVE A FEW *SECONDS* UNTIL THEY RECALIBRATE THEIR BLASTS TO PENETRATE THIS EQUIPMENT.
VMMMMM
HOW ARE WE GETTING OUT OF THIS, JOHN?
JOHN?
FOUR LEGS ON A TABLE.
FOUR WALLS ON A HOUSE.
FOUR SEATS IN A MUSTANG GT.
THE ONLY GOOD THING I EVER DID IS BE YOUR FRIEND.

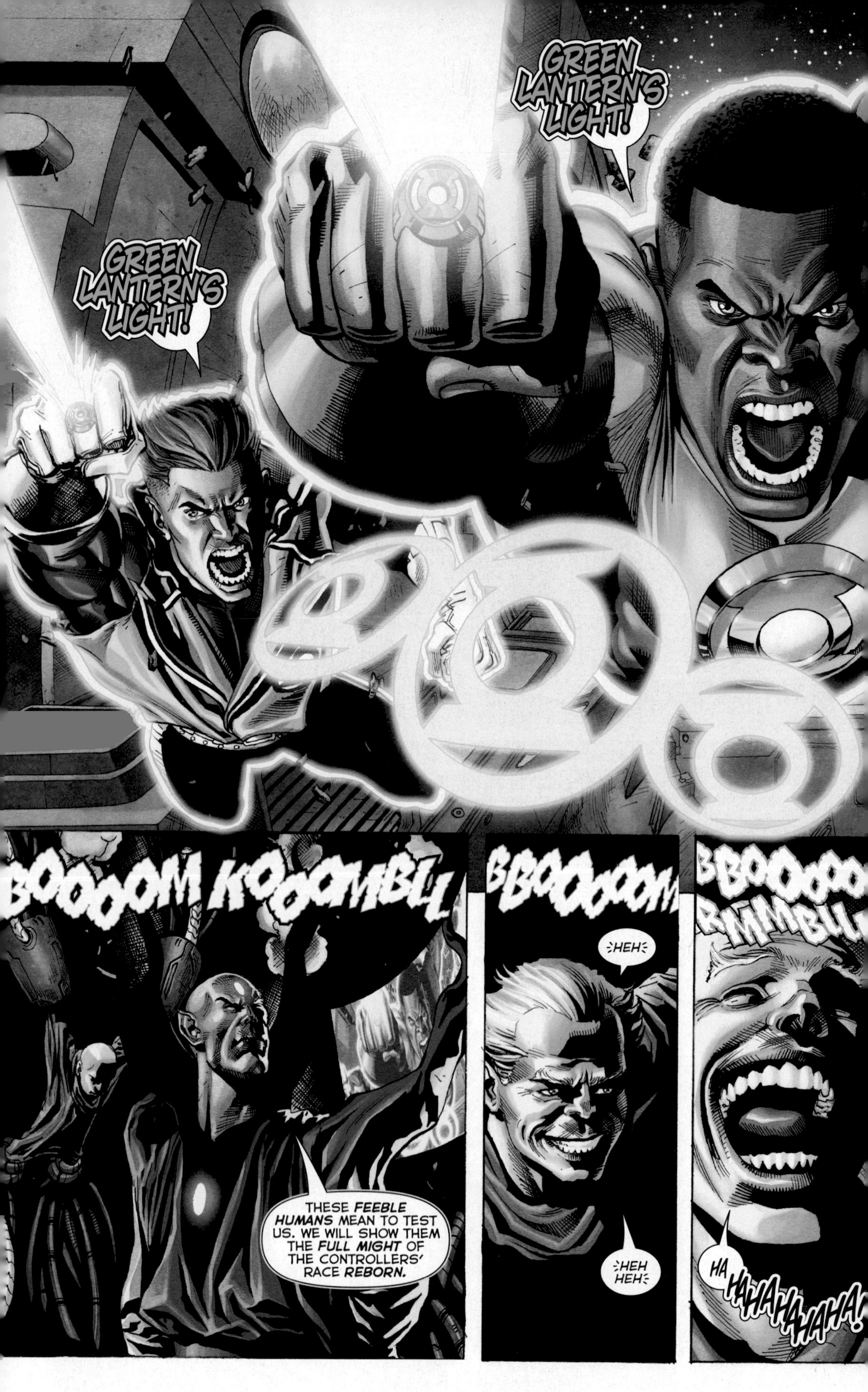

GREEN LANTERN'S LIGHT!
GREEN LANTERN'S LIGHT!
BOOOOOM KOOOOMBLL
THESE FEEBLE HUMANS MEAN TO TEST US. WE WILL SHOW THEM THE FULL MIGHT OF THE CONTROLLERS' RACE REBORN.
BBOOOOOOM
HEH
HEH HEH
BBOOOOOO RMMBLL
HA HAHAHAHAHAHA!

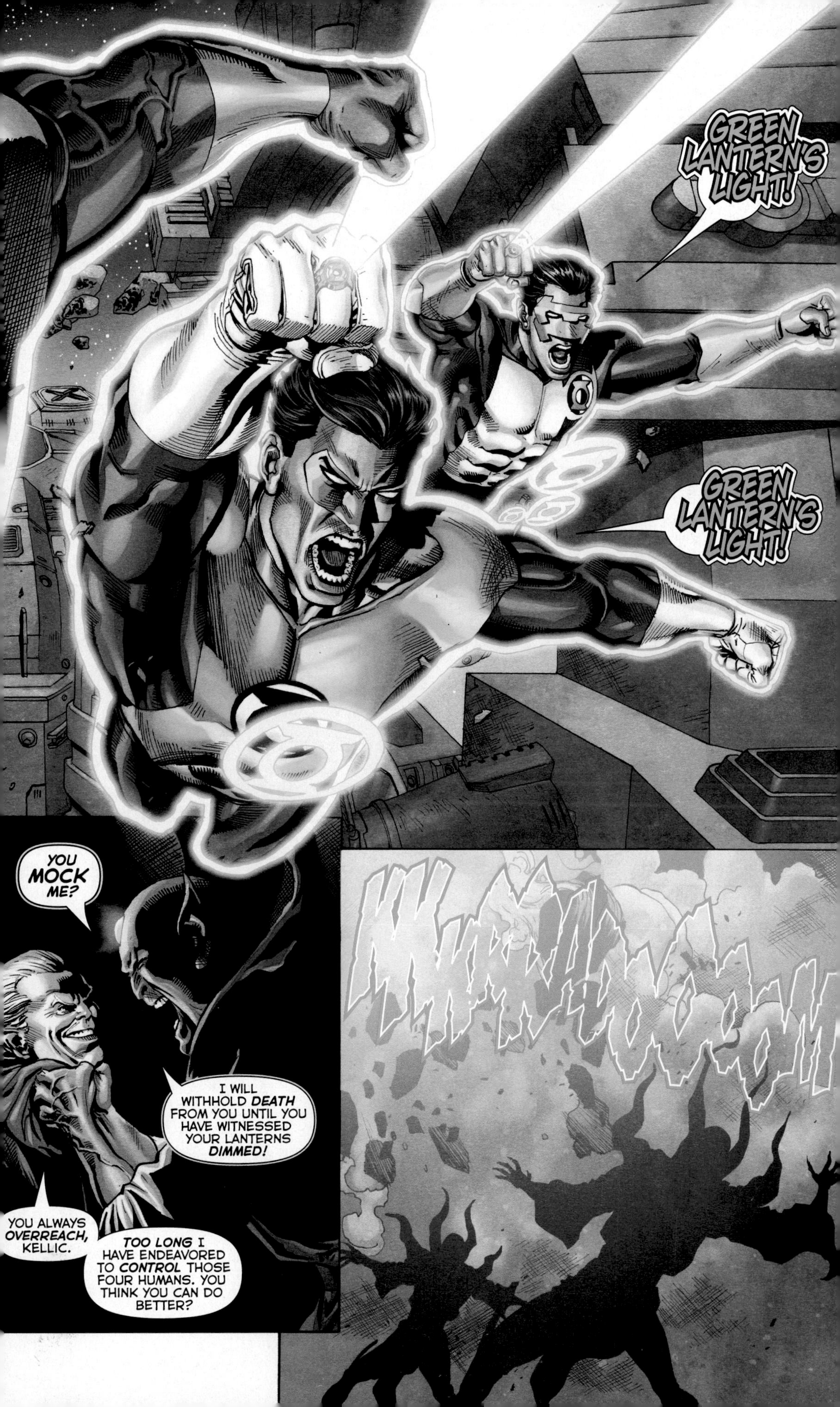
GREEN LANTERN'S LIGHT!
GREEN LANTERN'S LIGHT!
YOU MOCK ME?
I WILL WITHHOLD DEATH FROM YOU UNTIL YOU HAVE WITNESSED YOUR LANTERNS DIMMED!
YOU ALWAYS OVERREACH, KELLIC.
TOO LONG I HAVE ENDEAVORED TO CONTROL THOSE FOUR HUMANS. YOU THINK YOU CAN DO BETTER?
KKKRRAKKOOOOM

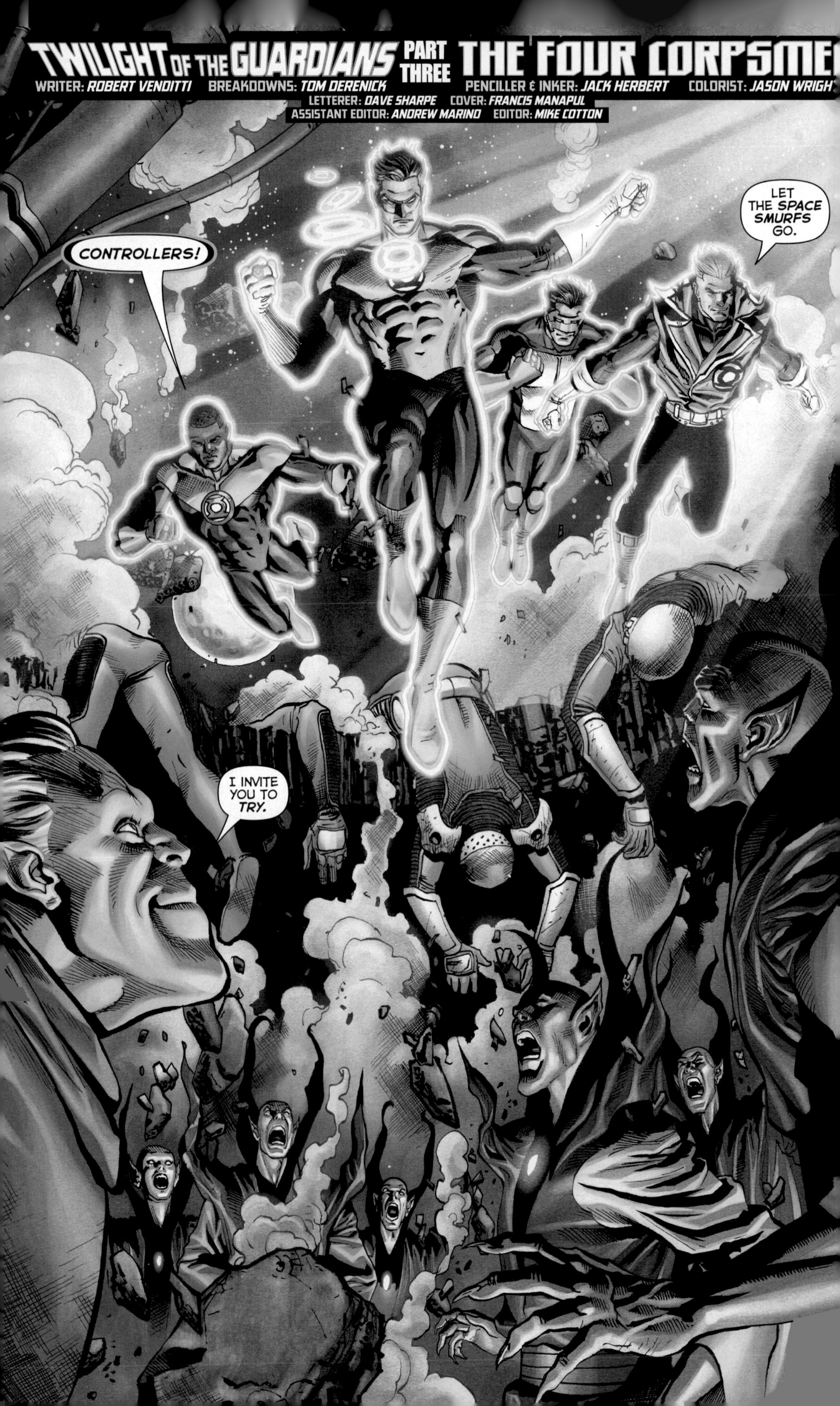

TWILIGHT OF THE GUARDIANS PART THREE THE FOUR CORPSMEN
WRITER: ROBERT VENDITTI BREAKDOWNS: TOM DERENICK PENCILLER & INKER: JACK HERBERT COLORIST: JASON WRIGHT
LETTERER: DAVE SHARPE COVER: FRANCIS MANAPUL
ASSISTANT EDITOR: ANDREW MARINO EDITOR: MIKE COTTON
CONTROLLERS!
LET THE SPACE SMURFS GO.
I INVITE YOU TO TRY.

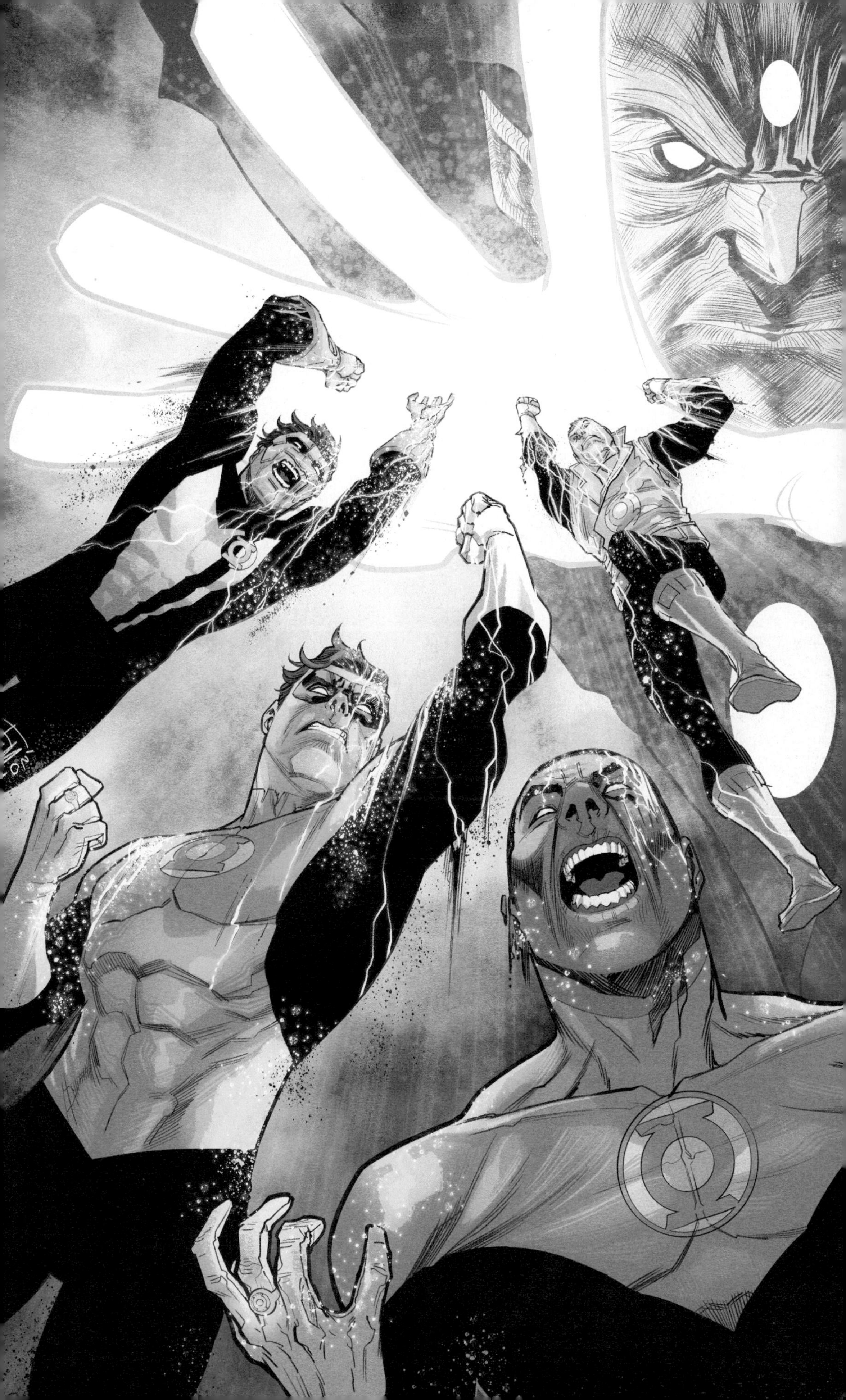

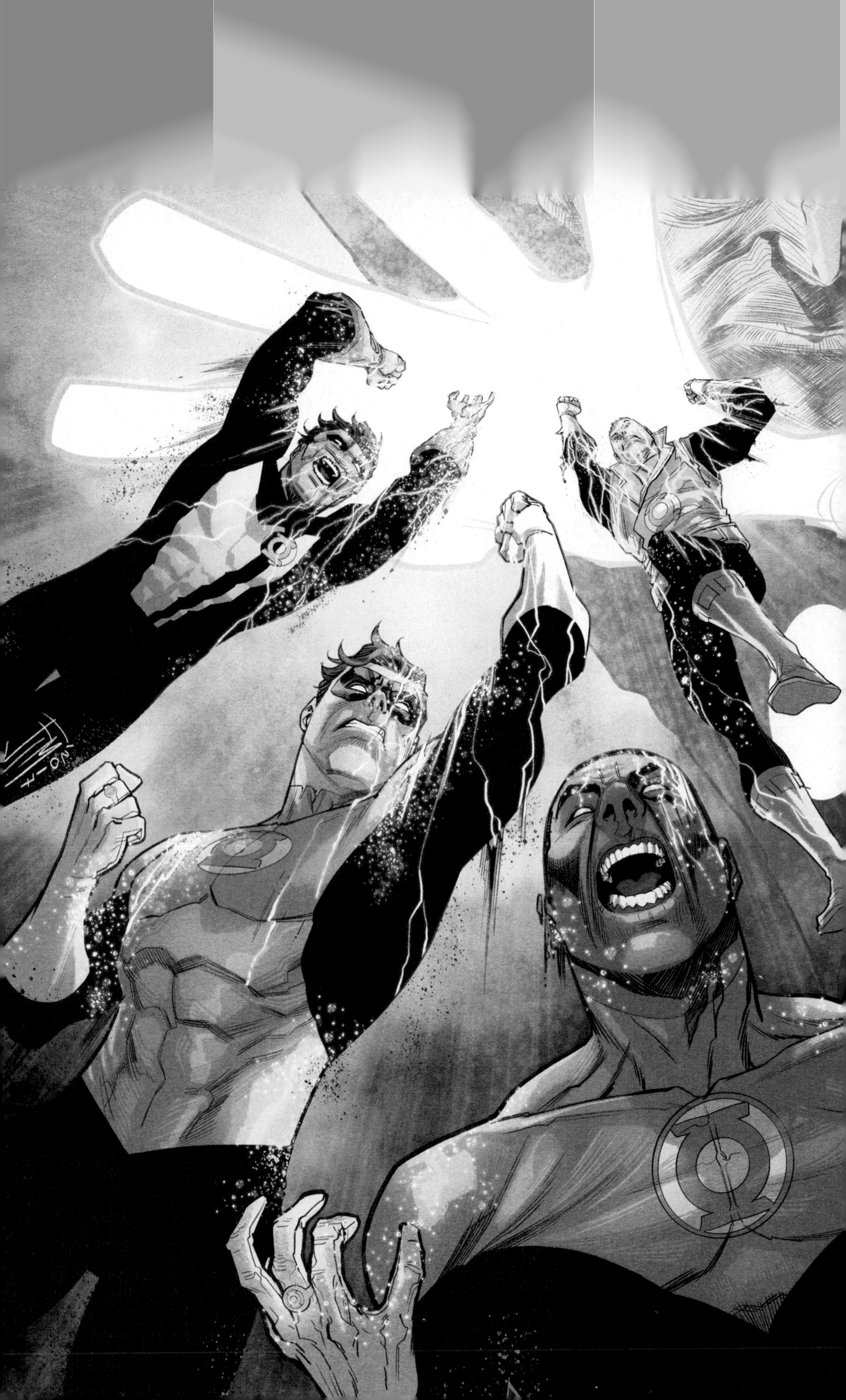

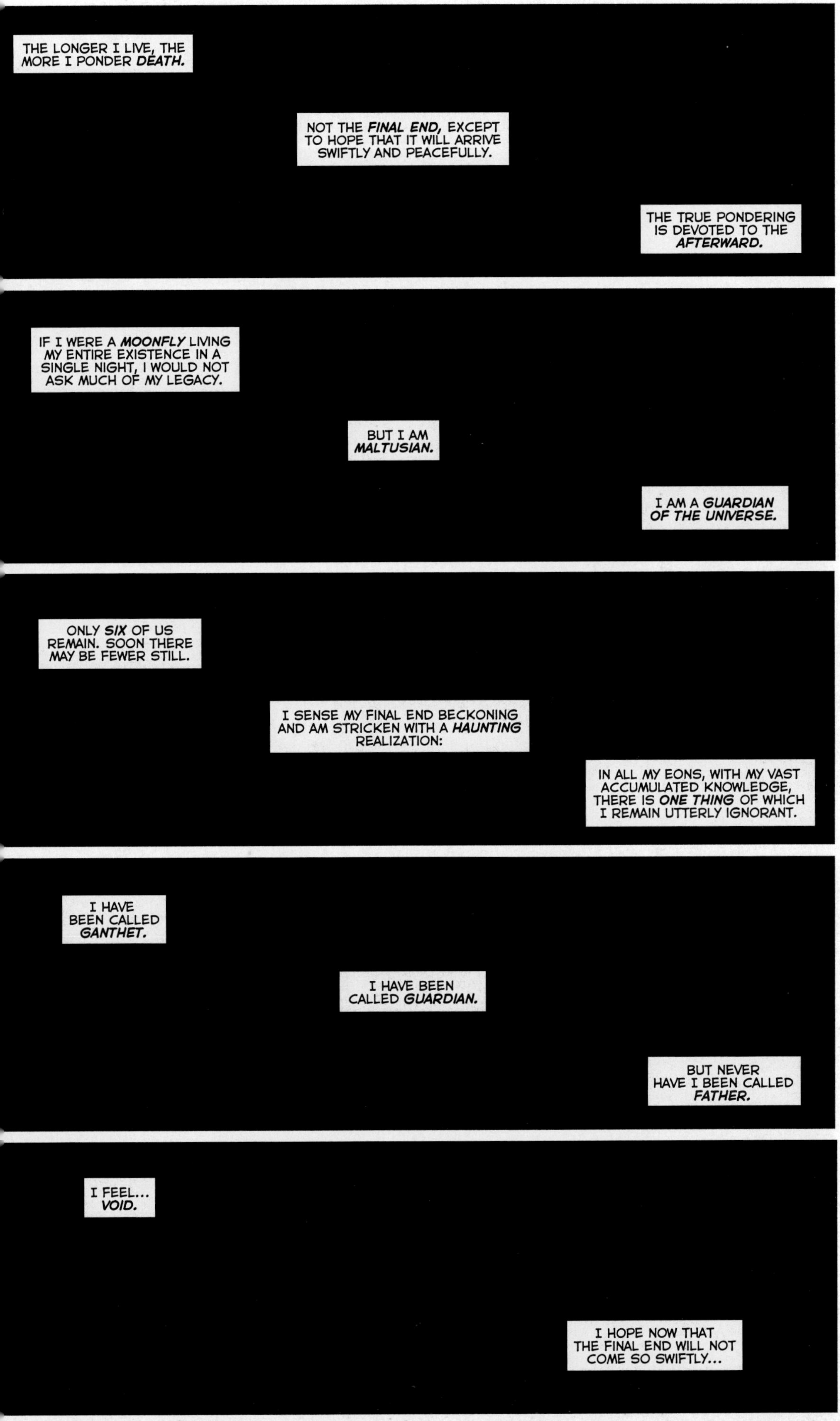
THE LONGER I LIVE, THE MORE I PONDER *DEATH.*
NOT THE *FINAL END,* EXCEPT TO HOPE THAT IT WILL ARRIVE SWIFTLY AND PEACEFULLY.
THE TRUE PONDERING IS DEVOTED TO THE *AFTERWARD.*
IF I WERE A *MOONFLY* LIVING MY ENTIRE EXISTENCE IN A SINGLE NIGHT, I WOULD NOT ASK MUCH OF MY LEGACY.
BUT I AM *MALTUSIAN.*
I AM A *GUARDIAN OF THE UNIVERSE.*
ONLY *SIX* OF US REMAIN. SOON THERE MAY BE FEWER STILL.
I SENSE MY FINAL END BECKONING AND AM STRICKEN WITH A *HAUNTING* REALIZATION:
IN ALL MY EONS, WITH MY VAST ACCUMULATED KNOWLEDGE, THERE IS *ONE THING* OF WHICH I REMAIN UTTERLY IGNORANT.
I HAVE BEEN CALLED *GANTHET.*
I HAVE BEEN CALLED *GUARDIAN.*
BUT NEVER HAVE I BEEN CALLED *FATHER.*
I FEEL... *VOID.*
I HOPE NOW THAT THE FINAL END WILL NOT COME SO SWIFTLY...

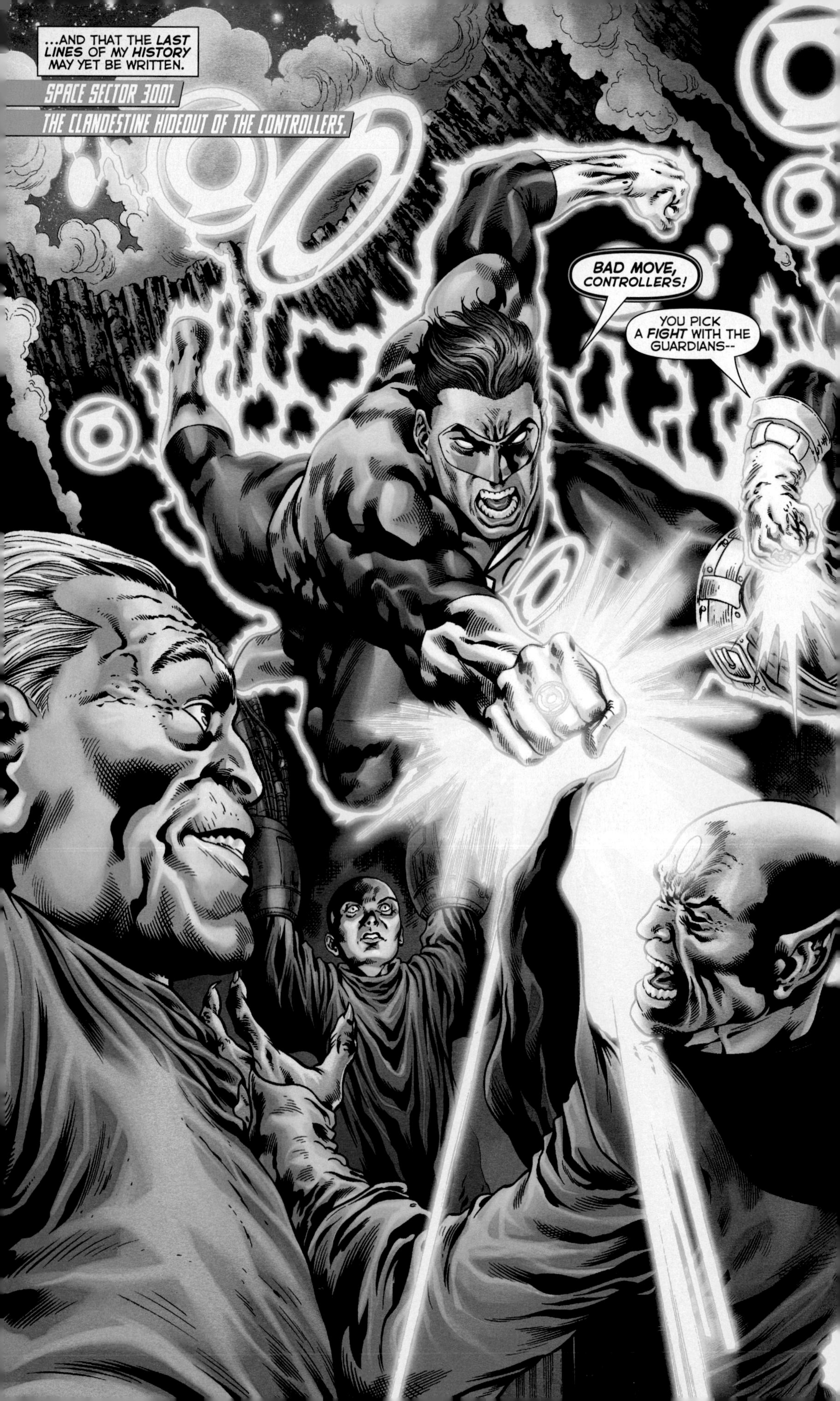
...AND THAT THE LAST LINES OF MY HISTORY MAY YET BE WRITTEN.
SPACE SECTOR 3001.
THE CLANDESTINE HIDEOUT OF THE CONTROLLERS.
BAD MOVE, CONTROLLERS!
YOU PICK A FIGHT WITH THE GUARDIANS--

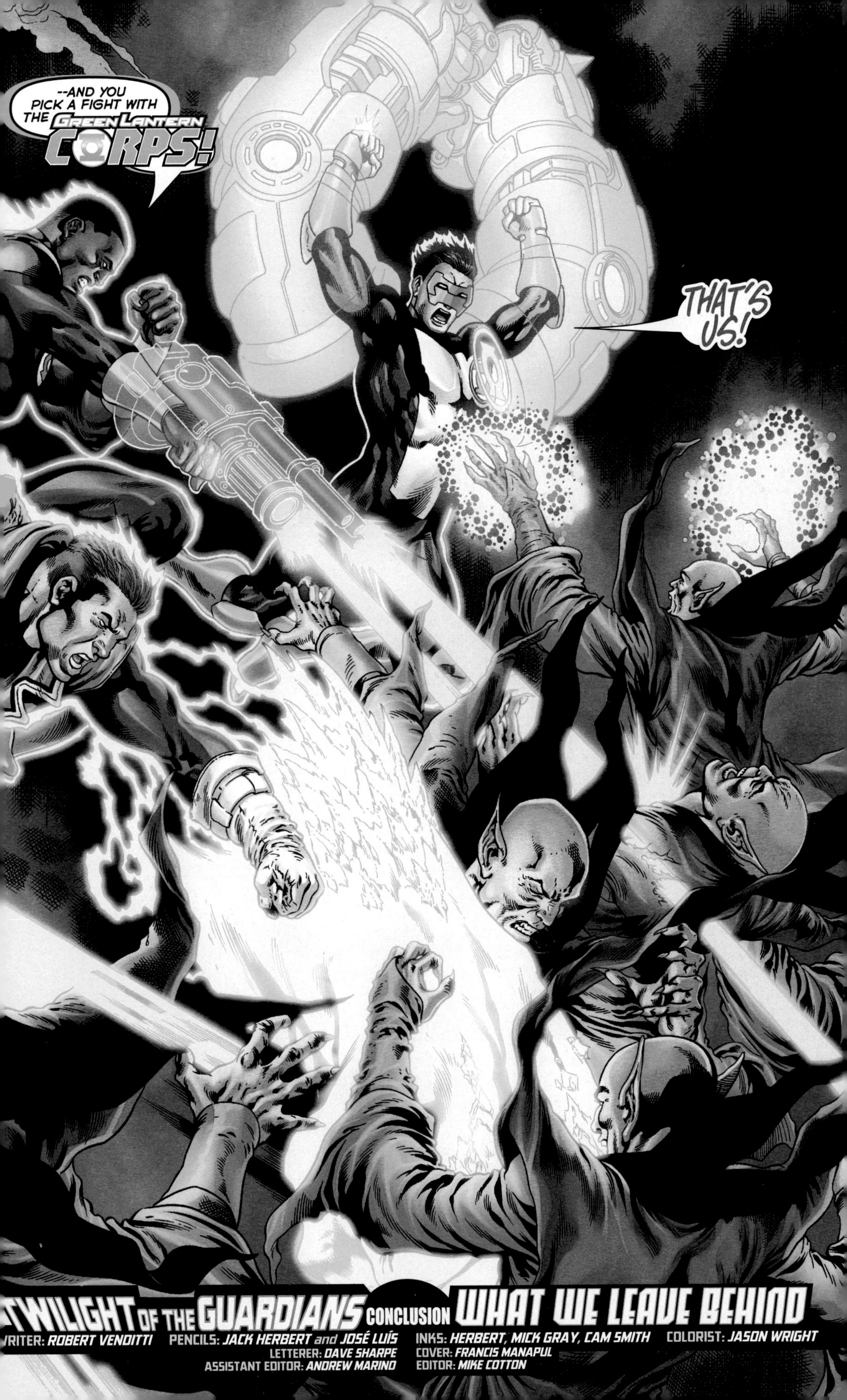
--AND YOU PICK A FIGHT WITH THE GREEN LANTERN CORPS!
THAT'S US!
TWILIGHT OF THE GUARDIANS CONCLUSION WHAT WE LEAVE BEHIND
WRITER: ROBERT VENDITTI PENCILS: JACK HERBERT and JOSÉ LUÍS INKS: HERBERT, MICK GRAY, CAM SMITH COLORIST: JASON WRIGHT
LETTERER: DAVE SHARPE COVER: FRANCIS MANAPUL
ASSISTANT EDITOR: ANDREW MARINO EDITOR: MIKE COTTON

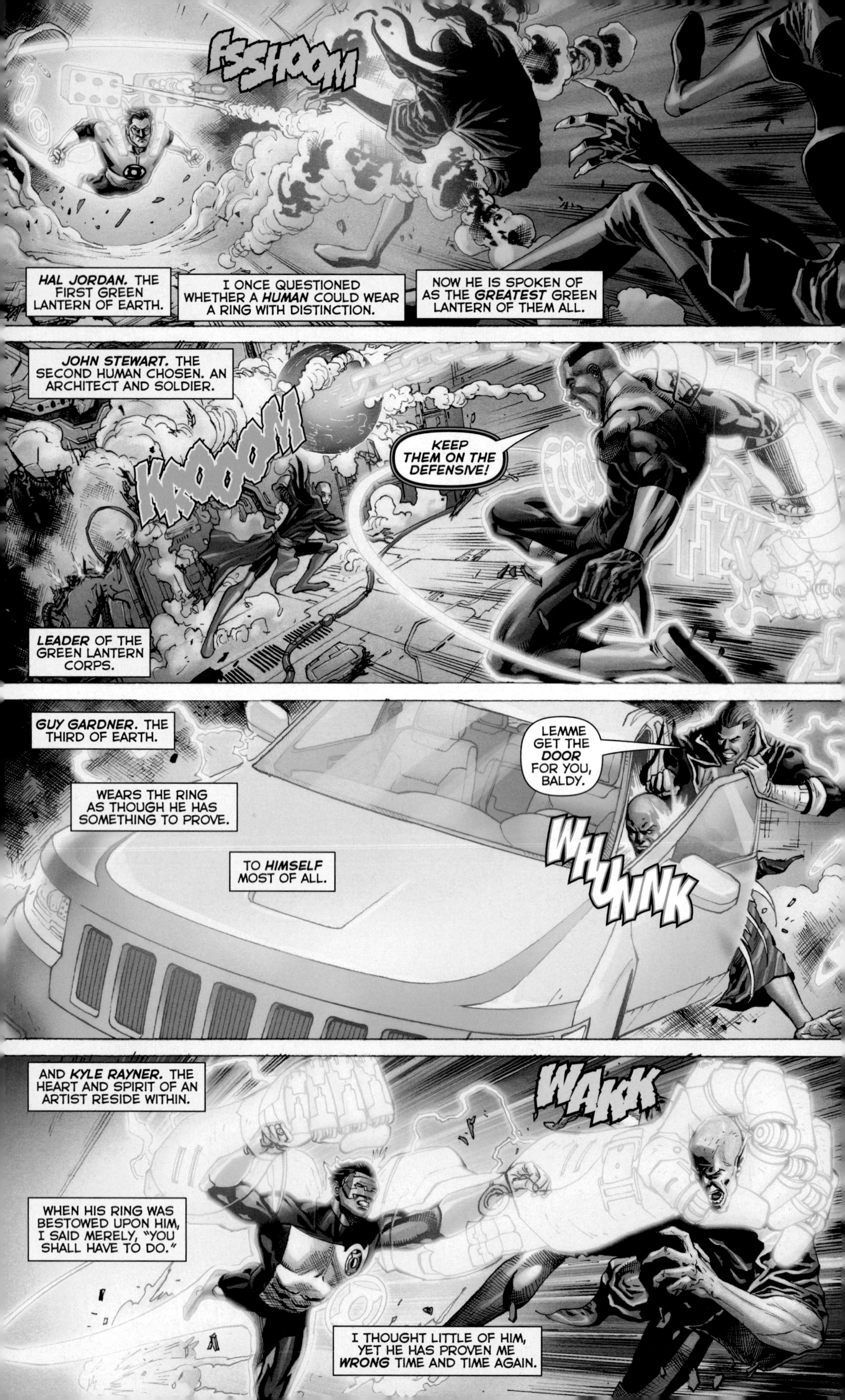
FSSHOOM
HAL JORDAN. THE FIRST GREEN LANTERN OF EARTH.
I ONCE QUESTIONED WHETHER A HUMAN COULD WEAR A RING WITH DISTINCTION.
NOW HE IS SPOKEN OF AS THE GREATEST GREEN LANTERN OF THEM ALL.
JOHN STEWART. THE SECOND HUMAN CHOSEN. AN ARCHITECT AND SOLDIER.
KROOOM
KEEP THEM ON THE DEFENSIVE!
LEADER OF THE GREEN LANTERN CORPS.
GUY GARDNER. THE THIRD OF EARTH.
WEARS THE RING AS THOUGH HE HAS SOMETHING TO PROVE.
TO HIMSELF MOST OF ALL.
LEMME GET THE DOOR FOR YOU, BALDY.
WHUNNK
AND KYLE RAYNER. THE HEART AND SPIRIT OF AN ARTIST RESIDE WITHIN.
WAKK
WHEN HIS RING WAS BESTOWED UPON HIM, I SAID MERELY, "YOU SHALL HAVE TO DO."
I THOUGHT LITTLE OF HIM, YET HE HAS PROVEN ME WRONG TIME AND TIME AGAIN.

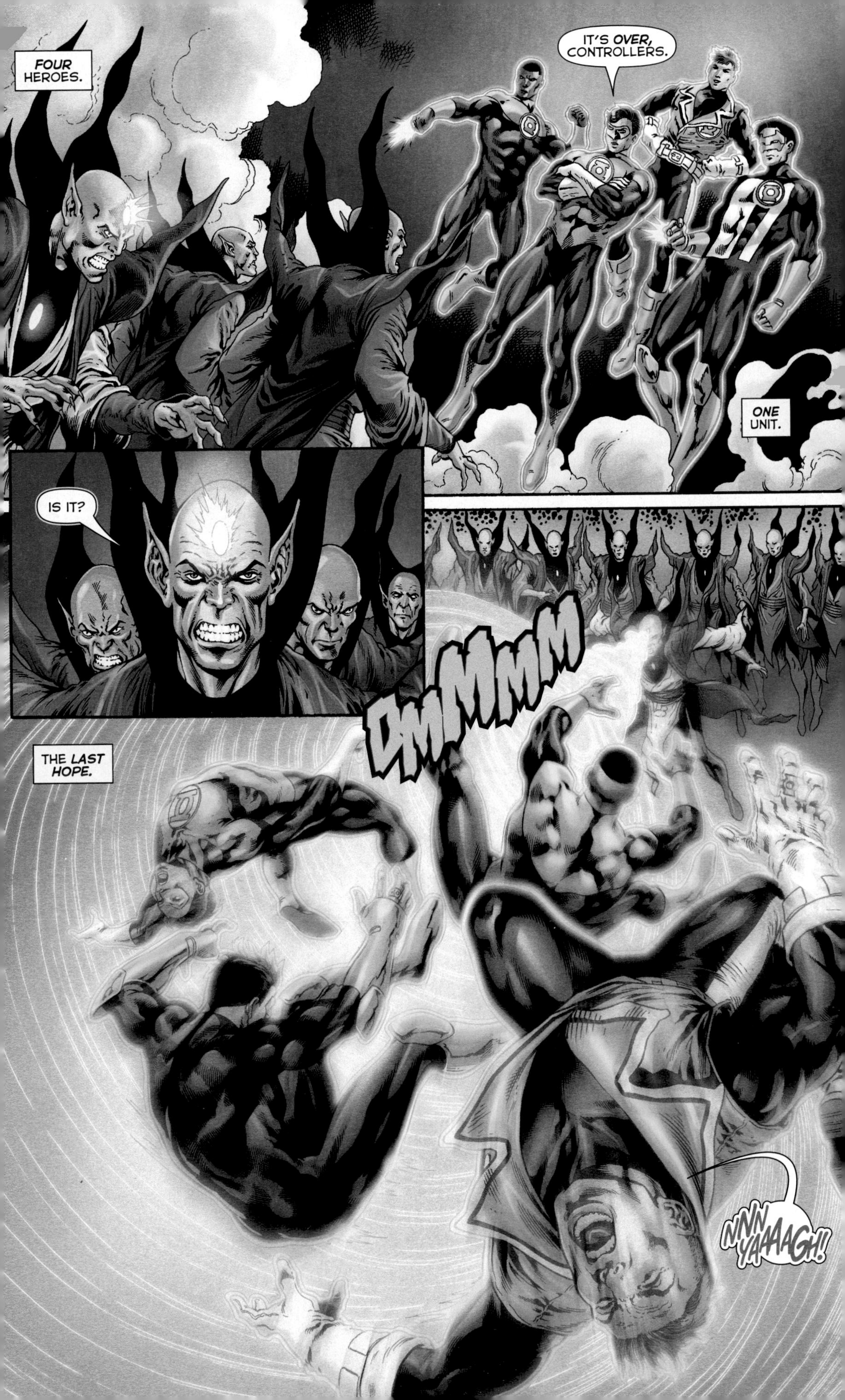
FOUR HEROES.
IT'S OVER, CONTROLLERS.
ONE UNIT.
IS IT?
OMMMM
THE LAST HOPE.
NNNYAAAAGH!

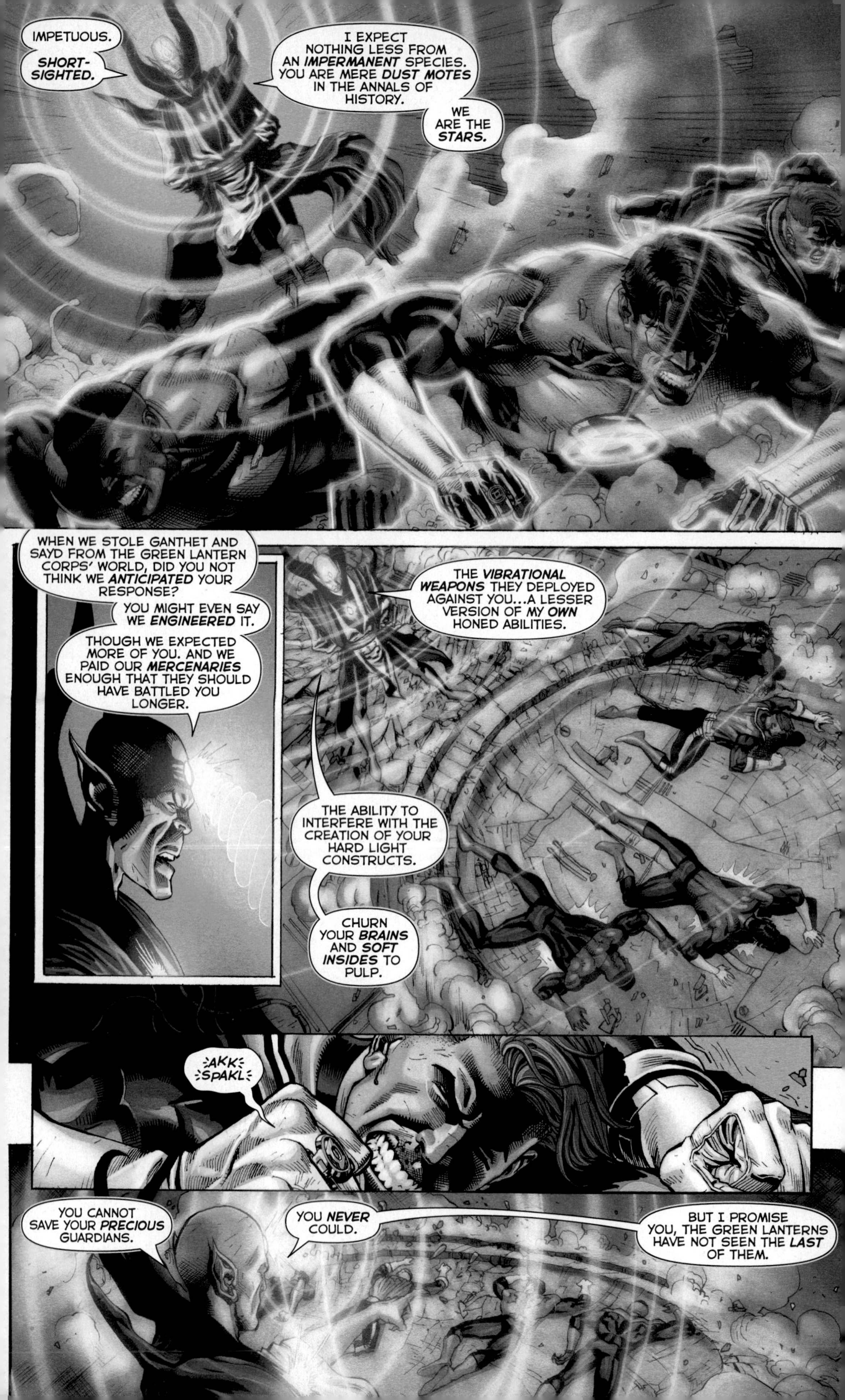
IMPETUOUS.
SHORT-SIGHTED.
I EXPECT NOTHING LESS FROM AN IMPERMANENT SPECIES. YOU ARE MERE DUST MOTES IN THE ANNALS OF HISTORY.
WE ARE THE STARS.
WHEN WE STOLE GANTHET AND SAYD FROM THE GREEN LANTERN CORPS' WORLD, DID YOU NOT THINK WE ANTICIPATED YOUR RESPONSE?
YOU MIGHT EVEN SAY WE ENGINEERED IT.
THOUGH WE EXPECTED MORE OF YOU. AND WE PAID OUR MERCENARIES ENOUGH THAT THEY SHOULD HAVE BATTLED YOU LONGER.
THE VIBRATIONAL WEAPONS THEY DEPLOYED AGAINST YOU...A LESSER VERSION OF MY OWN HONED ABILITIES.
THE ABILITY TO INTERFERE WITH THE CREATION OF YOUR HARD LIGHT CONSTRUCTS.
CHURN YOUR BRAINS AND SOFT INSIDES TO PULP.
AKK SPAKL
YOU CANNOT SAVE YOUR PRECIOUS GUARDIANS.
YOU NEVER COULD.
BUT I PROMISE YOU, THE GREEN LANTERNS HAVE NOT SEEN THE LAST OF THEM.

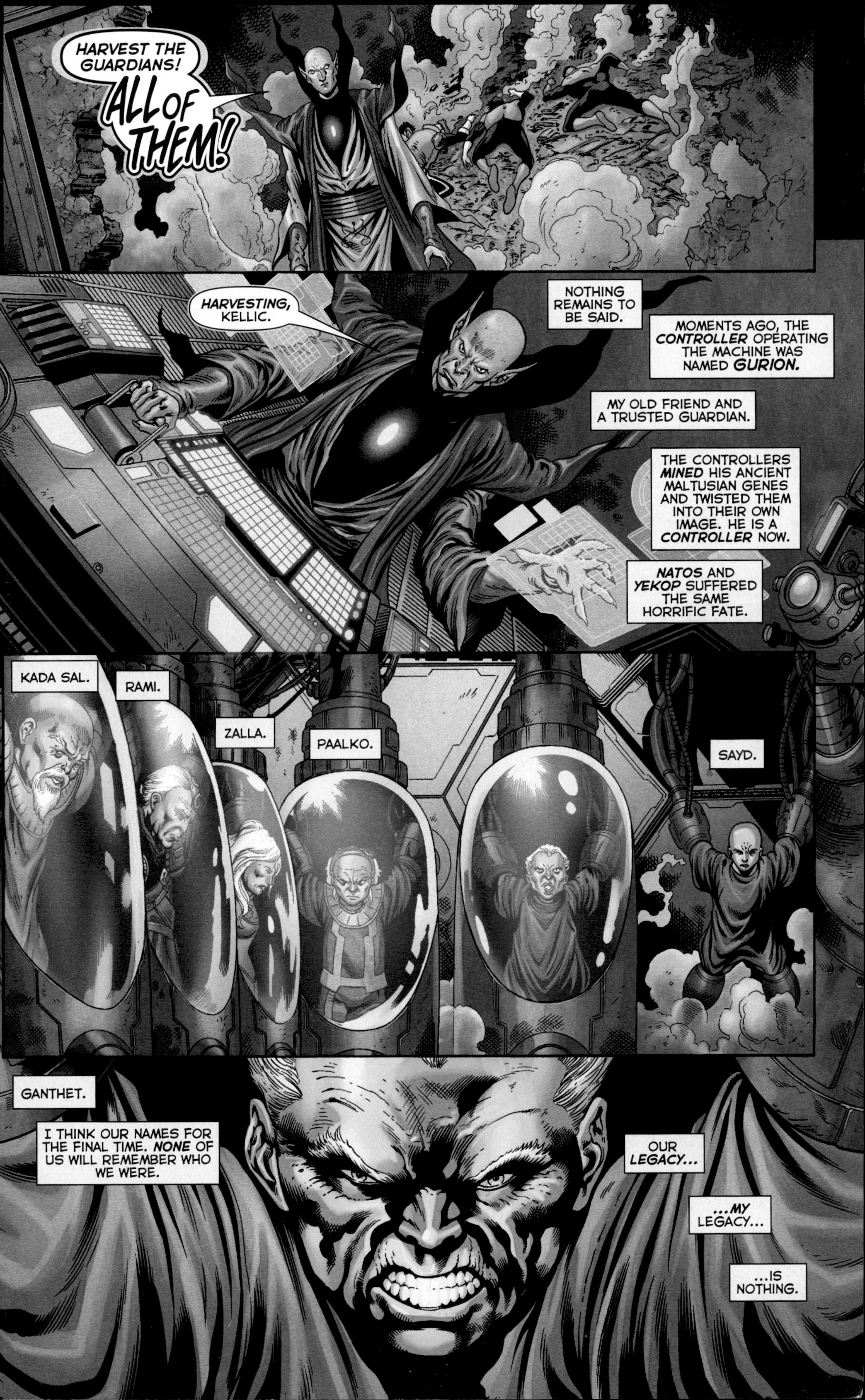
HARVEST THE GUARDIANS! ALL OF THEM!
HARVESTING, KELLIC.
NOTHING REMAINS TO BE SAID.
MOMENTS AGO, THE CONTROLLER OPERATING THE MACHINE WAS NAMED GURION.
MY OLD FRIEND AND A TRUSTED GUARDIAN.
THE CONTROLLERS MINED HIS ANCIENT MALTUSIAN GENES AND TWISTED THEM INTO THEIR OWN IMAGE. HE IS A CONTROLLER NOW.
NATOS AND YEKOP SUFFERED THE SAME HORRIFIC FATE.
KADA SAL.
RAMI.
ZALLA.
PAALKO.
SAYD.
GANTHET.
I THINK OUR NAMES FOR THE FINAL TIME. NONE OF US WILL REMEMBER WHO WE WERE.
OUR LEGACY...
...MY LEGACY...
...IS NOTHING.

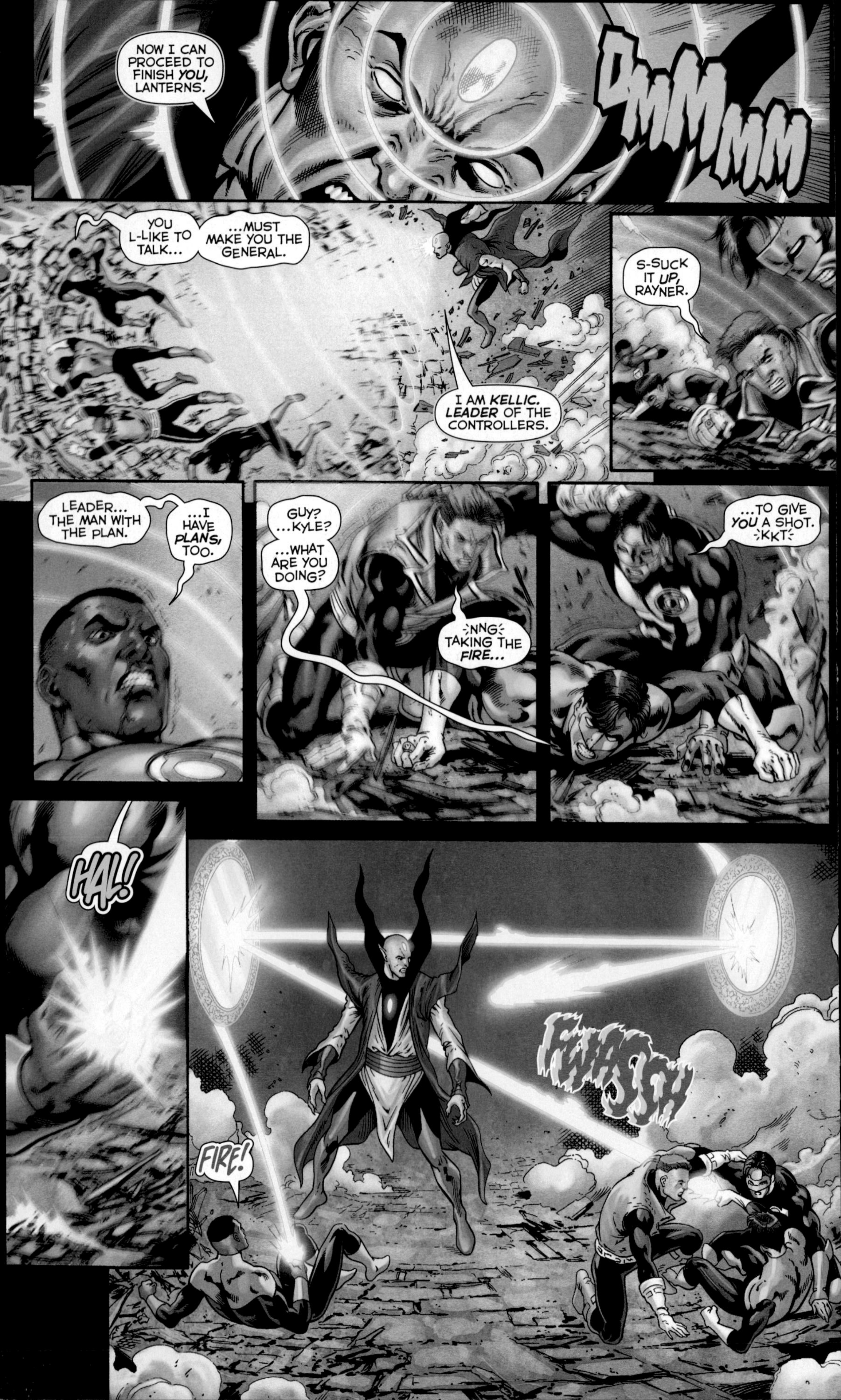
NOW I CAN PROCEED TO FINISH YOU, LANTERNS.
DMMMMM
YOU L-LIKE TO TALK...
...MUST MAKE YOU THE GENERAL.
I AM KELLIC. LEADER OF THE CONTROLLERS.
S-SUCK IT UP, RAYNER.
LEADER... THE MAN WITH THE PLAN.
...I HAVE PLANS, TOO.
GUY? ...KYLE?
...WHAT ARE YOU DOING?
NNG TAKING THE FIRE...
...TO GIVE YOU A SHOT. KKT
HAL!
FIRE!
FWASH

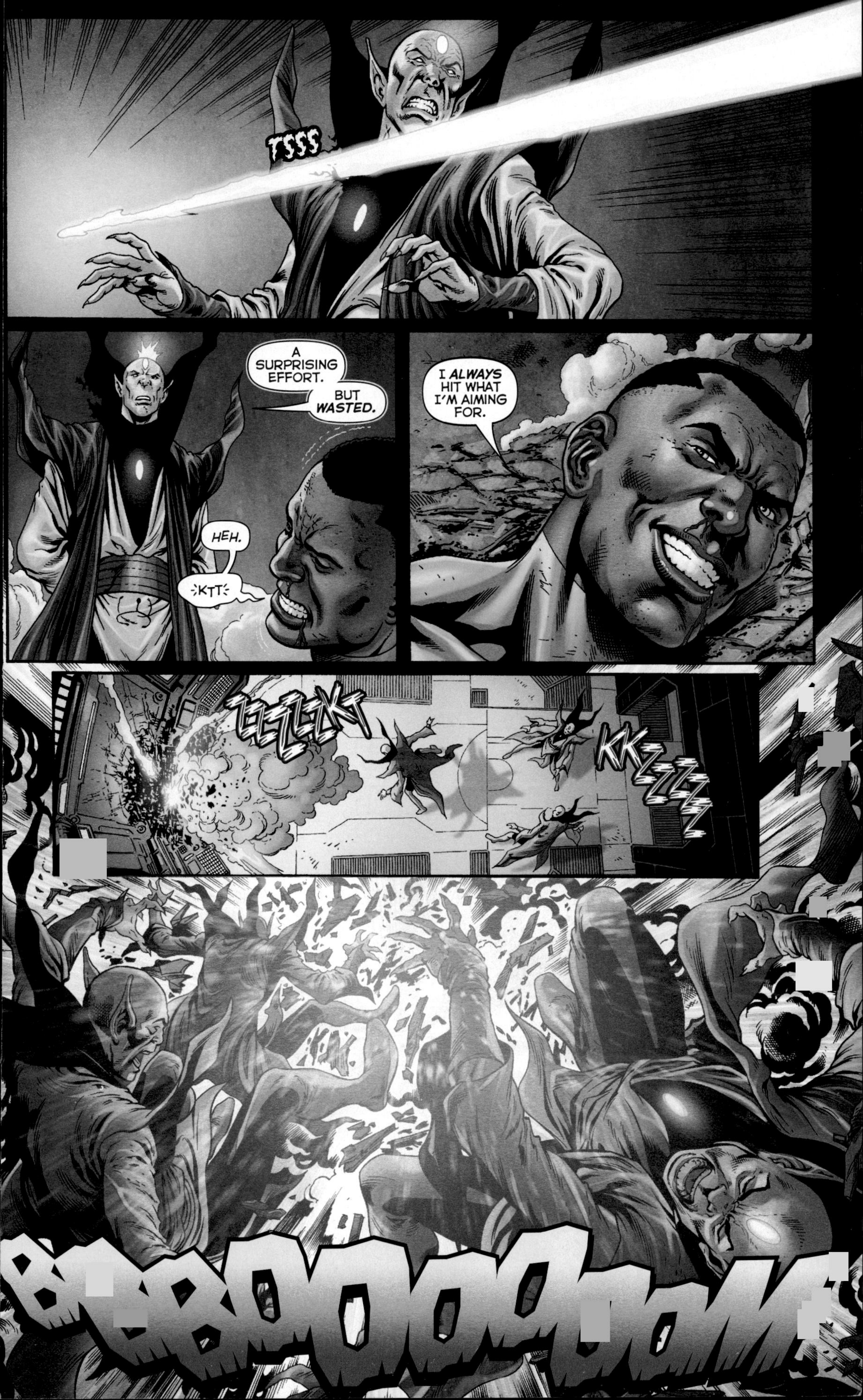
TSSS
A SURPRISING EFFORT.
BUT *WASTED.*
HEH.
KTT
I *ALWAYS* HIT WHAT I'M AIMING FOR.

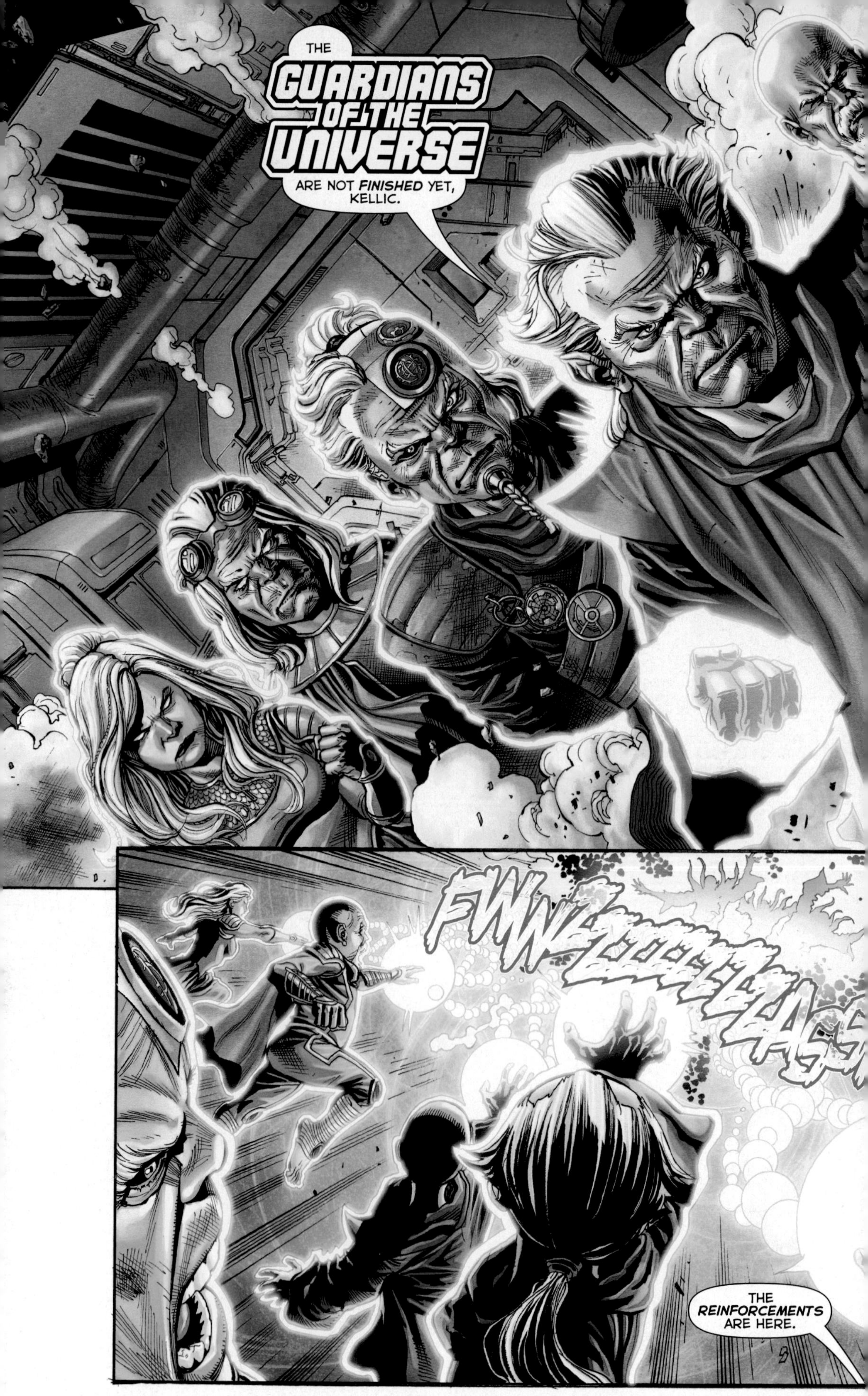
THE GUARDIANS OF THE UNIVERSE ARE NOT FINISHED YET, KELLIC.
THE REINFORCEMENTS ARE HERE.

RALLY, LANTERNS.

GRAARRRG!

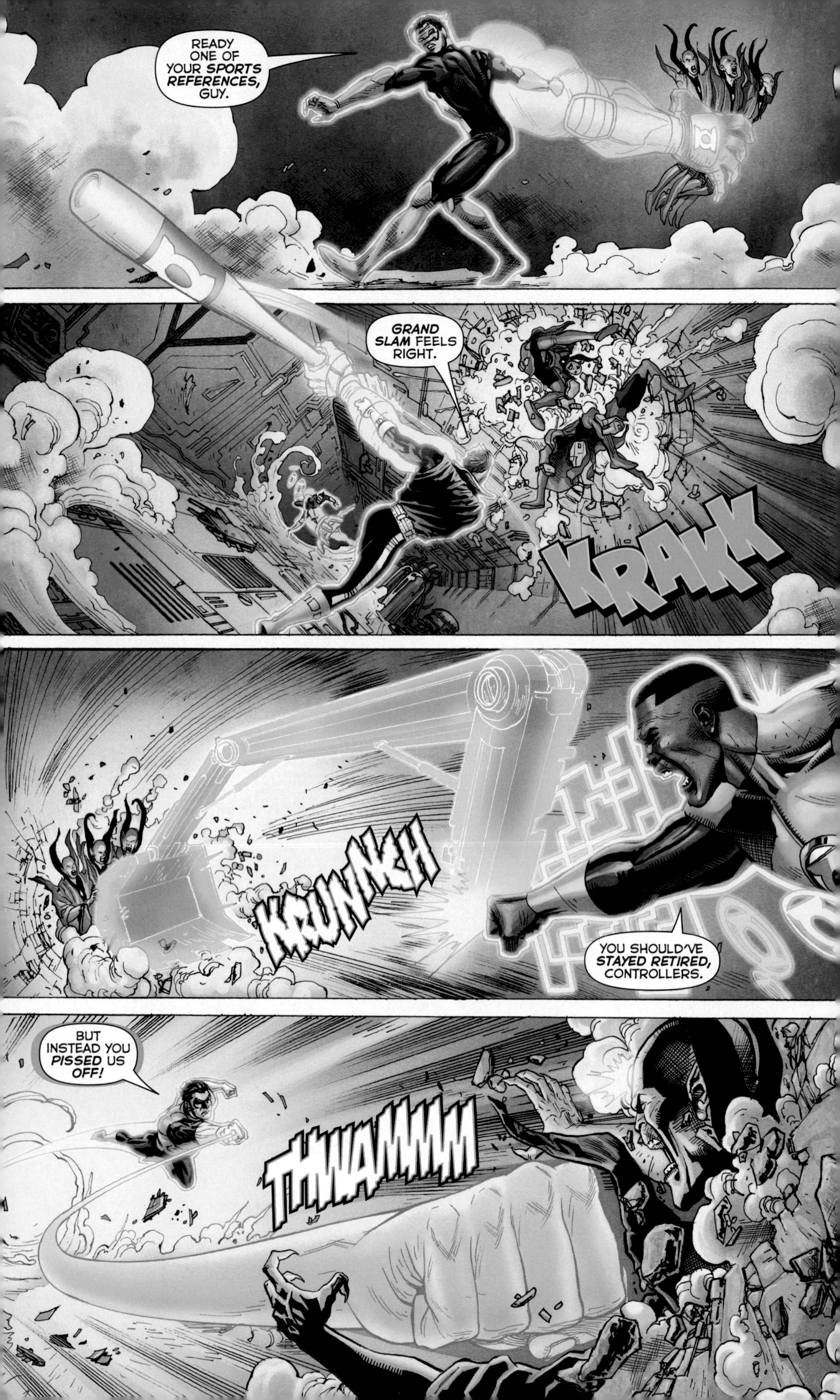
READY ONE OF YOUR SPORTS REFERENCES, GUY.
GRAND SLAM FEELS RIGHT.
KRAKK
KRUNKH
YOU SHOULD'VE STAYED RETIRED, CONTROLLERS.
BUT INSTEAD YOU PISSED US OFF!
THWAMMM

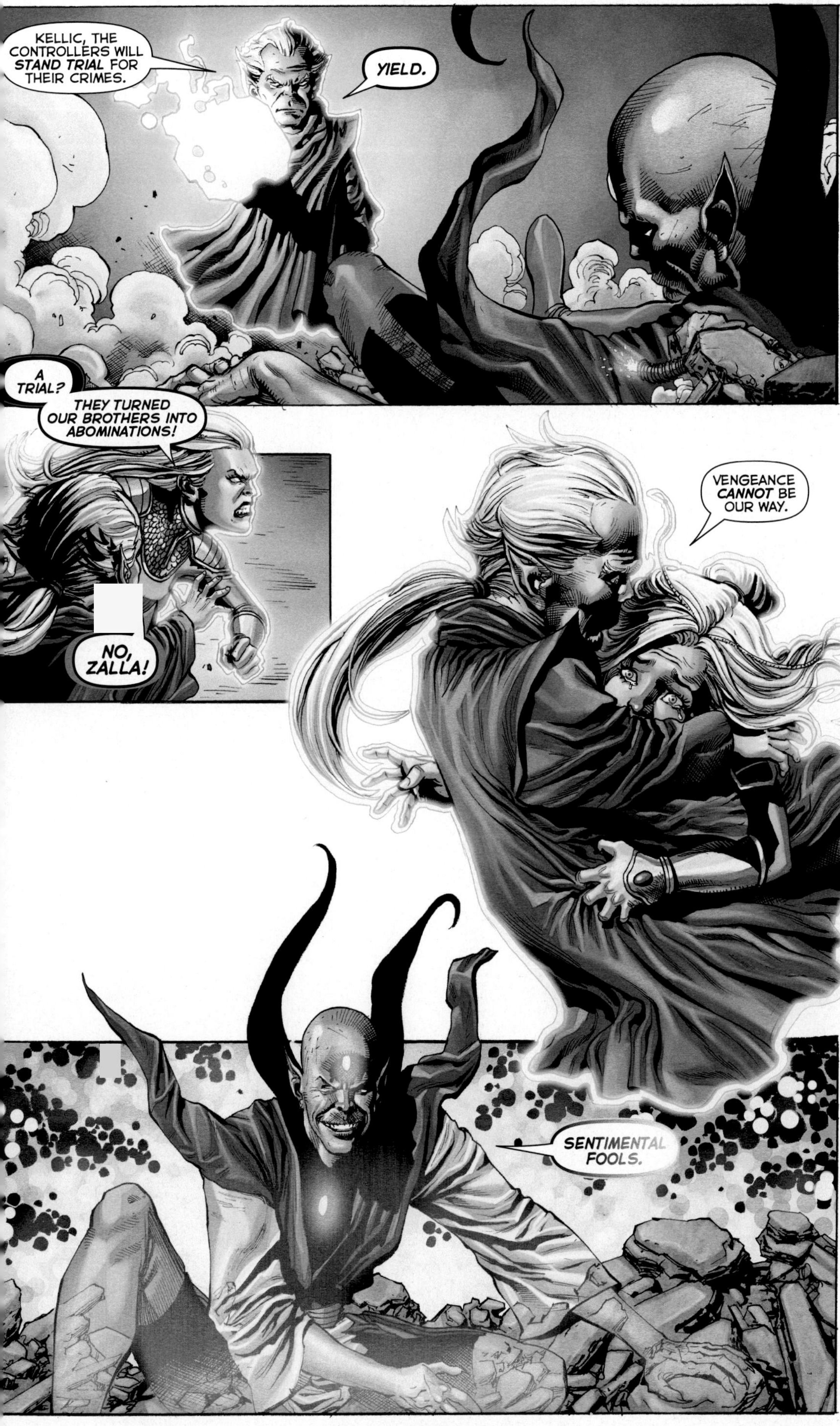
KELLIC, THE CONTROLLERS WILL STAND TRIAL FOR THEIR CRIMES.
YIELD.
A TRIAL?
THEY TURNED OUR BROTHERS INTO ABOMINATIONS!
NO, ZALLA!
VENGEANCE CANNOT BE OUR WAY.
SENTIMENTAL FOOLS.

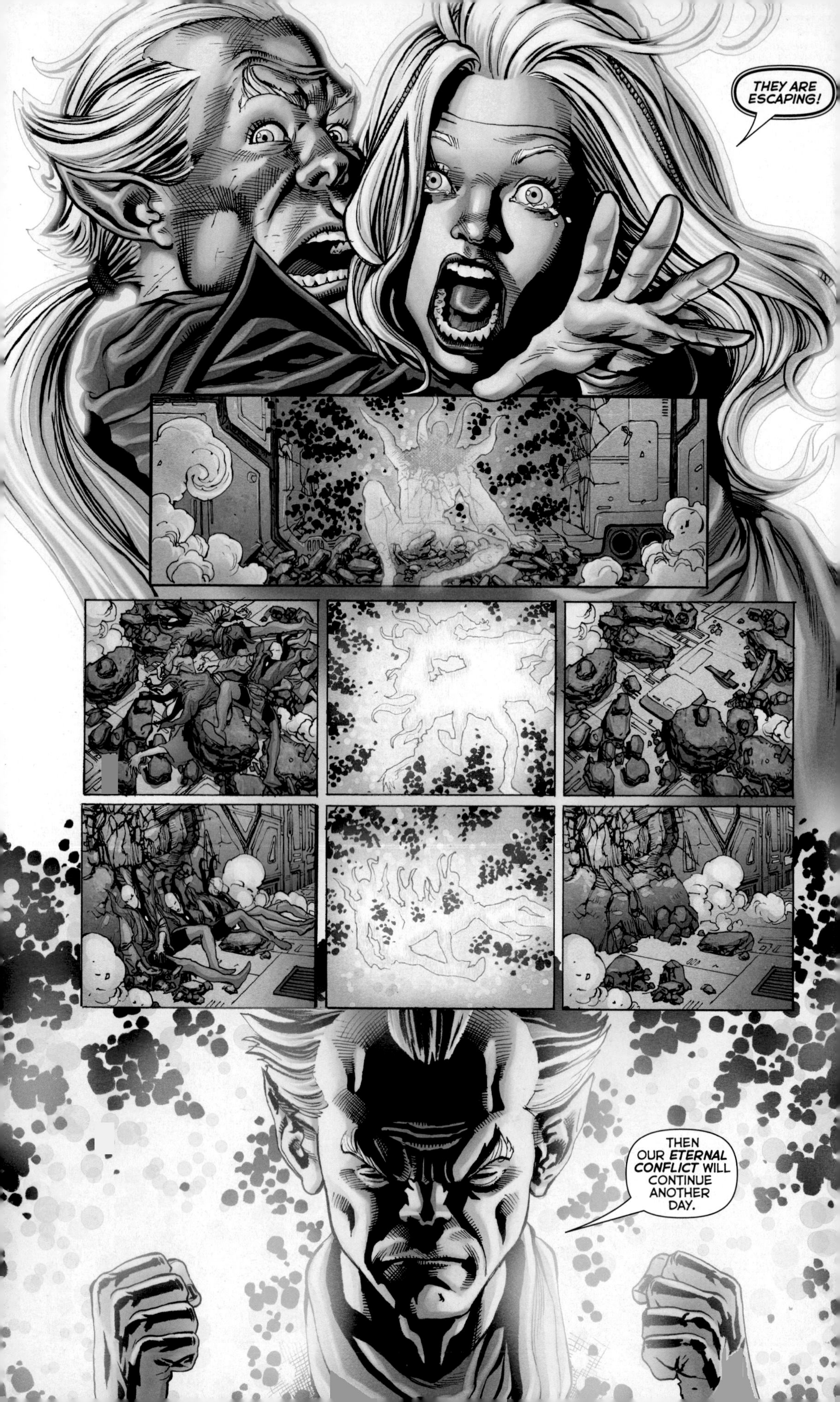
THEY ARE ESCAPING!
THEN OUR ETERNAL CONFLICT WILL CONTINUE ANOTHER DAY.

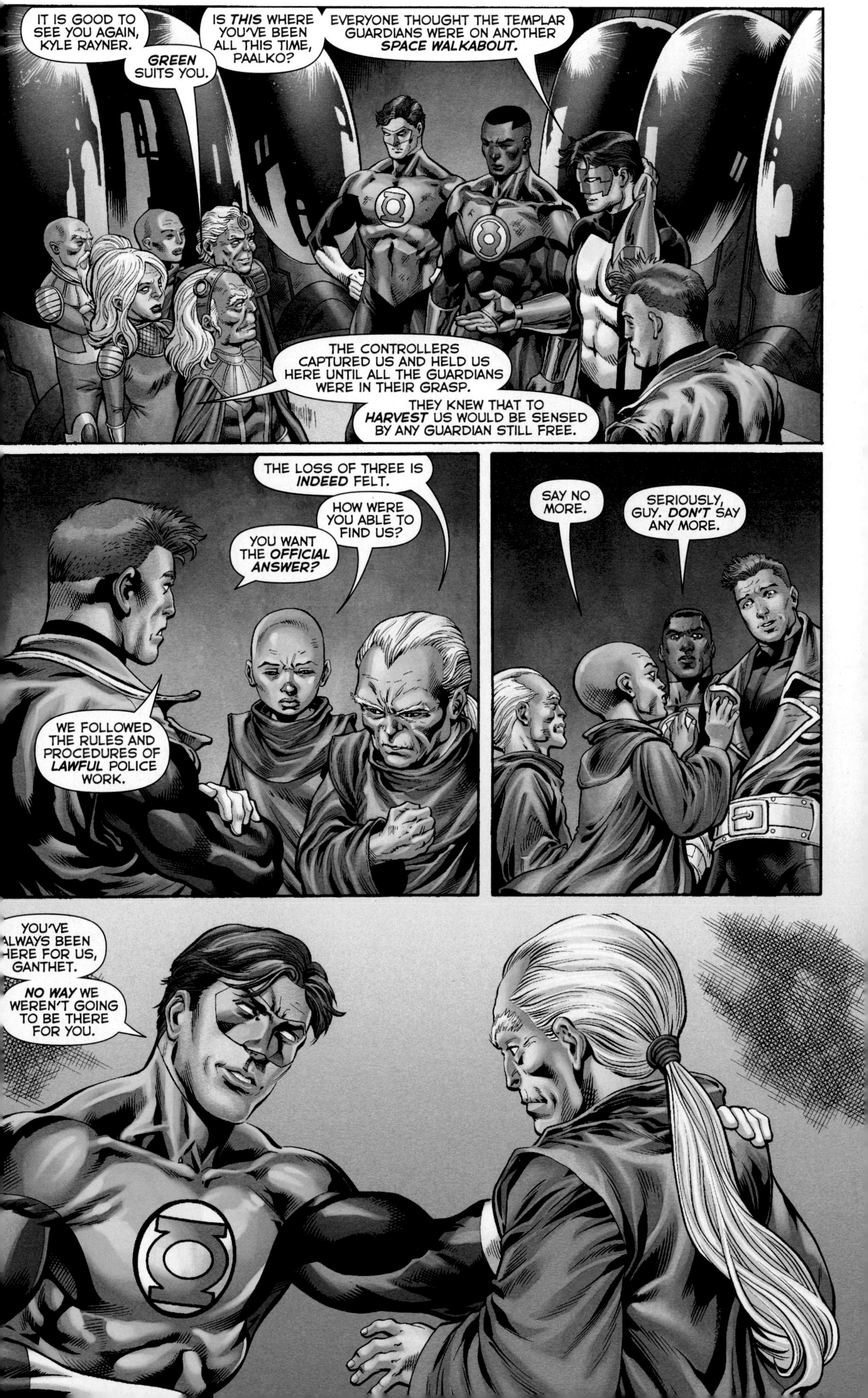

IT IS GOOD TO SEE YOU AGAIN, KYLE RAYNER.
GREEN SUITS YOU.
IS THIS WHERE YOU'VE BEEN ALL THIS TIME, PAALKO?
EVERYONE THOUGHT THE TEMPLAR GUARDIANS WERE ON ANOTHER SPACE WALKABOUT.
THE CONTROLLERS CAPTURED US AND HELD US HERE UNTIL ALL THE GUARDIANS WERE IN THEIR GRASP.
THEY KNEW THAT TO HARVEST US WOULD BE SENSED BY ANY GUARDIAN STILL FREE.
THE LOSS OF THREE IS INDEED FELT.
HOW WERE YOU ABLE TO FIND US?
YOU WANT THE OFFICIAL ANSWER?
WE FOLLOWED THE RULES AND PROCEDURES OF LAWFUL POLICE WORK.
SAY NO MORE.
SERIOUSLY, GUY. DON'T SAY ANY MORE.
YOU'VE ALWAYS BEEN HERE FOR US, GANTHET.
NO WAY WE WEREN'T GOING TO BE THERE FOR YOU.

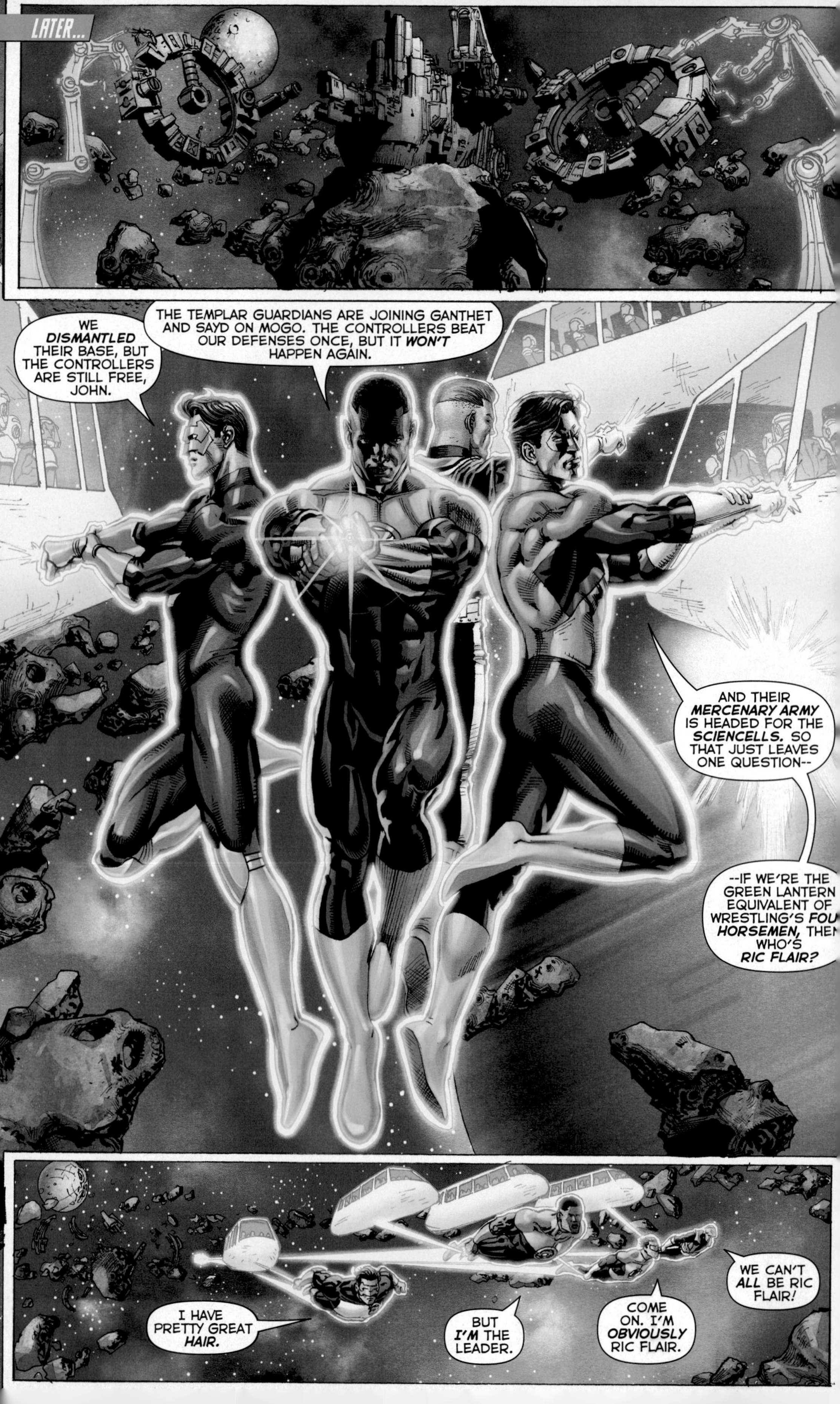
LATER...
WE DISMANTLED THEIR BASE, BUT THE CONTROLLERS ARE STILL FREE, JOHN.
THE TEMPLAR GUARDIANS ARE JOINING GANTHET AND SAYD ON MOGO. THE CONTROLLERS BEAT OUR DEFENSES ONCE, BUT IT WON'T HAPPEN AGAIN.
AND THEIR MERCENARY ARMY IS HEADED FOR THE SCIENCELLS. SO THAT JUST LEAVES ONE QUESTION--
--IF WE'RE THE GREEN LANTERN EQUIVALENT OF WRESTLING'S FOU HORSEMEN, THEN WHO'S RIC FLAIR?
I HAVE PRETTY GREAT HAIR.
BUT I'M THE LEADER.
COME ON. I'M OBVIOUSLY RIC FLAIR.
WE CAN'T ALL BE RIC FLAIR!

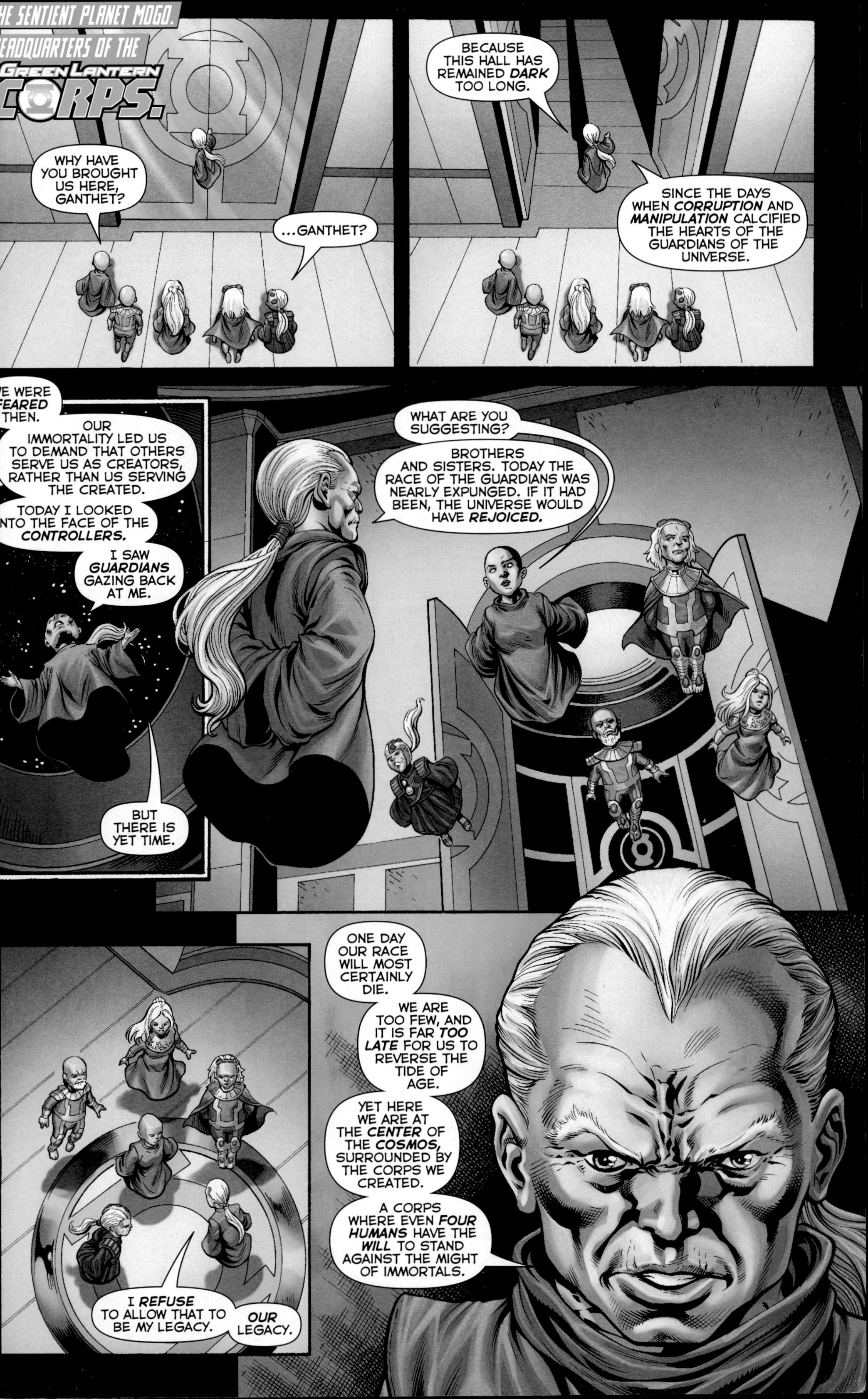

HE SENTIENT PLANET MOGO.
EADQUARTERS OF THE GREEN LANTERN CORPS.
WHY HAVE YOU BROUGHT US HERE, GANTHET?
...GANTHET?
BECAUSE THIS HALL HAS REMAINED DARK TOO LONG.
SINCE THE DAYS WHEN CORRUPTION AND MANIPULATION CALCIFIED THE HEARTS OF THE GUARDIANS OF THE UNIVERSE.
WHAT ARE YOU SUGGESTING?
BROTHERS AND SISTERS. TODAY THE RACE OF THE GUARDIANS WAS NEARLY EXPUNGED. IF IT HAD BEEN, THE UNIVERSE WOULD HAVE REJOICED.
E WERE FEARED THEN.
OUR IMMORTALITY LED US TO DEMAND THAT OTHERS SERVE US AS CREATORS, RATHER THAN US SERVING THE CREATED.
TODAY I LOOKED NTO THE FACE OF THE CONTROLLERS.
I SAW GUARDIANS GAZING BACK AT ME.
BUT THERE IS YET TIME.
ONE DAY OUR RACE WILL MOST CERTAINLY DIE.
WE ARE TOO FEW, AND IT IS FAR TOO LATE FOR US TO REVERSE THE TIDE OF AGE.
YET HERE WE ARE AT THE CENTER OF THE COSMOS, SURROUNDED BY THE CORPS WE CREATED.
A CORPS WHERE EVEN FOUR HUMANS HAVE THE WILL TO STAND AGAINST THE MIGHT OF IMMORTALS.
I REFUSE TO ALLOW THAT TO BE MY LEGACY.
OUR LEGACY.

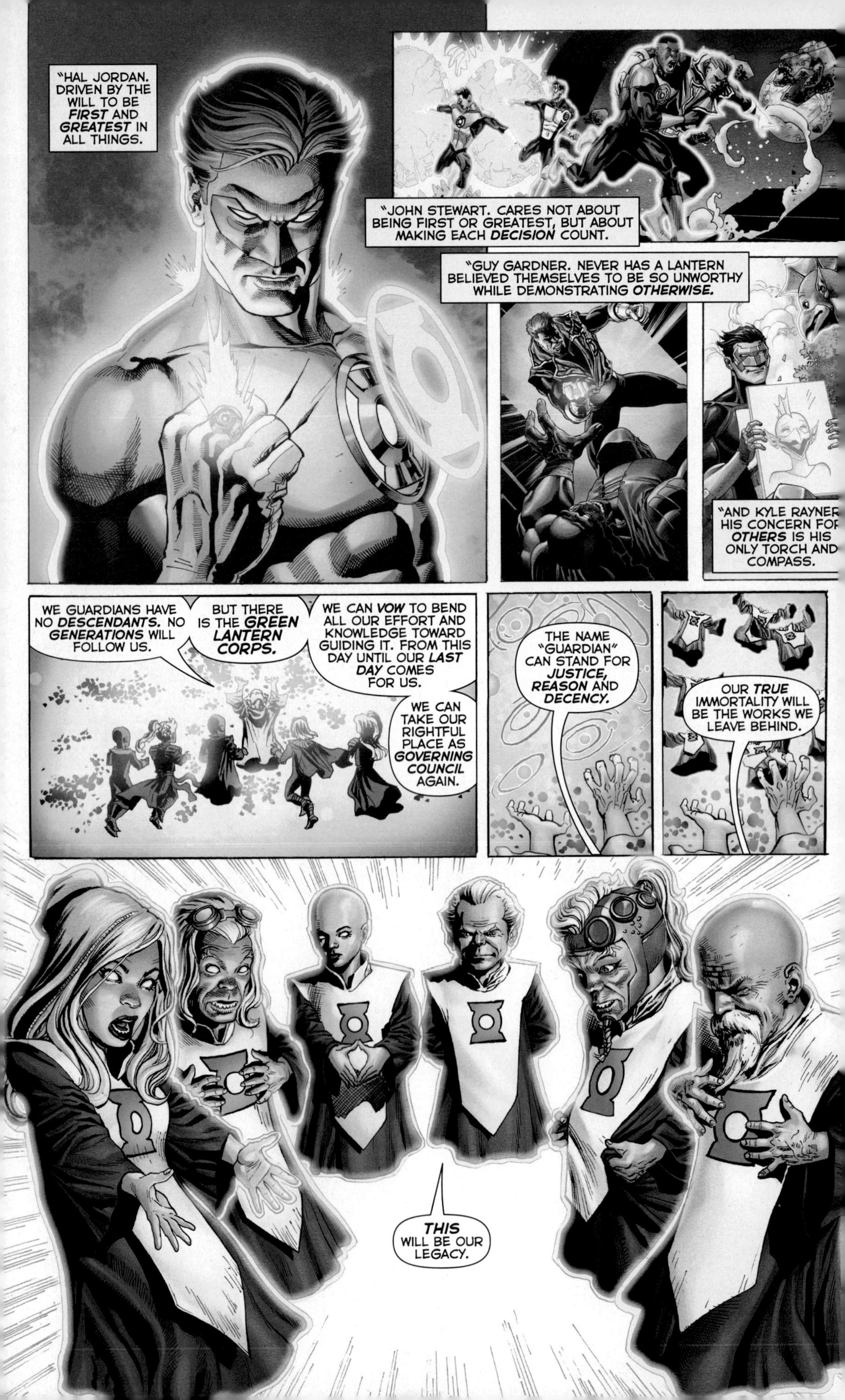
"HAL JORDAN. DRIVEN BY THE WILL TO BE FIRST AND GREATEST IN ALL THINGS.
"JOHN STEWART. CARES NOT ABOUT BEING FIRST OR GREATEST, BUT ABOUT MAKING EACH DECISION COUNT.
"GUY GARDNER. NEVER HAS A LANTERN BELIEVED THEMSELVES TO BE SO UNWORTHY WHILE DEMONSTRATING OTHERWISE.
"AND KYLE RAYNER HIS CONCERN FOR OTHERS IS HIS ONLY TORCH AND COMPASS.
WE GUARDIANS HAVE NO DESCENDANTS. NO GENERATIONS WILL FOLLOW US.
BUT THERE IS THE GREEN LANTERN CORPS.
WE CAN VOW TO BEND ALL OUR EFFORT AND KNOWLEDGE TOWARD GUIDING IT. FROM THIS DAY UNTIL OUR LAST DAY COMES FOR US.
WE CAN TAKE OUR RIGHTFUL PLACE AS GOVERNING COUNCIL AGAIN.
THE NAME "GUARDIAN" CAN STAND FOR JUSTICE, REASON AND DECENCY.
OUR TRUE IMMORTALITY WILL BE THE WORKS WE LEAVE BEHIND.
THIS WILL BE OUR LEGACY.

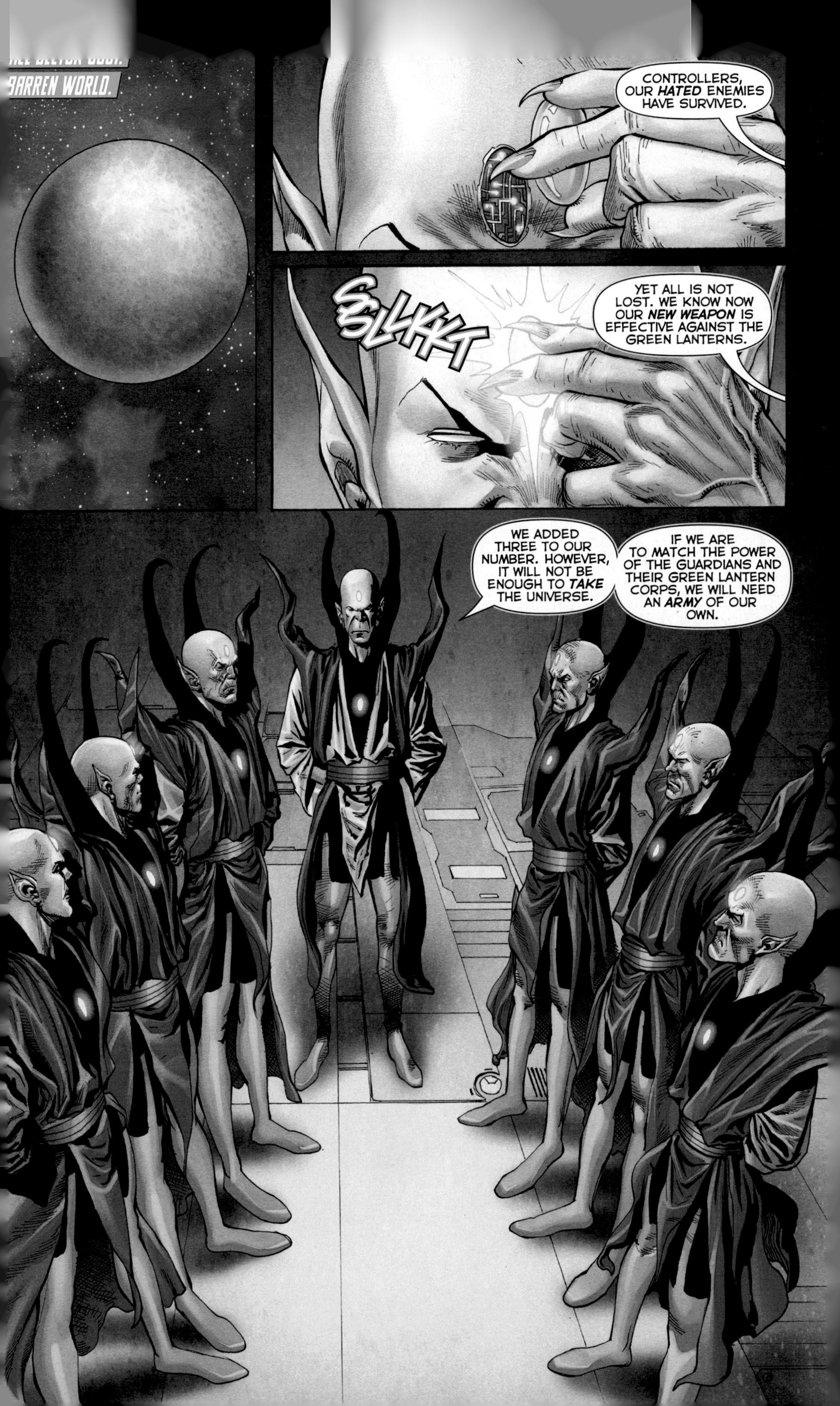
BARREN WORLD.
CONTROLLERS, OUR HATED ENEMIES HAVE SURVIVED.
SSLIKKT
YET ALL IS NOT LOST. WE KNOW NOW OUR NEW WEAPON IS EFFECTIVE AGAINST THE GREEN LANTERNS.
WE ADDED THREE TO OUR NUMBER. HOWEVER, IT WILL NOT BE ENOUGH TO TAKE THE UNIVERSE.
IF WE ARE TO MATCH THE POWER OF THE GUARDIANS AND THEIR GREEN LANTERN CORPS, WE WILL NEED AN ARMY OF OUR OWN.

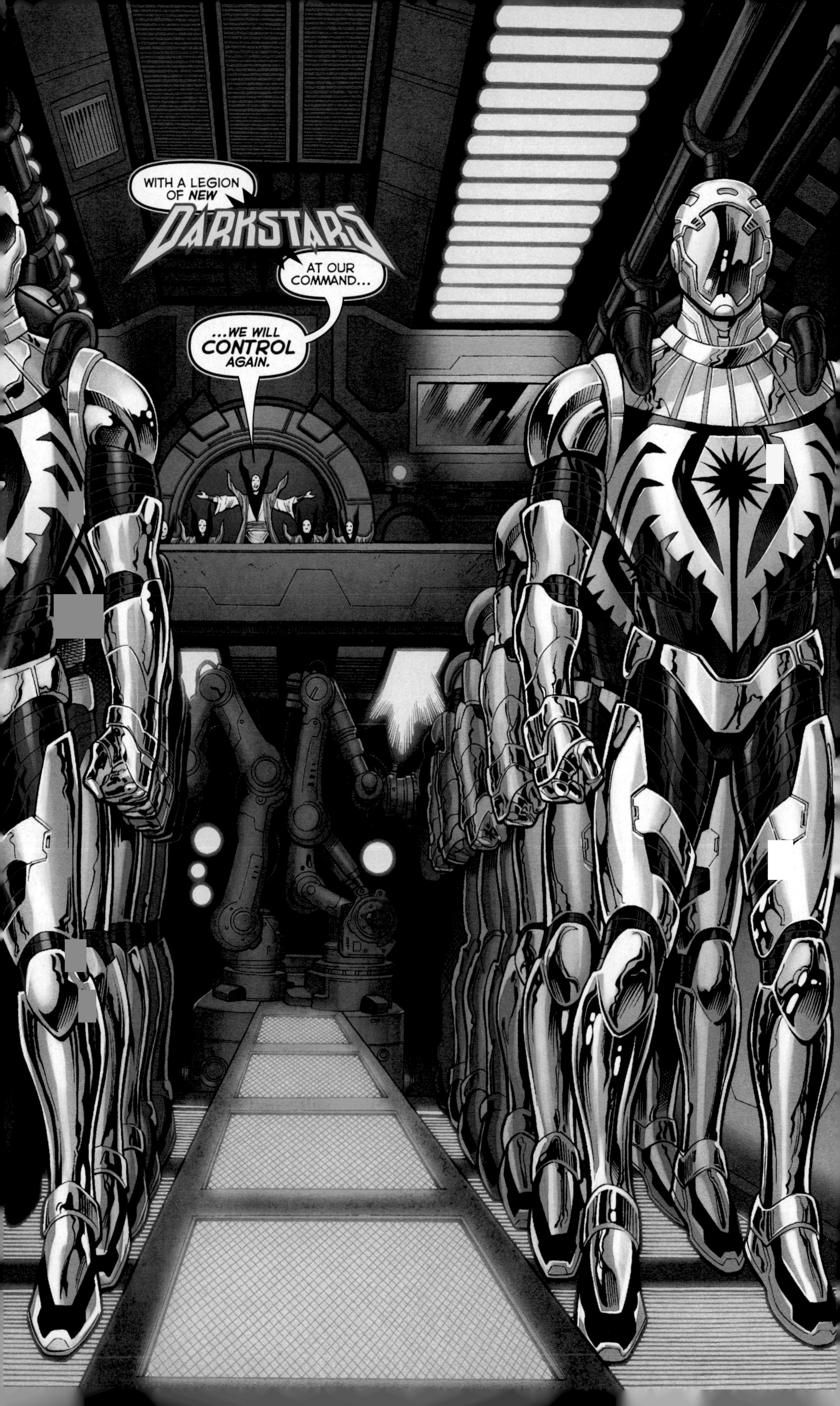
WITH A LEGION OF NEW DARKSTARS
AT OUR COMMAND...
...WE WILL CONTROL AGAIN.

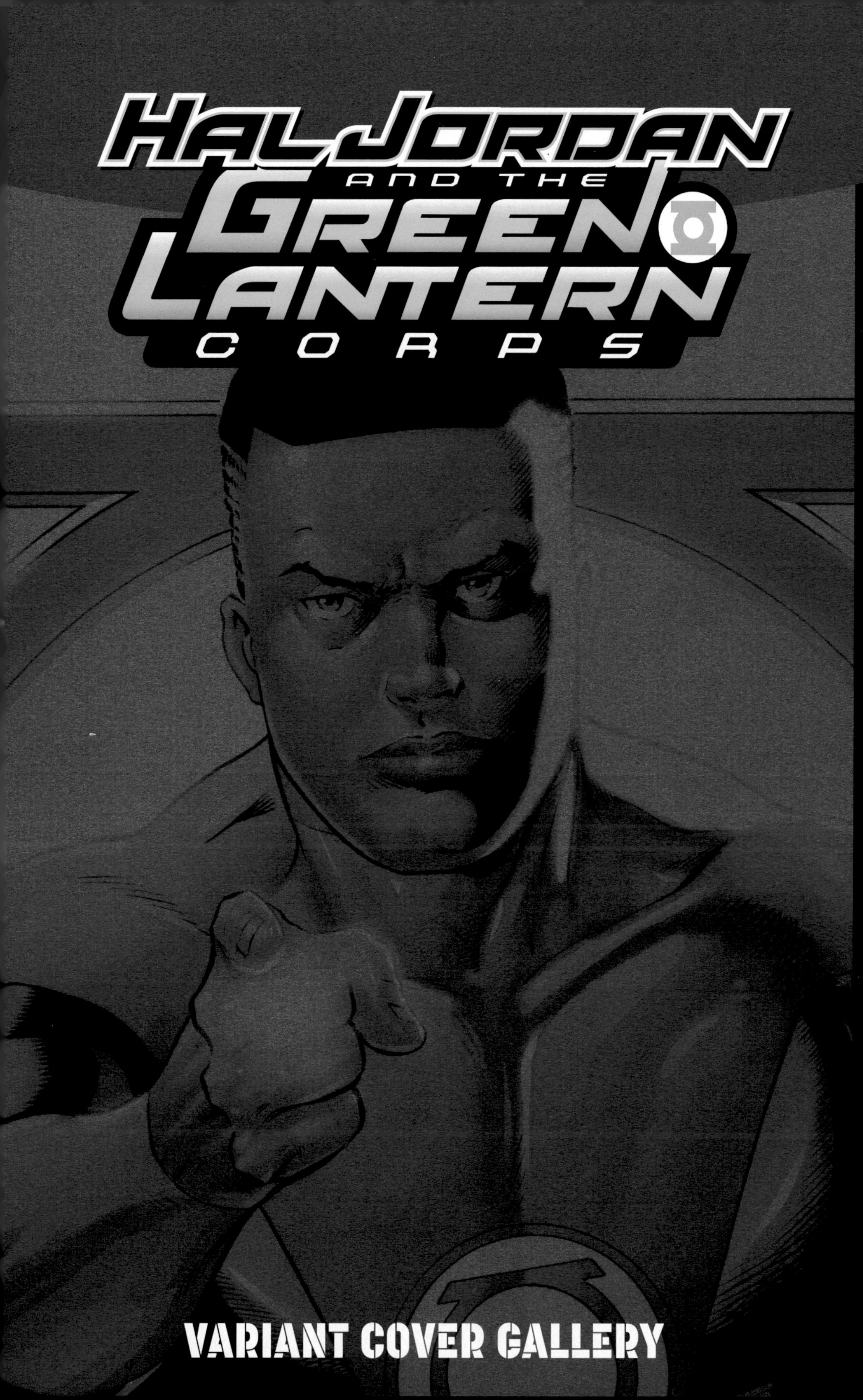
HAL JORDAN
AND THE
GREEN
LANTERN
CORPS

VARIANT COVER GALLERY

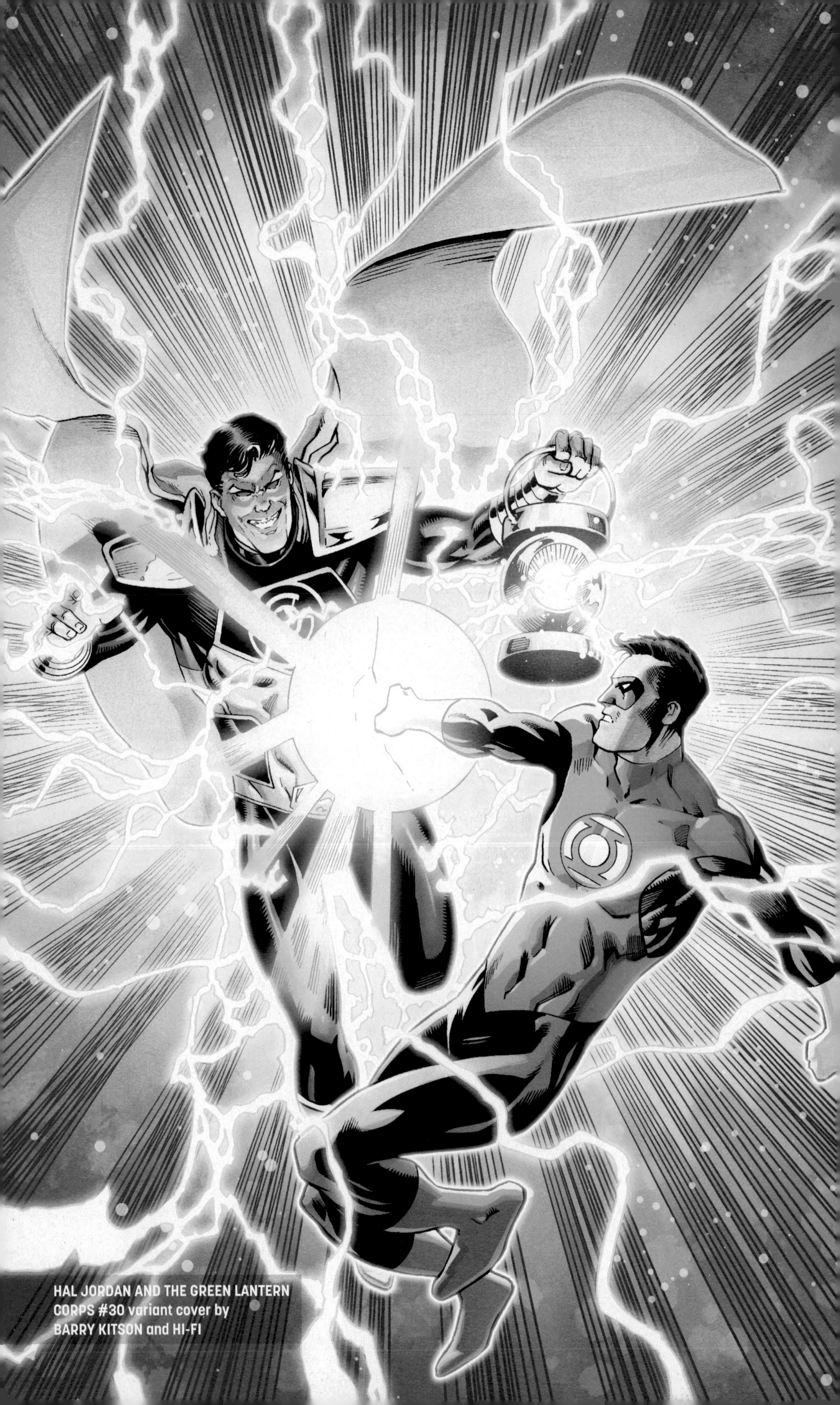

HAL JORDAN AND THE GREEN LANTERN
CORPS #30 variant cover by
BARRY KITSON and HI-FI

HAL JORDAN AND THE GREEN LANTERN CORPS #31 variant cover by BARRY KITSON and HI-FI

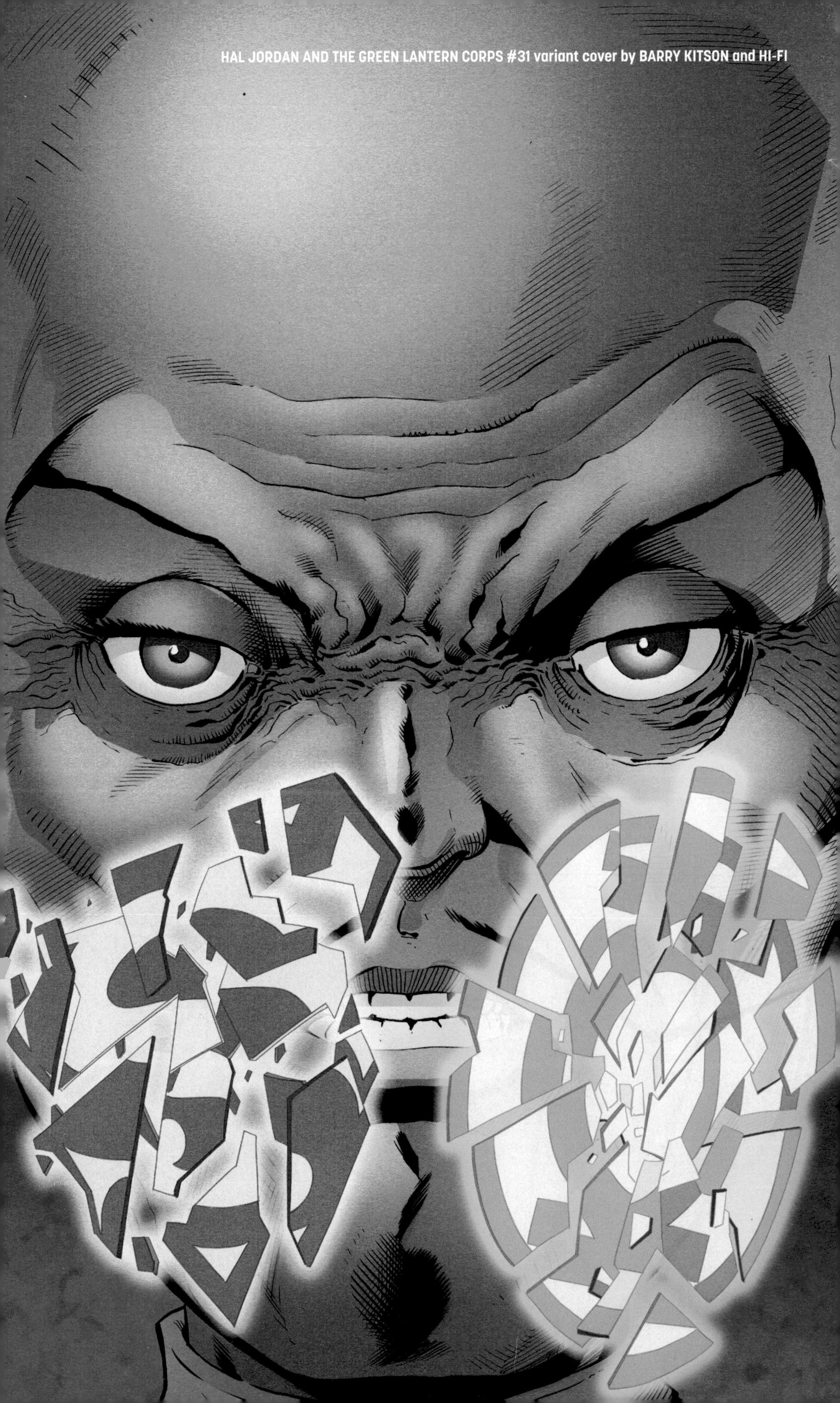

HAL JORDAN AND THE GREEN LANTERN CORPS #33 variant cover by BARRY KITSON and HI-FI

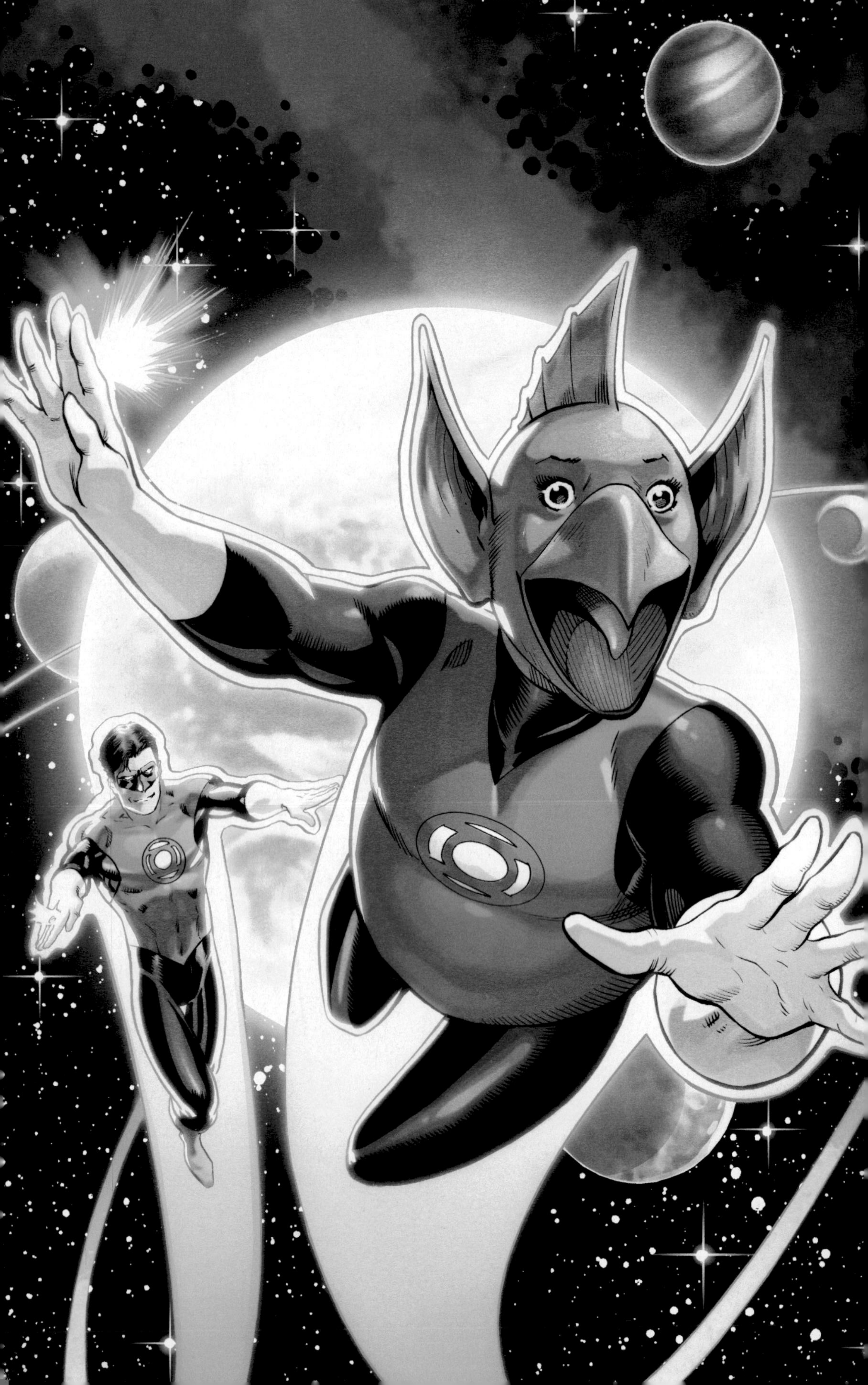

HAL JORDAN AND THE GREEN LANTERN CORPS #34 variant cover by BARRY KITSON and HI-FI

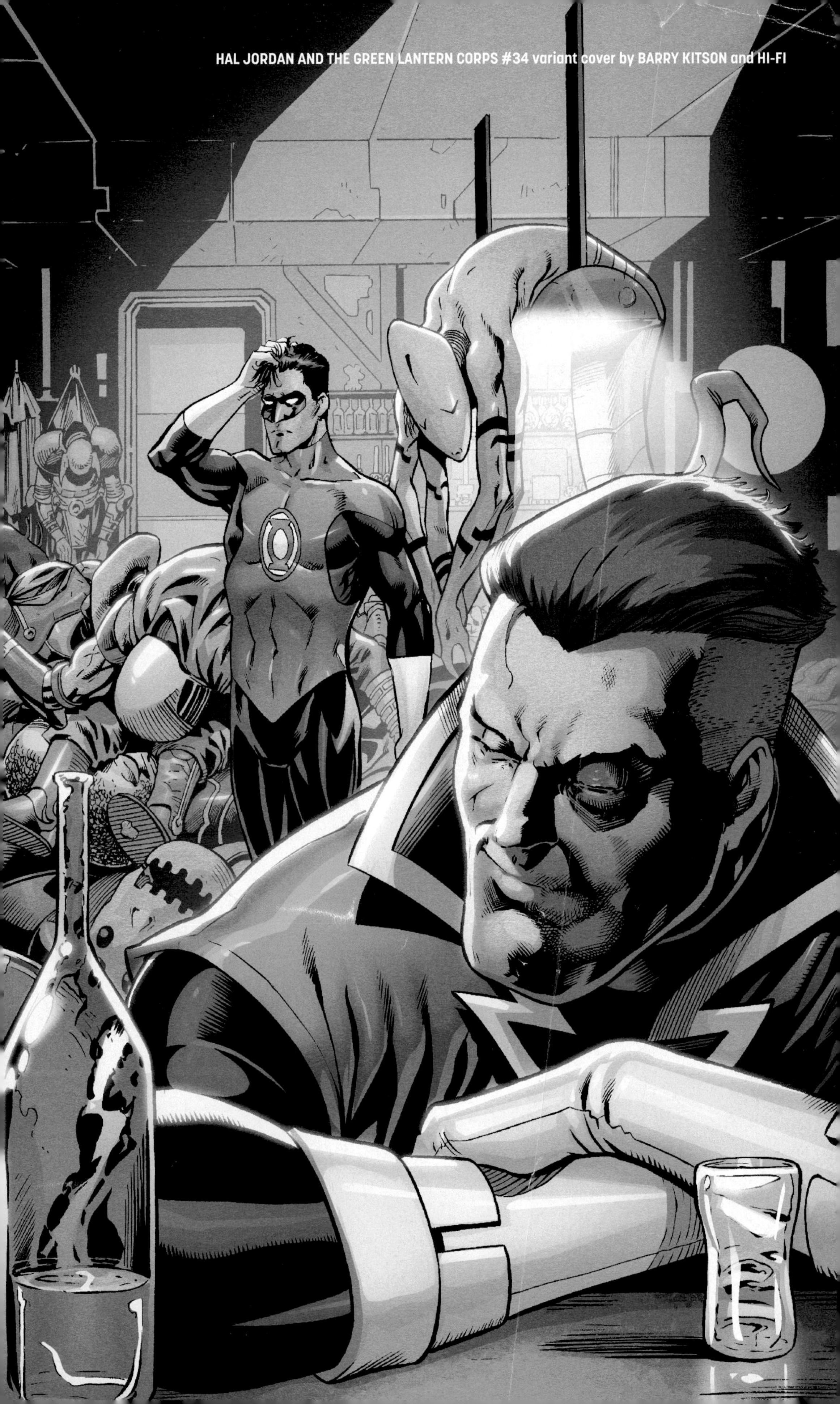

HAL JORDAN AND THE GREEN LANTERN CORPS #35 variant cover by BARRY KITSON and HI-FI

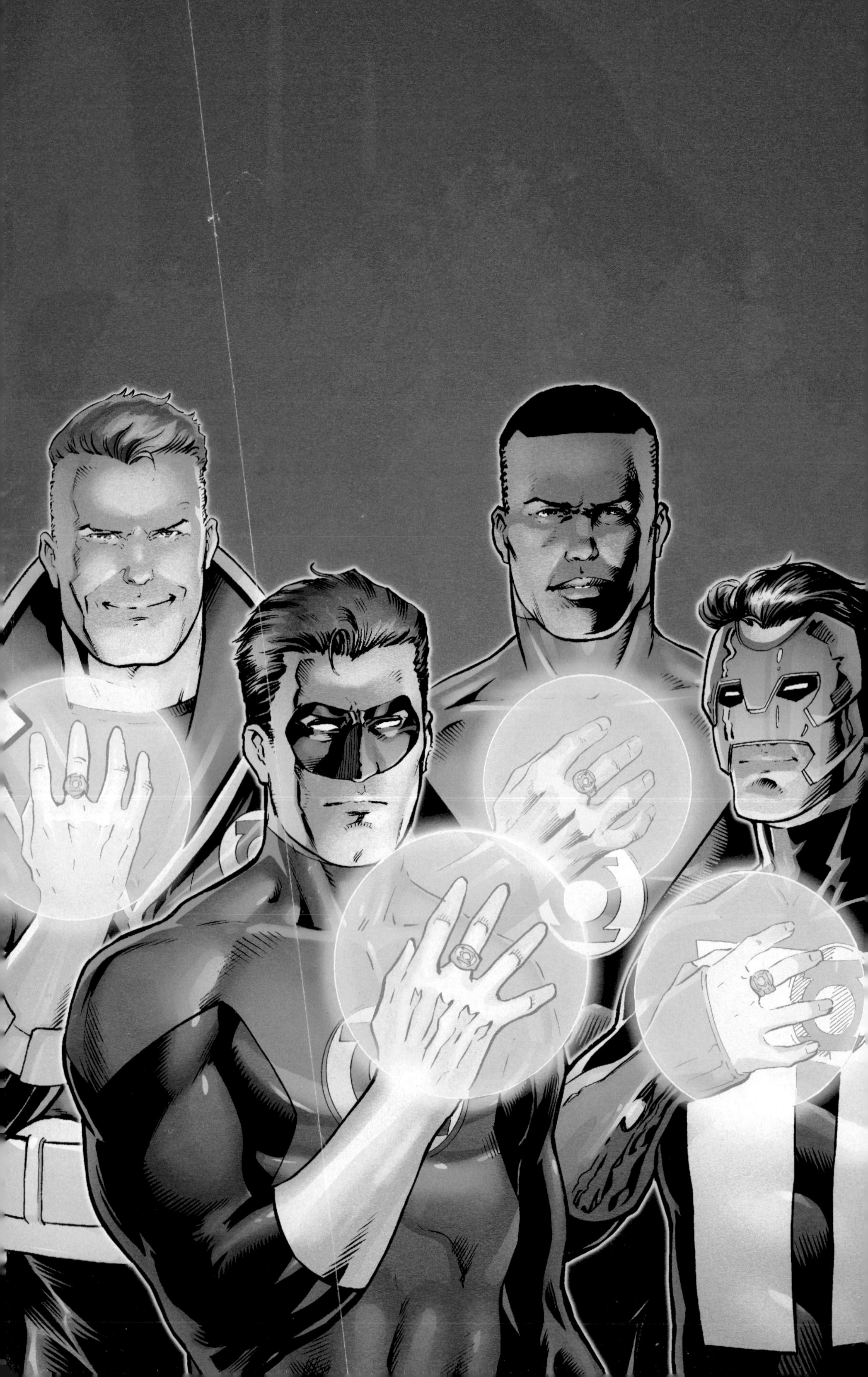

HAL JORDAN AND THE GREEN LANTERN CORPS #36 variant cover by BARRY KITSON and HI-FI

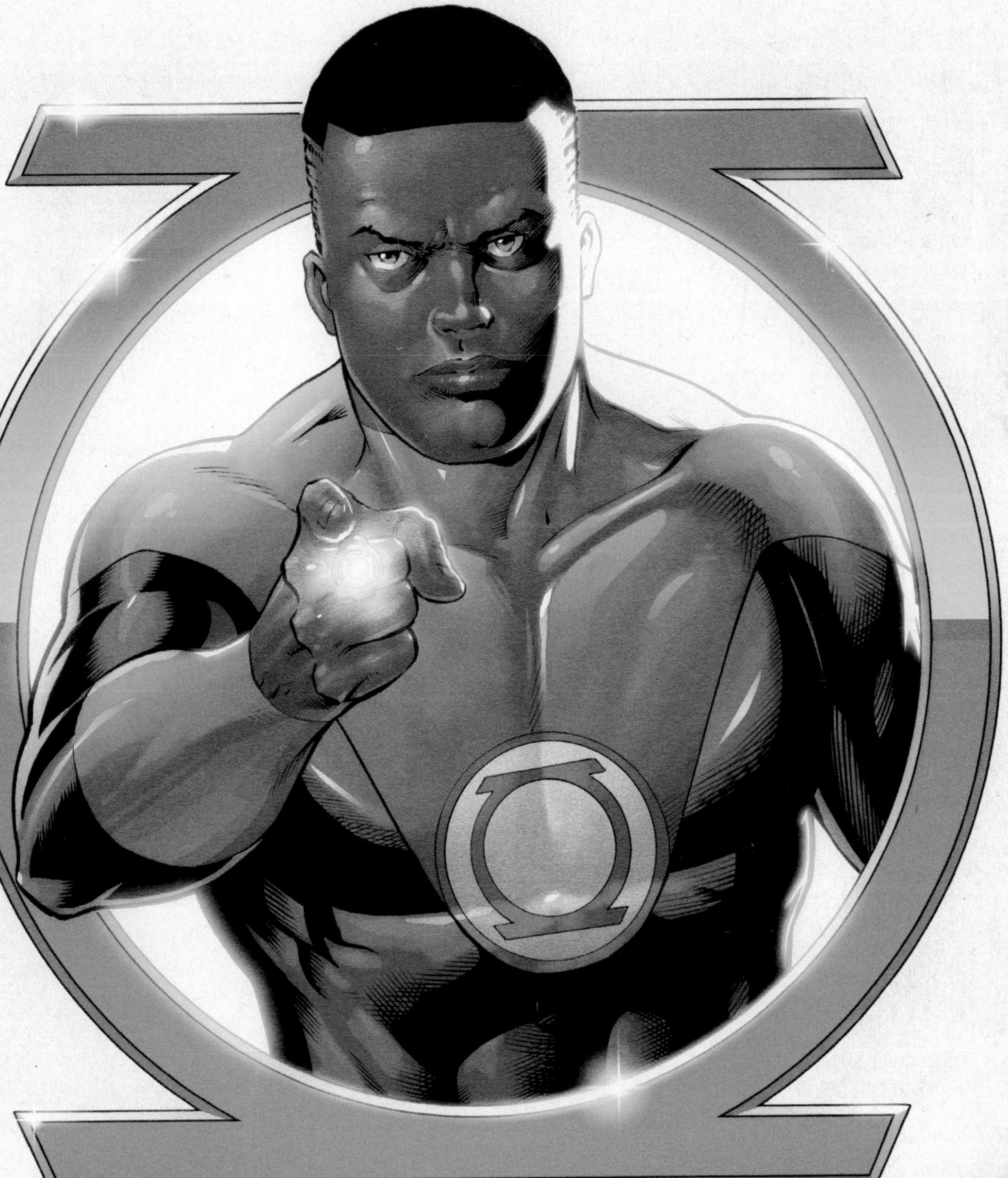

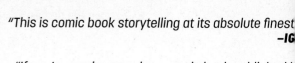

FROM THE WRITER OF
JUSTICE LEAGUE AND *THE FLASH*

GEOFF JOHNS

GREEN LANTERN: REBIRTH

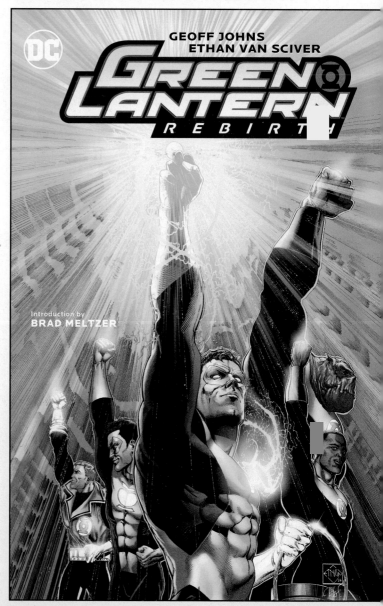